Praise for previous editions of

QUICK ESCAPES®
CHICAGO

"This is one of the best books around for quick getaways."
—*Travel Books Worldwide*

"Helps solve the problem of where to go for short, but full-fledged, breaks from the city."
—*Northwest Indiana Post Tribune*

Help Us Keep This Guide Up to Date

Every effort has been made by the authors and editors to make this guide as accurate and useful as possible. However, many things can change after a guide is published—establishments close, phone numbers change, facilities come under new management, etc.

We would love to hear from you concerning your experiences with this guide and how you feel it could be improved and kept up to date. While we may not be able to respond to all comments and suggestions, we'll take them to heart and we'll also make certain to share them with the author. Please send your comments and suggestions to the following address:

> The Globe Pequot Press
> Reader Response/Editorial Department
> P.O. Box 480
> Guilford, CT 06437

Or you may e-mail us at:
> editorial@globe-pequot.com

Thanks for your input, and happy travels!

QUICK ESCAPES® SERIES

QUICK ESCAPES®
CHICAGO

Fourth Edition

26 WEEKEND GETAWAYS
IN AND AROUND THE WINDY CITY

BY

BONNIE MILLER RUBIN
AND
MARCY MASON

The
Globe
Pequot
Press

GUILFORD, CONNECTICUT

Photo credits: pp. 1, 56: Ron Bailey, courtesy the *Chicago Tribune*; p. 5: Steve Stout, courtesy Starved Rock Lodge & Conference Center; p. 15: courtesy Maxon Manor; p. 38: Galena/Jo Daviess County Convention & Visitors Bureau; pp. 69, 90: courtesy Geneva Lake Area Chamber of Commerce; p. 76: courtesy Milwaukee Department of City Development; p. 119: courtesy of the Wisconsin Dells Visitor and Convention Bureau; p. 139: EAA photo; p. 158: Erol Reyal; pp. 167, 221: Balthazar Korab/Columbus Visitors Center; p. 172: courtesy LaPorte County Convention & Visitors Bureau; p. 184: courtesy Public Relations and Information, Notre Dame; p. 194: courtesy Elkhart County Convention & Visitors Bureau; p. 205: Delores Wright, courtesy The Indianapolis Project; pp. 227, 243: courtesy Lakeshore Convention & Visitors Bureau; p. 232: courtesy Harbor Country Chamber of Commerce; p. 254: J.O.L. Finucan, courtesy Saugatuck/Douglas Convention & Visitors Bureau; p. 263: courtesy Holland Convention & Visitors Bureau

Cover Photo by PhotoDisc, Inc.
Cover design by Laura Augustine
Text design by Nancy Freeborn
Maps by M.A. Dubé

Library of Congress Cataloging-in-Publication Data
Rubin, Bonnie Miller.
    Quick escapes Chicago : 26 weekend getaways in and around the Windy City / by Bonnie Miller Rubin and Marcy Mason.—4th ed.
    p. cm. — (Quick escapes series)
    Includes index.
    ISBN 0-7627-0628-7
    1. Chicago Region (Ill.)—Tours. I. Mason, Marcy. II. Title. III. Series.

F548.18 .R82 2000
917.73'110443—dc21   00-025055

Manufactured in the United States of America
Fourth Edition/First Printing

To Wayne and Gale, my brother and sister,
with whom I once shared the backseat of a station wagon
and now share some pretty terrific memories

—BONNIE MILLER RUBIN

CONTENTS

The prices and rates listed in this guidebook were confirmed at press time. We recommend, however, that you call establishments before traveling to obtain current information.

INTRODUCTION

Chicago has it all—from architecture to zoos. In between you'll find one world-class symphony, seven professional sports teams, fifty-five museums, and more than a hundred theaters (no wonder *Newsweek* calls it "the hottest theater town in America").

But sometimes you've just got to get out of town. So pack up the car, crank up the radio, and hit the road. A weekend escape can do wonders to clear your head—especially if you're short on time, money, or both. *Quick Escapes®Chicago* provides details of twenty-six cities or areas, some as close as 75 miles to Chicago and one as far away as 300 miles, to be seen on two- to four-day getaway trips. If you're a spa lover, antique hunter, art enthusiast, golfer, history buff, avid shopper, hiker . . . you name it, this book can point you in the right direction.

Each chapter is based on a different city or area to explore. The itinerary for each destination gives specifics on restaurants, lodgings, sights, and activities. Don't feel, however, that you must follow these itineraries verbatim. Just refer to them for some reliable suggestions about things to do and places to go. If you can't do it all in the time allotted, plan to return on another escape weekend.

At the end of each chapter, **There's More** suggests additional attractions and recreational activities. The **Special Events** section lists the area's noteworthy festivals and annual events. In case you want to try a different lodging or restaurant from the one we suggested, you'll find **Other Recommended Restaurants and Lodgings** at the end of each chapter. Finally, **For More Information** is your reference for names and addresses of chambers of commerce or tourism bureaus.

With many restaurant descriptions we've given price ranges for entrees, so you'll have an idea of what to expect. These are Inexpensive (under $12), Moderate ($12 to $18), and Expensive ($18 and up). Other rates and fees are given as precisely as possible throughout the book, but they often change. When you plan a trip, we recommend you call ahead for rate confirmation, reservations, and other specific information such as handicapped accessibility or smoking policy.

Most of these itineraries can be relied upon year-round, but a few, because of the location of the destination, may seem to be more suited to warm-weather travel. Nevertheless, every itinerary includes indoor activities and attractions that will come in handy on days when the weather just isn't cooperating.

Our itineraries can be as helpful to you as parents as they will be to couples traveling alone, and in several cases we've offered two alternatives for lodgings or attractions.

If you are going to take our recommendations, you should know something about us and our preferences. I did all my traveling with a husband and two children, while Marcy traveled on her own or with friends. Those differences aside, we both like the same things: firm mattresses, soft towels, thick walls, and thin pancakes. Antiques are lovely, but bathrooms should be strictly modern. To say that bed and breakfasts have been overly romanticized is an understatement. Not every old house is necessarily an inn, any more than the people who own them are innkeepers. (My husband and I once stood in the hall until the conclusion of *All My Children* so the proprietor could check us in.) Charm is great, but it is no substitute for professionalism.

The best advice is to zero in on what you want. Sometimes it will be old-fashioned quilts, a screened porch, and sharing lively conversation with fellow travelers. Other times it will be a heated pool, wall-to-wall carpeting, and the blessed anonymity of a national chain.

Food should never be treated as mere fill, which, unfortunately, is what you'll find all too often—especially once you leave the city. Pass up the safe franchise for a local gem—the kind of place that's been in the same family for generations. It doesn't have to be fancy; a bowl of homemade soup and crusty bread beats a microwaved duck a l'orange any day.

Of course, chefs change—as do prices—and the place that was extraordinary a year ago may be merely ordinary now. What we have attempted to do here is to be both comprehensive and discriminating. Let us know if we've succeeded.

If you would like to make a correction or suggest a new find that should be considered for a future edition, please let us know. In the meantime, we hope you will enjoy these twenty-six quick escapes from Chicago as much as we have.

Bonnie Miller Rubin

THE BEST

OF THE MIDWEST

In a region as delightfully diverse as the Midwest, there's something for everyone. But here are a few favorites that still remain standouts, even after months of travel.

REGIONAL DINING DELIGHTS:

A fish boil in Door County, Wisconsin

Any breakfast with blueberries at North Beach in South Haven, Michigan

A hearty German meal in Milwaukee

The house salad at The Sea Wolf in South Haven, Michigan

A hot fudge sundae at Beernsten's, Manitowoc, Wisconsin

A sinful scoop of ice cream at Sherman's Dairy, South Haven, Michigan, or Babcock Hall at the University of Wisconsin, Madison

The Blackhawk Chocolate Trail through the Rock River Valley, Illinois

HISTORICAL HIGHLIGHTS:

Museum of Science and Industry, Chicago

Abraham Lincoln's home, Springfield, Illinois

The homes of Marshall, Michigan

The Victorian cottages of Bayfield, Michigan

QUIRKY ATTRACTIONS:

Circus World Museum, Baraboo, Wisconsin

The Musical Fountain, Grand Haven, Michigan

House on the Rock, Spring Green, Wisconsin

LODGING:

The American Club, Kohler, Wisconsin

The Four Seasons, Chicago

Eagle Ridge Inn & Resort, Galena, Illinois

The Fairmont, Chicago

Harbor Grand, New Buffalo, Michigan

Yelton Manor, South Haven, Michigan

NATURAL WONDERS:

Cave of the Mounds, Blue Mounds, Wisconsin

The Dunes (either in Chesterton, Indiana, or Warren Dunes State Park, Bridgman, Michigan)

Migration of Canada geese, Horicon Marsh, Wisconsin

Autumn leaves in Brown County, Indiana

CHILDREN'S DELIGHT:

Indianapolis Children's Museum

Water Parks, Wisconsin Dells

Chicago Children's Museum

ILLINOIS
ESCAPES

Starved Rock State Park

TAKE A HIKE

1 NIGHT

*Cycling • Winter sports • Hiking • Camping
Bird-watching • Fall foliage*

If the idea of spending any time at all in a government-supported park lodge sounds like reliving Boy Scout camp, then it has probably been a while since you've been a guest of the state.

In 1984 Governor James Thompson pumped $100 million worth of renovations into Illinois' sixty-seven state parks. Seven of them—Starved Rock, Illinois Beach, White Pines Forest, Père Marquette, Eagle Creek, Giant City, and Cave-in-Rock—are equipped with lodges.

Starved Rock, one of the state's most popular attractions, now includes a complex that could compete with some of the best luxury resorts from Lake Geneva to Upper Michigan, and at a fraction of the price. Swimming is no longer relegated to some slippery riverbank; the lodge's new wing, completed in 1989, offers an Olympic-size pool, flanked by whirlpool, sauna, and kiddie pool. Thirty new rooms have been added, too, along with cable TV.

But the face-lift has not altered Starved Rock's rustic charm, which has been in place since the Civilian Conservation Corps built the lodge back in the 1930s. Douglas fir logs (some nearly 3 feet in diameter) and a 700-ton double fireplace still dominate the Great Room, where it seems downright quaint to see families playing board games. (It doesn't take kids too long, however, to discover the video games on the second floor.)

Another big factor in Starved Rock's favor is its proximity. Located on the Illinois River, the park is a mere 95 miles southwest of Chicago (just off I–80),

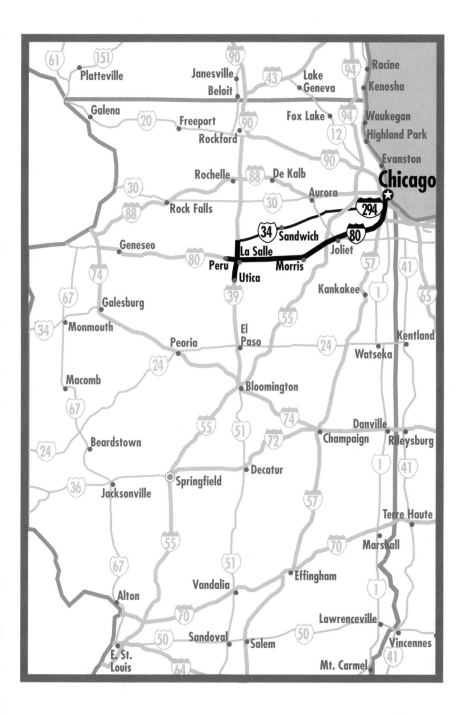

in Utica. You can leave downtown at five on a Friday afternoon and easily make dinner at seven. Because it is so close, it also makes a very nice daylong excursion.

DAY 1

Morning

Take I–80 west. Just as the suburbs turn to countryside, make a stop in Morris at **Gebhard Woods State Park.** The thirty-acre park has four ponds for fishing, including one for kids' fishing only. Bass, bluegill, and sunfish are the catches of the day.

Gebhard Woods is part of the Illinois–Michigan State Canal Trail. The I & M was dug in the 1840s to link Chicago to St. Louis, and it helped clinch the Windy City's reputation as a commercial center. Today a 61½-mile section—from Rockdale to Peru—provides excellent recreational facilities for hikers, bikers, and cross-country skiers.

This scenic area is heavily forested with oak, maple, walnut, and ash. In fact, trivia experts may note that the largest tree in the state, a 120-foot-tall cottonwood, is located 1 mile west of Gebhard Woods. The area doesn't offer much in the way of food service, but there are fine picnic facilities, so plan on bringing your lunch. If you want to leave the park or the weather isn't cooperating, there are a couple of good Morris alternatives (see "Other Recommended Restaurants and Lodgings"). For more information contact the park at (815) 942–0796.

Afternoon

Get back on I–80 and continue west another 30 miles or so to **Starved Rock State Park.** Legend has it that during the 1760s a group of Illinewek Indians, under attack by an Ottawa-Potawatami war party, sought refuge atop the rock. The Illini were surrounded and eventually starved—hence the name.

The infamous rock, a 125-pound sandstone butte, is still the park's main attraction, and you can explore it yourself. There are also trickling waterfalls, rock formations, and eighteen canyons formed during the glacial drift; the biggest rock formations are in St. Louis, French, and LaSalle Canyons. There are more than 600 species of plants, making the park a veritable feast for everyone from photographers to botanists. The well-marked trails offer easy

The natural beauty of Starved Rock makes for exhilarating hiking.

accessibility for young children, but the rugged terrain will challenge even the most advanced hiker. Stop at the Visitors Center, which is open daily, for information.

Depending on the season, you also can paddle a canoe, fish, cross-country ski, or explore the scenery by horseback.

As you return to the lodge, be sure to notice the wood carvings that dot the landscape. The bald eagles, ducks, and black bear cubs are the work of Larry Jensen, one of the best chain saw sculptors in the country.

DINNER: The Starved Rock lodge dining room is where you'll probably end up eating all your meals. And given the limited number of dining choices in the area, it's a lot better than it has to be. The chef serves up honest fare: fried chicken, fish, steaks. The prime rib and red-jacketed potatoes are better than what you'd find at many city restaurants. And who would ever expect to see a dessert tray, complete with flourless chocolate torte and caramel pecan cheese-cake, at a state park dining hall? Dinners are in the $10 to $15 range, but there is a child's menu with little portions and prices to match. Insider's tip: Make your dining reservations as soon as you arrive.

LODGING: Since your tax dollars help defray operating expenses, room rates at the lodge are a bargain that even budget motels would find hard to match. Accommodations range from about $75 per night for a double in the main wing to $91 for a deluxe cabin with a fireplace and a king-size bed. The most difficult part is booking a room, not affording it. It is not unusual to hear about waiting lists of a year or more. If you find yourself thwarted by the reservations desk, play hooky during the week, when the demand for rooms is much less. The lodge also deserves high marks for being totally handicapped-accessible (including the pool). For reservations, call (815) 667–4211 or (800) 868–7625.

DAY 2

Morning

BREAKFAST: The lodge dining room offers the usual choice of pancakes, waffles, eggs. Prices range from $5.00 to $8.00.

The **Waterway Visitors Center** (Starved Rock Lock & Dam, Dee Bennett Road and Route 178, Utica) presents an audiovisual display on early Midwestern river travel. A visit to the center is especially worthwhile if you're a transportation buff or it's a rainy day and you have kids in tow. The observation deck offers a great view of the locks along the 327-mile Illinois Waterway, which forms a link between the Great Lakes and the Mississippi River. Open 9:00 A.M.–8:00 P.M. from Memorial Day to Labor Day; 9:00 A.M.–5:00 P.M. from the day after Labor Day to mid-December and from March 1 until the day before Memorial Day. Closed between mid-December and March 1. Call a park ranger at the U.S. Army Corps of Engineers at (815) 667–4054.

There's still another state park to hit. **Matthiessen,** southeast of Starved Rock, is smaller, but take a look at the upper dells, which include a staggered series of waterfalls that plunge into the Vermilion River. This park is made for winter activities. The terrain is challenging, and equipment (skates, skis, even snowshoes) can be rented at a nominal charge.

If your timing is good, return to Chicago via I–39. Travel north to Highway 52 and go east to Sandwich, about 60 miles west of the city. Take the

Sugar Grove exit to Hinkley and then follow the signs to **Sandwich Antiques Market.** The market is open only five Sundays a season, from May to October, but it's worth a detour. It has a national reputation for top-quality furniture and collectibles and was recently listed in *Metropolitan Home* as one of the best antiques markets in the country. Call (815) 786–3337. Food service here is better than you'd expect, too. The fare is simple (charbroiled chicken sandwiches, fresh lemonade, for example), but better than the franchise offerings in the city. (Note: If you're making this a day trip from Chicago, take I–88 west to the Sugar Grove exit to Hinkley.)

THERE'S MORE

Antiques. The Princeton area (about 25 miles west of Starved Rock off I–80) has really developed a following among serious antiquers in recent years. The new Sherwood Antique Mall, along with Princeton Point and Midtown Mall, guarantees enough browsing for the day. Also, don't miss Hoffman's Patterns of the Past, 513 South Main Street, which has achieved a national reputation for locating discontinued china patterns. Call (815) 875–1944.

Red Covered Bridge, 1863 Highway 26, Princeton. The last covered bridge in the state to still carry traffic.

LaSalle County Historical Museum, north of Starved Rock on Highway 178, LaSalle; (815) 667–4861. Artifacts and relics from the Prairie State.

Reddick Mansion, 100 West Lafayette, Ottawa (east of Starved Rock; south off I–80); call the Ottawa Chamber of Commerce at (815) 433–0084. This ornate Italianate mansion, one of the most elaborate ever built in northern Illinois, was a stop on the Underground Railroad.

SPECIAL EVENTS

Starved Rock State Park offers a number of theme weekends, which are very popular. For exact dates and reservations, call (815) 667–4906.

Mid-January. Winter Wilderness Weekend. Cross-country skiing with basic instruction. Ski rentals are available.

Early February (first weekend). Cross-Country Ski Weekend. Similar to Winter Wilderness Weekend, but at Matthiessen State Park, which is 2 miles south of Starved Rock on Route 178.

Early May. Annual Wildflower Pilgrimage. An outstanding area for wildflowers. Guided hikes take place twice daily.

Mid-September. Turn-of-the-Century Celebration. Arts and crafts, stage shows, hot-air balloons.

Mid-October. Fall Colors Weekend. Guided hikes to view Mother Nature's grandest annual show.

Elsewhere

September. Mendota Sweet Corn Festival. There are literally tons of the stuff. Festivities include a corn-shucking contest.

October. Utica Burgoo Bash. Burgoo is a stew of meat, fowl, and vegetables that simmers in large kettles for as long as eighteen hours. The name comes from the combination of seasonings that is known only to the burgoomaster. Such festivals are common in the South, but this one may be the closest to Chicago. Call (815) 667–4861.

OTHER RECOMMENDED RESTAURANTS AND LODGINGS

LaSalle

Uptown Bar and Grill, 601 First Street; (815) 224–4545. Salads, sandwiches. Local folks recommend the sizzling fajitas. Choose a frosty brew from the bar's large selection of domestic and imported beers.

Morris

Rockwell Inn, 2400 West Route 6; (815) 942–6224. About a half hour from Starved Rock, the Rockwell Inn offers straightforward food (steaks, chops, seafood) in a pleasant setting, which features World's Fair memorabilia and lots of art by its namesake, Norman Rockwell.

R-Place, I–80 and Highway 47; (815) 942–3690. The R-Place is that rarity: no-nonsense, truck-stop food (good breakfasts, sandwiches, steaks) with charming ambience. Owners Larry and Kathie Romines collect old-time toys and Americana, such as Disney and Coke memorabilia. That's not the only gimmick: The four-pound hamburger sells for $17, but it's free if you can finish it.

Peru

Red Door Inn, 1701 Water Street; (815) 223–2500. This is a lovely restaurant, located in a restored 1850 river house in nearby Peru. Fine dining, with steak Diane the signature dish. Three miles south of I–80. Reservations recommended.

Princeton

Downtown Cafe, 529 South Main Street; (815) 872–9951. People come from all over for the legendary pies, baked fresh each morning. Open for breakfast, lunch, and dinner (until 8:00 P.M.).

Utica

The Cajun Connection, downtown Utica; (815) 667–9855. Offers authentic Cajun food straight from Louisiana; the owner flies down weekly to get it. Don't miss the roasted pecan pie or the Cajun fries. Closed Monday, Tuesday, and Wednesday.

Duffy's, downtown Utica, across from the LaSalle County Historical Museum; (815) 667–4324. An Irish pub on the prairie, where you can get a tasty burger.

FOR MORE INFORMATION

Heritage Corridor Convention and Visitors Bureau, 81 Chicago Street, Suite 103, Joliet, IL 60431; (800) 535–5682.

Starved Rock Visitors Center, Box 116, Utica, IL 61673; (815) 667–4906.

Rock River Valley

COUNTRY ROADS COME ALIVE

1 NIGHT

Antiques • Historical sites • Canoeing • Fishing
Horseback riding • Fall foliage • Hiking • Camping • Golfing

It was rumored that after a visit to the Rock River Valley, the late John Denver wrote his 1970s hit song "Country Roads." Whether that's true or not, this little cradle of tall trees and limestone bluffs shrouded in an almost eerie quiet is a well-kept secret—rather remarkable, considering that it's barely 100 miles from Chicago.

It's also the home of three state parks—White Pines, Castle Rock, and Lowden—so you would think it would attract a steady stream of daytrippers. Not so. In addition, it has just enough quirky tourist attractions, such as the homes of John Deere and Ronald Reagan, to make it a popular destination. To our good fortune, the masses have not made those same discoveries—yet—although its highly touted chocolate tour may change that.

If you're lucky enough to be traveling during the time that the leaves are turning, don't miss the ride on Highway 2 north from Dixon to Rockford. It follows the Rock River shoreline and is considered by many veteran leaf-peepers to be the most scenic route in the state.

DAY 1

Morning

Take Highway 64 west into Oregon. An early start is recommended, as you'll want to make it into town by 11:00 A.M. for the ***Pride of Oregon*** paddleboat

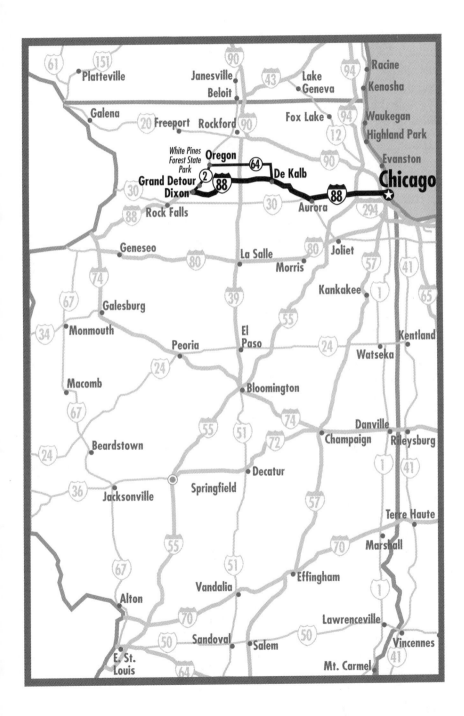

ride, which departs from Maxson Riverside Restaurant at 11:30. If you're late, though, don't worry. There are two more departures, one at 3:00 P.M. and one at 6:30 P.M.; the latter includes dinner while the other two include luncheon and sightseeing, respectively. This two-hour cruise is a visual feast, especially in the fall. Prices range from $10 to $30 (depending on whether a meal is included). Call (800) 468–4222.

LUNCH: Lunch is served on board the *Pride of Oregon*. The scrumptious orange rolls are almost as famous as the scenery.

Afternoon

Head over to **White Pines Forest State Park** (6712 West Pines Road, Mt. Morris; 815–946–3717; the official address is Mt. Morris, but it's 8 miles west of Oregon). The park offers unlimited recreation and is significant for being the southernmost stand of virgin white pine in the Midwest, which means something to botanists, if not tourists.

Explorers will find an area rich in Indian history, as well as an abundance of natural resources spread over 385 acres. The park has seven well-marked hiking trails running through it. The Chicago-Iowa trail, which borders the south side of the park, once served as the main east-west road through Illinois. White Pines is the most popular of the area's three parks, primarily because it offers the most amenities, including a lodge, cabins, a gift shop, and a restaurant (see "Other Recommended Restaurants and Lodgings" at the end of this chapter).

Castle Rock (Route 2, Oregon; 815–732–7329) is the largest of the three state parks, with 2,000-plus acres, and attracts more die-hard nature lovers. Rock hounds, take note: This is one of the few places where you can see St. Peter sandstone, which underlies nearly all of Illinois, at its surface. For a panoramic view of the river, climb the wooden stairs to the top of Castle Rock.

Lowden State Park encompasses 207 peaceful acres just across the river from Oregon. It is situated on a bluff. Sharing that vantage point is *Black Hawk,* a stern, 48-foot statue that stands guard over the Rock River Valley. The statue is the most famous work by Lorado Taft, who, along with a few fellow artists, set up an artists' colony here during the 1920s called Eagles Nest. To reach the park, go north on River Road from Route 64 to Route 2 (815–732–6828).

Regardless of where you choose to do your hiking, be sure you end up in front of the White Pines Inn just in time for dinner.

DINNER: Like most state-run properties, the menu at the **White Pines Inn** is a terrific value. Entrees lean heavily toward baked chicken, fresh fish, and barbecued ribs—fare that fits nicely with the knotty pine decor. After dinner take your coffee out onto the porch and settle into a wicker rocker or browse the gift shop, stocked with equal parts Illinois crafts and tacky souvenirs. For reservations, call (815) 946–3817.

LODGING: Pinehill Bed & Breakfast, 400 Mix Street, Oregon; (815) 732–2067. Innkeeper Susan Koppes is very proud of her 1874 Italianate villa, with its five charming rooms, all with private baths and three with original, working marble fireplaces. The rooms have whimsical names, such as the Somerset Maugham (Maugham often visited Pinehill during the 1930s). During the holidays Koppes puts on lavish Christmas teas and stocks the dining room table with her homemade fudge. Guests can savor the creamy confections during their stay or take one home. Pinehill is just one stop on the Blackhawk Chocolate Trail. (See "There's More.") Rates: $110–$195.

DAY 2

Morning

BREAKFAST: A full breakfast at Pinehill may include eggs and homemade blueberry or banana-chocolate chip muffins, cinnamon sticky buns, crumpets, and hot entrees such as granola pancakes with real maple syrup or cheese blintz soufflé.

Drive down Highway 2 to the **John Deere Home,** Grand Detour (5 miles north of Dixon). Grand Detour is to agriculture what Detroit is to transportation. This prairie hamlet is where a blacksmith named Deere built a plow that would forever change the way people farmed. Much of the original shop was destroyed by fire, but it has been carefully restored, right down to the white picket fence. Admission charge of $3.00 for ages 12 and over. Call (815) 652–4551.

You can swing back onto Highway 2 and head up to DeKalb, home to Cindy Crawford and **Northern Illinois University,** the second-largest school in the state. If you would like a tour, call the university at (815) 753–1000.

LUNCH: Good Vietnamese food beyond the 312 area code? Believe it. **Bea's Wok 'n Roll,** 1402 Sycamore Road, DeKalb (815–756–1660), turns out a mean crab rangoon, spring rolls, and beef lemongrass. Don't be put off by the cutesy name or the hole-in-the-wall decor; this is the real stuff.

Afternoon

If your time is short, limit your touring to two architecturally important sites in DeKalb. The first is **Ellwood House Museum,** 509 North First Street. Colonel Isaac Ellwood, who made his money in barbed wire (it was invented here, an ironic touch in such rural surroundings), built a grand Victorian mansion and furnished it in an equally grand manner. It's open from April to early December every day except Monday and major holidays. Admission: $1.00; children under 6, free. Call (815) 756–4609.

Your other stop should be the **Egyptian Theater,** 135 North Second Street (near Lincoln Highway). The terra-cotta exterior and Egyptian Revival style (circa 1929) will recall a time when vaudeville was king, despite the fact that touring companies still play here. For a schedule, call (815) 758–1215.

THERE'S MORE

Antiques and crafts. Conover Square, corner of Third and Franklin, Oregon; (815) 732–2134. Renovated piano factory, consisting mostly of crafts and antiques shops. Silo Antiques (on Route 2, a little more than a mile north of Oregon) for oak and walnut furniture, china, pottery, and glass. Holly's Homespun (corner of Route 2 and Fifth Street, Oregon) is a quilter's delight, with hard-to-find patterns and more than 500 bolts of fabric. Heart in Hand (across from the courthouse in Oregon) features primitive folk art. Merlin's Florist and Greenhouse (300 Mix Street, Oregon) sells collectibles and furniture amid the blooms.

Blackhawk Chocolate Trail. An odyssey through four counties in Northwestern Illinois, from muffins to mousse, pies to pastries. Stay at an all-chocolate B&B, enjoy an old-fashioned chocolate soda, plan a chocolate teatime, or sample homemade fudge. For a brochure, call (800) 678–2108.

Lowden Miller State Forest. In 1992 the Illinois Department of Conservation purchased 1,186 acres of Sinnissippi Forest to create a new state forest, which includes several miles of Rock River shoreline, wetland, deer and turkey hunting grounds, and hiking trails. For information, call (815) 732–7329.

Moe's Bait Shop, 123 North Second Street, Oregon; (815) 732–2311. One of the most popular spots in town. A gathering place where you can learn just where the fish are biting, as well as hear local gossip. Boat launch.

The Pride of Oregon *paddleboat affords views of pristine scenery.*

White Pines Ranch, 3581 Pines Road, Oregon; (815) 732–7923. This ranch (one of two working ranches in the state) offers horseback riding and an outdoor education program for kids that teaches everything from reading headstones to searching for fossils. By reservation only.

Silver Ridge Golf Course, Highway 2 (1½ miles north of Oregon); (815) 734–4440. This is a serenely beautiful course, high up on the ridge, overlooking the Rock River.

Sinnissippi Forest, 3122 South Lowden Road, Oregon; (815) 732–6240. If the season's right, this is the perfect spot to cut down your own Christmas tree. Here the job is done so well that the experience is turned into a Currier & Ives print. A horse-drawn wagon takes you into the 290-acre tree farm. After you've cut down your tree, sip a cup of cocoa while you warm your toes by the fire. (For Scrooges, there are also precut trees.)

SPECIAL EVENTS

June. Canoe Rally. Pleasure canoeing and breakfast. Rock River near Maxson Manor.

July. Ogle County Airport Open House. Antique planes and rides.

July. Petunia Festival, Dixon. Dutch Reagan's hometown pulls out the stops with more than 7 miles of petunias.

October. Autumn on Parade, Oregon. One of Northern Illinois' oldest and largest festivals. Food, crafts, and games on the main square.

November. Candlelight Forest Walk. Decorated homes, crafts, etc. Downtown Oregon. Starts at Ogle County Historic Courthouse with the lighting of the tree.

OTHER RECOMMENDED RESTAURANTS AND LODGINGS

DeKalb

Crystal Pistol, 1312 West Lincoln Highway; (815) 751–1000. Steaks and seafood in a New Orleans decor at moderate prices. Locals chow down on the sixteen-ounce sirloin. Closed Monday.

Dixon

Best Western Brandywine Lodge, 443 Highway 2; (815) 284–1890. A full-service motel with pool and all other amenities. Four rooms have whirlpools. Rates: $57 to $99 per night.

Grand Detour

Colonial Rose Inn, 8230 South Green Street; (815) 652–4422. An 1850 red-brick Italianate house of twelve rooms (four with private bath), with lots of period furniture, such as iron-rail and brass beds. Some rooms have fireplaces. The continental breakfast includes fresh fruits and croissants. Rates start at $80 per night.

Mt. Morris

White Pines Inn, 6712 West Pines Road; (815) 946–3817. Like Starved Rock, this state park lodge has undergone extensive renovation and is a steal. The lodge has twenty-five cabins, each with gas fireplace and accommodations for four people. Closes mid-December through February. Rates: $66–$77 per night. Stay for lunch and enjoy a light entree with Sweet Street Snickers cream pie or chocolate bar peanut butter pie. White Pines also runs a dinner theater, with productions on periodic Thursday and Friday. Like most dinner theaters, the repertoire is on the frothy side. Prices range from $22 to $26, which also includes dinner.

Kable House, Sunset Hill; (815) 734–7297. This sort-of B&B (no breakfast served) is located right in the middle of a nine-hole golf course. That's right, you walk out and you're on the fairway. Six rooms. Rates: $65 to $100 per night.

Oregon

Blackhawk Steak Pit, Highway 2; (815) 732–2500. Just as it sounds. A place to indulge in prime Midwestern beef, which is charbroiled before your eyes. Moderate.

Maxson Riverside Restaurant, Highway 2, about 2 miles north of Highway 64; (800) 468–4222. Although this popular restaurant burned down in 1993, it opened bigger and better a year later. The famous prime rib and orange rolls haven't changed a bit; they're also offered on the *Pride of Oregon,* which docks here. Moderate.

Patchwork Inn, 122 North Third Street; (815) 732–4113. Indulge in slow-paced elegance and sophistication. The twelve guest rooms are decorated with antiques and quilts. Stay in the room where Abraham Lincoln stayed. Rates (including breakfast): $75 to $115 per night.

La Vigna Restaurant, 2190 South Dausville Road; (815) 732–4413. Fine Northern Italian cuisine in a quaint, romantic atmosphere. Features pasta, seafood, and steaks. Homemade desserts and a large wine selection. Moderate.

FOR MORE INFORMATION

Blackhawk Waterways Convention and Visitors Bureau, 201 North Franklin Avenue, Polo, IL 61064; (800) 678–2108. The bureau has information on Carroll, Lee, Ogle, and Whiteside Counties.

Northern Illinois Tourism Council, 419 South State Street, Belvidere, IL 61008; (815) 547–3740.

Gilman

THE ULTIMATE MIDWESTERN SPA

2 NIGHTS

Health • Fitness • Self-indulgence

At the first sign of a few extra pounds, half of Hollywood retreats to the Golden Door in California or flies off to Switzerland for an injection of sheep's cells. But for many Midwesterners, luxury is in Gilman, Illinois, just 20 miles south of Kankakee.

The Heartland Spa may be just an hour and a half from Chicago, but it could just as easily be a world away. This fourteen-year-old spa, situated on thirty-one acres of lush central Illinois countryside, offers equal parts clean living and indulgence.

The short drive is pleasant, not only because it clears your head as you get out into the country, but also because it lets you explore some interesting stops along the way.

DAY 1

Afternoon

If you're an antiques buff, take I–94 to Highway 1 and stop in **Crete.** This far-southern suburb doesn't get half the attention of other Chicago area antique "meccas" such as Long Grove, St. Charles, or Geneva; therefore, it has twice the bargains.

Start at **Marketplace Antiques** (550 West Exchange; 708–672–5556). It has about a dozen dealers and is filled to the rafters with china and glass primitives, quilts, furniture, and jewelry.

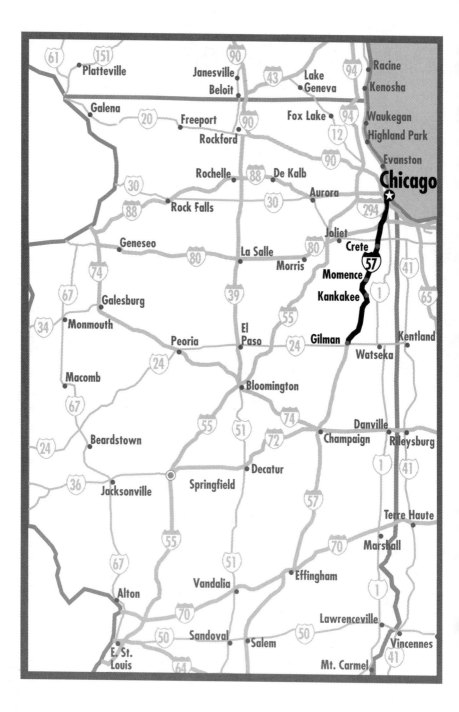

Continue on Highway 1 to the Heartland Spa in Gilman. (If you're going straight to Gilman and bypassing Crete, I–57 is the most direct route.)

The Heartland Spa is a beautiful country estate with every conceivable amenity and an attentive, knowledgeable staff. There is just the right combination of health without hysteria, luxury without snobbery, and gain without pain.

The weekend we were there, a quick look around at the other twenty-seven guests confirmed that this was a place for real people, and there were few washboard-flat abdomens among us. One woman came to celebrate a 75th birthday; another was there to hide out from a 50th. Some guests came with their spouses, others with their mothers, and quite a few came alone. One woman was a waitress who decided that she needed to break the milk shake-a-day habit she had acquired on the job. Another, an accountant, was trying to wean herself from a nasty candy bar habit, a result of too much anxiety during tax season.

Stress is considered as much a no-no as a hot fudge sundae. Consequently, everything is designed to achieve maximum mellowness. The rooms are comfortably appointed, and there are no phones or TVs to break the mood.

Perplexed about what to wear? Everything is provided, from sweat suits to bathrobes. As for laundry, you just drop your clothes on your doormat and the "laundry fairies" whisk them away and replace them with a new stack. (Alas, one woman took her doormat with her, only to find that the magic does not work at home.)

The Heartland offers a two-for-one program, priced at $378 ($430 weekend) per night for two people. One massage is included but other services are extra. Single rates: $340 per person per night ($378 weekend). Weeklong stays are also available, for people who are lucky enough to have that unbeatable combination of time and money.

The moderate tone is set right on the first page of the spa's manual: "Try as much or as little as is comfortable for you. This is your time to concentrate on yourself and nothing else."

DINNER: Moroccan-style fish and couscous are so delicious you don't even miss the fat. There's always plenty of fresh fruit to get you back on the straight and narrow.

DAY 2

Morning

A typical morning at the Heartland starts with stretching exercises and a brisk 2-mile walk through pastoral farmland. If you'd rather sleep in, however, no one will come pounding on your door.

After breakfast (plum coffee cake or broccoli and cheddar frittatas) you can participate in a scheduled activity, such as Bodyworks (a conditioning class for exercise dropouts), weight training, water exercises, or advanced aerobics.

Lunch is a high point of the day. It can be a Caesar salad with grilled chicken or a mouth-watering portobello mushroom sandwich. It is surprisingly satisfying.

Afternoon

Lunch may be followed by more activity, maybe on such high-tech equipment as StairMaster, NordicTrack, or Elliptical Crosstrainers. Or perhaps you'd like to take a yoga class or head for the sauna and whirlpool. You can turn the self-indulgence up a notch with a therapeutic aroma massage, a manicure, or a soothing facial.

After a dinner of grilled swordfish, an evening walk feels just right. In the summer you can play a few sets of tennis or take a paddleboat out on shimmering Kam Lake; in the winter guests don cross-country skis.

A series of educational programs, called "The Heartland Institute," takes place every night in a cozy library complete with fireplace and overstuffed furniture. Topics range from "how to read food labels" to "stress management." You can skip class and retire to your room with a steamy novel if you want to; class—and guilt—are not required.

DAY 3

After saying good-bye, get back to I–57 (the Heartland will give you directions) and head north. At Kankakee, you can keep up the healthy life-style with an easy canoe trip on the **Kankakee River,** considered by many to be the best canoeing river in the state. **Reed's Canoe** trips will outfit you completely, from the boat itself to the life jackets. After your two-hour trip, buses are waiting at your destination to take you back to your car. There are longer options as well; some last as long as two days. Prices start at $30 for two adults

(children under 12 cost $3.00 each) for a three-hour trip. This makes a wonderful day trip as well. April to October (815–932–2663).

Canoeing not your thing? Stop off at **Kankakee River State Park,** with its beautiful bike and walking trails (815–933–9036).

LUNCH: Take a short jog east on Highway 17, before hitting Highway 1 for the drive home. Stop at **Dionne's** in Momence, at the intersection of Route 1 (Dixie Highway) and Sixth Street (815–472–6081). You may have learned a lot about nutrition over the last two days, but who can resist French onion soup with a thick blanket of cheese? It goes especially well with a crisp salad and a basket of crusty bread. If you go for the chocolate mousse, no one will ever tell. Open for dinner, too, but only on weekends.

What the tulip is to Holland, the gladiola is to **Momence.** There are several major growers here that produce about sixty varieties of blossoms, which are shipped all over the country. An annual three-day festival, held usually the second weekend of August—when some 500 acres of flowers are in bloom— is alone worthy of a day trip.

THERE'S MORE

Kankakee County Historical Society Museum, Eighth Avenue at Water Street; (815) 932–5279. The French and Indian heritage of the Kankakee River Valley is on display here, as are housewares, furniture, and Civil War memorabilia.

Fishing, hiking, snowmobiling (3 miles of designated trails). Kankakee River State Park, 8 miles northwest of Kankakee on Highway 102; (815) 933–1383.

Plum Creek Nursery, 1255 East Bemes Road, Crete; (708) 672–7999. In the fall, this is a lovely destination, with hayrides out to the pumpkin patch, a petting zoo, and pony rides. If you're looking for a quiet, rural alternative to commercialized haunted houses, this is it.

SPECIAL EVENTS

Mid-July. Kankakee Fishing Derby. Anglers from all over the Midwest compete for cash prizes. Held throughout the county on the Kankakee River.

August. Kankakee County Fair and Rodeo Exposition. Carnival, entertainment, food.

OTHER RECOMMENDED RESTAURANTS AND LODGINGS

Wilmington

Andrews Manor Bed and Breakfast, 116 South Kankakee Street; (815) 476–1055. Stop at this historic Victorian home in the antiques center of Will County for afternoon tea, or stay overnight in one of four elegant guest rooms. Rates: $65 to $95 per night.

Grant Park

Bennett-Curtis House, 302 West Taylor; (815) 465–2288. Senator Edward C. Curtis built this stately Victorian home in 1900. Senator George Bennett bought it in 1919. The specialty is prime rib, and all pastries are baked in the kitchen. Open for lunch, dinner, and Sunday brunch. Reservations required.

FOR MORE INFORMATION

The Heartland Spa Corporate Office, 1237 East 1600 North Road, Gilman, IL 60938; (800) 545–4853; www.heartlandspa.com.

Kankakee Convention and Visitors Association, 4 Dearborn Square, 2nd floor, Kankakee, IL 60901; (815) 935–7390.

Springfield

LAND OF LINCOLN

2 NIGHTS

Sightseeing • Architecture • Historic sites

It's amazing to consider the number of adults who have been to Paris, London, and Rome but somehow have never made it to Springfield.

Lacking both the proximity and cachet of, say, Lake Geneva, Springfield is easy to overlook. And while it's true that there are no beautiful beaches or sunset cruises to seduce you, the sheer dignity of Abraham Lincoln's life will provide more than enough sightseeing fodder for one weekend.

A trip to Springfield, however, is not just a glorified history lesson. You'll find several surprises strictly of the hedonistic variety. For example, the Springfield Renaissance Hotel is one of the best in the Midwest. Not only does it have every creature comfort one would expect from Michigan Avenue accommodations, but it is also an incredible bargain. On weekends—when lobbyists on fat expense accounts have left town—rooms go for nearly half the weekday rate. (More on lodging later.) With virtually all the historic and government buildings free of charge, Springfield can be a lot cheaper than a getaway closer to home.

You'll also find that despite the many attractions that capitalize on the popularity of its most famous citizen, the town still retains an unpolished quaintness. While you will see Mr. Lincoln's Campgrounds, Abe's Antiques, and even Abe Lincoln Barber College, the landmarks, at least, are remarkably scrubbed of crass commercialism and are disarmingly accessible. No lines, no barrage of billboards, no one hawking T-shirts. Just the Lincoln legacy—even kids raised on Nintendo come away impressed.

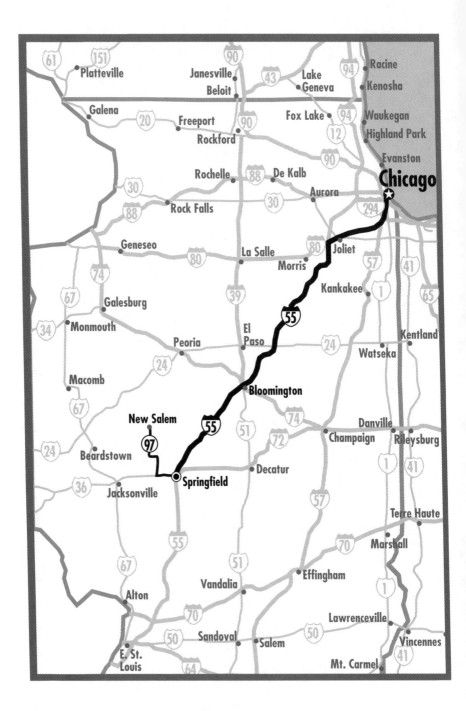

A few postscripts: While there are more than twenty attractions, many would be of interest only to the most passionate history buff. The top draws—Lincoln's home, Lincoln's tomb, the state capitol, the Illinois State Museum, the Dana-Thomas House—can be accomplished in a weekend. While the Governor's Mansion is undoubtedly worth a stop, hours are limited to Tuesday, Thursday, and Saturday mornings.

DAY 1

Take I–55 south to Springfield, about a 200-mile trip. You might want to put in a few hours of driving before stopping for breakfast in the Bloomington/Normal area, about 75 miles north of your final destination. (The usual selection of Bob Evans, Denny's, etc., can be found right off the highway.)

The break will also allow you to visit the **David Davis Mansion State Historic Site** (1000 East Monroe Street, Bloomington; 309–828–1084), a large, exquisite Victorian home built in 1872 for Judge David Davis and his wife. The home of this wealthy landowner and crony of Abraham Lincoln has been faithfully restored and contains a great many period furnishings. Fans of Victoriana will find it especially worth a stop at Christmas, when it is decked out for the holiday season. Admission: free, though there is a $2.00 suggested donation.

Back onto I–55, Springfield is a little more than an hour away. Not only will you find the Lincoln sites close together, but the block of Eighth Street between Capitol Avenue and Jackson Street is closed to auto traffic, so travelers can immerse themselves in nineteenth-century history without any twentieth-century intrusions. The gaslights and wooden sidewalks add to the ambience, as well.

Stop first at the **Lincoln Home Visitors Center** to pick up tickets for the tour of Lincoln's home, just a block away. Tickets are free but are dispensed on a first-come basis. It's worth a stop to check availability when you come into town. If tickets are gone, make this the first stop of the day tomorrow. Tickets are stamped with the time of your tour; this way you can visit other stops and return in time for the tour. The visitors center is also a good place to get oriented. You'll find special exhibits and an excellent bookstore, with a wealth of material on the Lincoln years and the Civil War. The Lincoln Home Visitors Center is located at 426 South Seventh Street. Hours are 8:30 A.M.–5:00 P.M., with extended summer hours. Call (217) 492–4241, ext. 221. Free.

When you tour Abraham Lincoln's home, where the family lived for the seventeen years before Lincoln was elected president, you'll actually feel good about your tax dollars at work. Beautifully restored and impeccably maintained, the home sits squarely in the middle of a four-square-block area. Tours, conducted by knowledgeable park rangers, are about twenty minutes in length—short enough to hold the interest of even a five-year-old, but still substantial enough to satisfy adults. The home—the only one Lincoln ever owned—is furnished (mostly with reproductions) as it appeared in 1860. A black silk top hat hangs on a rack just inside the door. The Lincoln Home National Historic Site, Eighth and Jackson Streets, is open daily 8:30 A.M.–5:00 P.M., April through October. Call for winter hours; (217) 492–4244. Free.

When you leave Lincoln's home, head north on Ninth Street to Monroe. Turn right and you'll find the **Lincoln Depot,** where president-elect Lincoln said good-bye to Springfield and boarded a train for Washington, D.C. The depot contains restored waiting rooms and offers a multimedia presentation. Open daily, 10:00 A.M.–4:00 P.M., April through August. Call (217) 544–8695. Free.

Head west on Monroe a couple of blocks and stop at the **First Presbyterian Church** (Seventh and Capitol Streets; 217–528–4311) to view the Lincoln Family pew and lovely Tiffany stained glass windows. Another block to the northwest, at Sixth and Adams, is the **Lincoln-Herndon Law Offices.** Lincoln practiced law here for ten years. It is the only surviving structure in which he maintained working law offices. Open Monday through Friday, 8:30 A.M.–4:30 P.M. Free.

That's a lot for one day. Time to break for dinner.

DINNER: Alexander's Steak House, 620 Bruns Lane; (217) 793–0440. Carnivores will think they've died and gone to heaven at Alexander's, where T-bones weigh in at twenty-five ounces. The gimmick of picking out your steak and cooking it over a charcoal grill adds to the fun. Moderate.

LODGING: The Renaissance Springfield Hotel, 701 East Adams Street; (217) 544–8800. The furnishings are lovely, the service impeccable, and the food exceptional, which is not quite typical of central Illinois. Use of the clean, comfortable health club is included in your room rate (during the week it's often used by legislators). You'll find small, unexpected touches everywhere, from complimentary newspapers to a jigsaw puzzle-in-progress in the lobby, just waiting for you to sit down and add a piece. Weekend rates start at $69 per night.

DAY 2

Morning

BREAKFAST: Renaissance Springfield Hotel.

If you didn't see the Lincoln home, go to the visitors center as early as possible and get your tickets. If you've already seen it, then pick up the Lincoln trail where we left off.

Go 2 blocks north and 1 block west from the First Presbyterian Church to the **Old State Capitol.** This is where Lincoln served as a state representative and made his famous "House Divided" speech. The Capitol is completely furnished and restored to duplicate his legislative years. There is also a tour, called "Mr. Lincoln's World," provided by costumed interpreters every Friday and Saturday. The Old State Capitol, located at the Downtown Mall, on the corner of Adams and Washington, is open daily March through October, 9:00 A.M.–5:00 P.M. November through February, 9:00 A.M.–4:00 P.M. Call (217) 785–7961. Donation.

If you want to view modern-day government in action, the new **State Capitol** houses the Illinois state legislature and constitutional offices. The capitol complex includes the Michael J. Howlett Building, which houses the Hall of Flags. Built in 1868, the capitol offers free guide service. The Illinois State Capitol Building, Second Street and Capitol Avenue, is open to visitors Monday through Friday, 8:00 A.M.–4:00 P.M.; Saturday and Sunday, 9:00 A.M.–3:00 P.M. Call (217) 782–2099. Free.

Just next to the capitol is the **Illinois State Museum** (Spring and Edwards Streets; 217–782–7386). For kids who have access to the Field Museum, this will seem a bit tame. The emphasis is on the state's history, geology, and anthropology. Art galleries feature photography and fine and decorative arts, but easily the most popular displays are the Carson miniatures and a mastodon skeleton. There is also a special hands-on discovery room for kids. The museum is open Monday through Saturday, 8:30 A.M.–5:00 P.M.; Sunday, noon–5:00 P.M. Free.

LUNCH: Maldaner's, 222 South Sixth Street; (217) 522–4313. A Springfield establishment, where as much state business is conducted as on the capitol

floor. This restaurant features a light menu of salads, soups, and sandwiches. Springfield's most famous culinary contribution is the horseshoe sandwich, which was created in the late 1920s at the Leland Hotel. Variations abound, but the basic formula is the same: ham, cheese sauce, and French fries on toast. The name comes from the ham's resembling a horseshoe and the fries' representing the nails. Other places that still serve the horseshoe include Norb Andy's (518 East Capitol Avenue; 217–523–7777) and the Red Coach Inn (301 North Grand Avenue West; 217–522–0198).

Afternoon

If you feel as if you're burned out on government and need to shift gears, about 3 blocks away, at 301 East Lawrence Avenue, is the **Dana-Thomas House.** After a three-year restoration project, the Dana-Thomas House reopened in 1990 to rave reviews. Designed and built by Frank Lloyd Wright in 1902–1904, the house and its contents have been brought back to a time when Springfield socialite Susan Lawrence Dana entertained dignitaries there with great flourish.

This is the Wright mother lode, containing the largest collection of original Wright-designed oak furniture and art glass (about 450 windows, skylights, light fixtures, lamps, and door panels). Fully narrated tours last about one hour and are preceded by a slide show. Visitors should also take note of the Sumac Book Shop, which offers architectural books, gifts, and home furnishings of superb quality. The house is open Wednesday through Sunday, 9:00 A.M.–4:00 P.M. Admission: free, but donations are suggested. Call (217) 782–6776.

LODGING: Return to the Renaissance Springfield for some swimming and a soak in the whirlpool before dinner.

DINNER: Lindsay's, Renaissance Springfield Hotel. Lindsay's, named after Springfield's own Vachel Lindsay, offers casual fare for tourists. Basics such as chicken, steak, and fish range from $6.00 to $17.00. Call (217) 544–8800.

DAY 3

Morning

BREAKFAST: Renaissance Springfield Hotel.

Start your day with a visit to **Lincoln's Tomb,** about a ten-minute drive from downtown. This is the final resting place of Lincoln, his wife, and three of their four sons. (A fourth son, Robert Todd Lincoln, is buried at Arlington National Cemetery.) Inside the tomb are statuettes of Lincoln that celebrate various periods of his life. The nose of the popular bust of Lincoln that stands at the tomb's entrance has been rubbed smooth by visitors for luck. Despite this one bit of folly, the tomb is as dignified a monument as you'll see, mercifully free of anything but solitude. The tomb attracts international visitors, and along with Lincoln's home, it should be a priority for any Springfield visitor. While you're at the cemetery, take a moment to view the Vietnam Veterans Memorial, which pays tribute to all Illinois residents who served in the war, as well as the Illinois Korean War Memorial. Also buried here is poet Vachel Lindsay.

The Lincoln Tomb State Historic Site is located at Oak Ridge Cemetery. Entrance is at 1500 North Monument Avenue or at North Walnut Street. The monument is open daily March through October, 9:00 A.M.–5:00 P.M. November through February, 9:00 A.M.–4:00 P.M. Call (217) 782–2717. Free.

Springfield offers a number of other attractions, which are listed below. To fit everything into a weekend, however, start making your way back home, so you can hit **Lincoln's New Salem State Historic Site,** which is about 20 miles northwest of Springfield on Highway 97 near Petersburg.

Lincoln lived and worked in New Salem for six pivotal years of his life. He arrived at this tiny hamlet in 1831 as an awkward youngster and left in 1837 as an adult poised for a career in law and politics. In between, he worked as a store clerk, postmaster, surveyor, and steamboat pilot.

Ironically, the years Lincoln spent here almost entirely encompass the town's brief history. Shortly after Lincoln left, the county seat was moved to nearby Petersburg, and New Salem blew off the map like a tumbleweed. Today the restoration is virtually all that is here, but that is more than enough to warrant a detour.

About two dozen buildings—from the tavern to the church—have been reconstructed and furnished to take you back to the 1830s. The only original building is the Henry Onstot Cooper Shop; this is the place where Lincoln pored over his law books. Children will enjoy the horse-drawn carriage that rolls through the village.

Hours: March through October, 9:00 A.M.–5:00 P.M.; winter hours, 8:00 A.M.–11:00 P.M. Call (217) 632–4000 for admission fees and other information.

Friday through Saturday night the original musical *Abraham* is performed at the **Theatre in the Park,** New Salem's outdoor amphitheater. For information and reservations, call (217) 632–5440.

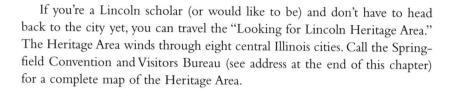
If you're a Lincoln scholar (or would like to be) and don't have to head back to the city yet, you can travel the "Looking for Lincoln Heritage Area." The Heritage Area winds through eight central Illinois cities. Call the Springfield Convention and Visitors Bureau (see address at the end of this chapter) for a complete map of the Heritage Area.

THERE'S MORE

Governor's Mansion, Fifth and Jackson Streets; (217) 782–6450 or (217) 789–6950. Home to Illinois' first family, this is the third oldest continually occupied governor's mansion in the country. Of the fourteen rooms open to the public, the state dining room, Lincoln bedroom, and library are especially worth noting. So are the antiques, which grew impressively during the years Jim Thompson was governor, thanks to Big Jim's passion for collecting. While this is a splendid stop, note that its hours are abbreviated, especially on the weekend. Open Tuesday and Thursday, 9:30–11:00 A.M. and 2:00–3:30 P.M.; Saturday, 9:30–11:00 A.M. Free.

Vachel Lindsay Home, 603 South Fifth Street; (217) 524–0901. This home gets overshadowed by the magnificence of the Dana-Thomas House, but if you love house tours, you'll enjoy viewing its original fixtures, furnishings, and artwork, as well as writings of this poet, known as the "Prairie Troubadour." Call ahead for hours.

Lincoln Memorial Garden & Nature Center, 2301 East Lake Drive; (217) 529–1111. Lush gardens designed by Jens Jensen, America's leading landscape architect in the early twentieth century. Five miles of trails, blanketed with wildflowers, which give their peak performance in late April and May. In winter try the cross-country skiing. The nature center will be of interest to the little ones. Open Tuesday through Saturday, 10:00 A.M.–4:00 P.M.; Sunday, 1:00–4:00 P.M. Free. The garden is open daily from sunrise to sunset.

Washington Park Botanical Gardens, Springfield; (217) 753–6228. For serious gardeners, Washington Park features a domed conservatory, formal rose garden, and seasonal floral shows. Open Monday through Friday, noon–4:00 P.M.; Saturday–Sunday, noon–5:00 P.M. Free.

Henson Robinson Zoo, 1100 East Lake Drive; (217) 753–6217. This fourteen-acre zoo, which includes a nifty reptile house and nocturnal animal building, is a good place to visit when the kids have endured just about all the educational stuff they can stand. Open late March to mid-October; Monday through Friday, 10:00 A.M.–5:00 P.M.; Saturday and Sunday, 10:00 A.M.–6:00 P.M.; some summer evenings until 8:00 P.M.

Antiques. Springfield has a lot to offer the antiquer, and prices aren't inflated, either. Try the Antique Mall, 3031 Reilly Drive; (217) 522–3031. Sixty dealers, with an impressive selection of estate jewelry. Open 10:00 A.M.–5:30 P.M. daily.

Golf. Springfield has nine public courses. Reservations accepted but not required. Call the Springfield Convention and Visitors Bureau.

Knight's Action Park, Bypass 36 and Chatham Road; (217) 546–8881. Includes eighteen-hole miniature golf courses, driving range, batting cages, gameroom, river ride, and waterslide. Call for hours.

SPECIAL EVENTS

Mid-February to early March. Maple Syrup Time, Lincoln Memorial Gardens & Nature Center. Get some pancakes ready as you watch the process from sap to syrup. Weekends only.

Mid-August. Illinois State Fair (Sixth to Ninth Streets and Sangamon Avenue). A good excuse to pig out on corn dogs and cotton candy. (During the fair hotel accommodations can be tough, so plan accordingly.) For fair information, write Box 576, Springfield, IL 62705.

OTHER RECOMMENDED RESTAURANTS AND LODGINGS

Springfield

Cafe Brio, 524 East Monroe; (217) 544–0574. Choose from a variety of Mexican and Carribean dishes. Also popular for its eclectic Sunday brunch. Moderate.

Sebastian's Hideout, 221 South Fifth Street; (217) 789–8988. Known for its delicious homemade soups, but its steak, salmon, pork, and pasta are also favorites. Come for the food and stay for the jazz bar downstairs.

Hampton Inn of Springfield, 3185 South Dirksen Parkway; (217) 529–1100. Heated indoor pool, whirlpool. Rates: $62 to $67 per night.

Hilton, 700 East Adams Street; (217) 789–1530. Recently renovated, the Hilton offers indoor pool, sauna, and all the other extras you'd expect from this upscale chain. Weekend rates. Like the Renaissance, the Hilton is within walking distance of all the major sights. Rates: $78 to $185 per night.

Holiday Inn East Conference Center, 3100 South Dirksen Parkway; (217) 529–7171. Two heated pools, sauna, whirlpool, putting green, playground. Rates start at $78 per night.

FOR MORE INFORMATION

Springfield Convention and Visitors Bureau, 109 North Seventh Street, Springfield, IL 62701; (217) 789–2360 or (800) 545–7300.

Galena

A TRIP BACK IN TIME

2 NIGHTS

Antiques • Architecture • Historical sites • Museums
House tours • Golfing • Horseback riding • Shopping
Downhill skiing • Cross-country skiing
Riverboat gambling • Hiking • Camping

When you tire of all the high-tech gadgetry and helter-skelter of this century, pack a bag for Galena and take a trip back in time. Cradled in the rolling countryside and wooded hills of Illinois' great northwest lies a land of quintessential quaintness. A real-life nineteenth-century Brigadoon, Galena is a haven for the historic-minded, with 85 percent of its buildings listed on the National Register of Historic Places.

During the mid–1800s the town was the largest Mississippi River port north of St. Louis and a thriving capital of commerce. This was the site of America's first mining rush, an 1820s boom town in search of lead (or *galena,* the ore's name in Latin). As Galena's star rose, its wealth was transformed into elegant mansion's and other architecturally distinct buildings. Today virtually every street boasts fine period examples (many beautifully preserved), ranging from Federal, Greek Revival, and Italianate styles to Queen Anne, Second Empire, and Gothic Revival (to name a few).

Galena was also the hometown of President Ulysses S. Grant. Oddly enough, it was at about the time Grant and his family arrived here (shortly before the Civil War broke out) that the seeds of Galena's demise were sown. Among the contributing factors was the decision to relocate the Illinois Cen-

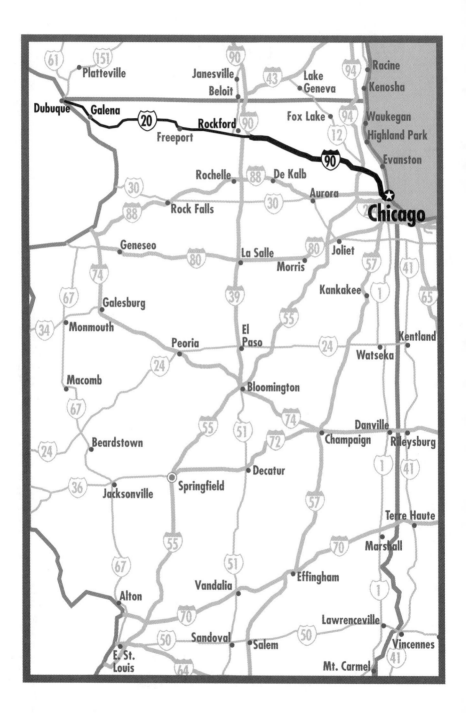

tral Railroad terminal to neighboring Dubuque, Iowa, which has charms of its own and the makings of a nice detour if you have the time.

Ironically, it was the town's slumber that renewed its prominence. After Chicago and Springfield, Galena, population less than 4,000, is considered the third most popular destination in Illinois.

Keep in mind that reservations are a must in Galena; be sure to contact restaurants and bed and breakfasts well in advance. The Convention and Visitors Bureau staff monitors weekend and holiday availabilities; call (800) 747–9377. Parking can be troublesome, too, so plan on doing a lot of walking, and bring a comfortable pair of shoes. Casual attire is appropriate; don't worry about dressing up. And although there is much to be enjoyed by young and old alike, Galena is primarily a getaway for adults with a hankering to experience a little history.

DAY 1

Morning

The drive to Galena, roughly three hours, is picturesque, especially as you approach Jo Daviess (pronounced day-veez) County in the state's far northwest corner, where Galena is situated. Lovely farm vistas stretch for miles, and the panorama, particularly in autumn, is invigorating.

Head west out of Chicago on I–90 until you get to U.S. Highway 20. (Business 20 will take you into downtown Rockford, Illinois—So Beware.) Take U.S. Highway 20 into Galena.

LUNCH: As you enter town (off U.S. Highway 20) heading north on Main Street, you'll find **Grant's Place** (515 South Main Street; 815–777–3331). This adorable pub is just upstairs from the Galena Cellars Winery (both are housed in a restored 1840s granary). Hamburgers and big sandwiches are specialties of the house, as are the servers, the real novelty here. The costumed crew are dressed as Civil War soldiers, complete with Union blues and forage caps.

Note: If you opt to tour the winery, plan on spending forty-five minutes at **Galena Cellars** (4746 North Ford Road; 815–777–3330). You'll learn via video how the family-run winery presses, ferments, and ages its wines. Tasting is also part of the tour, but you'll have to savor your sample. The guides teach you how to extract three different tastes from a single serving. Tours of the Galena Cellars Vineyard are also available. Friday, Saturday, and Sunday for $2.50 per person. Tours are one hour long and begin at 2:30 P.M.

Galena is a town still very much rooted in the nineteenth century.

Afternoon

Exploring Galena is hardly an activity you'll accomplish in a single afternoon. And while there are touring services that will take you past the historic sites by trolley or bus, you may want to rely on your own resources and set off on foot.

Begin your introduction to the town at the **Galena/Jo Daviess County Historical Society and Museum** (211 South Bench Street; 815–777–9129). Along with the lead-mining, steamboating, and Civil War exhibits housed in this nineteenth-century mansion is a concise slide presentation that will give you a fairly good overview of Galena's history. The museum also offers self-guided walking tours that take roughly forty-five minutes to complete. Open daily, 9:00 A.M.–4:30 P.M.; closed on major holidays. Admission: adults, $3.50; students 10–18, $2.50; children under 10, free.

Next walk across the Galena River (over the footbridge) to the **Galena/Jo Daviess County Convention and Visitors Bureau,** a train depot built in 1857 (101 Bouthillier Street; 800–747–9377). This is the same station from which Colonel U.S. Grant first departed on his way to war. Today you can sit on one of the long wooden benches and watch the freight trains go by. You'll also be able to stock up on maps, brochures, and plenty of pamphlets. Admission is free. Note: If you're having trouble finding parking, this is a good place to leave your car. The visitors center has an ample lot with no time restrictions.

At this point, check out the **Ulysses S. Grant Home,** which is just a short walk up the street. The house is located on a hill at 500 Bouthillier Street (815–777–3310 or 815–777–0248). Certainly not the largest or grandest home in Galena, this two-story Italianate brick house was a gift presented to Grant upon his heroic return from the Civil War in 1865. Although Grant actually spent little time in the home (he was elected to the presidency in 1868 and returned only briefly to Galena in 1879), it contains many of the family's possessions. Additionally, most of the home's original furnishings are still intact. Open daily, 9:00 A.M.–4:45 P.M.; closed major holidays. Donations are strongly suggested: adults, $2.00; children, $1.00.

Retrace your steps down Bouthillier Street, turn north on Park Avenue, and venture into **Grant Park** for a leisurely stroll. Straddled alongside the Galena River, the park provides an excellent vantage point from which to view the town. The park's highlights are a statue of its namesake, a Civil War monument, and a charming gazebo where you'll be tempted to linger.

Try to visit the **Old Market House State Historic Site** (423 North Commerce Street; 815–777–2570 or 815–777–3310). Built in 1845, this is one of the oldest remaining market houses in the Midwest. During Galena's most prosperous years, it was the hub of the town's community life. Fully restored, the building houses seasonal exhibits. Also housed here is the **Old General Store Museum,** a replica of a nineteenth-century general store with authentic artifacts. Open daily 9:00 A.M.–noon, 1:00–5:00 P.M.; closed major holidays. Donations are requested: adults, $2.00; children, $1.00. Allow a minimum of thirty minutes.

DINNER: Cafe Italia (301 North Main Street; 815–777–0033). As the name suggests, Italian cuisine is the specialty here, with an accent on seafood (great baked clams). A noteworthy side dish is the Sicilian grilled tomatoes. Open daily for lunch and dinner, May through October. If you have a hankering for something spicier, in the rear of Cafe Italia is the **Twisted Taco Cafe,** which serves authentic Mexican fare (dinner only). Reservations recommended at both restaurants. Moderate.

LODGING: The **DeSoto House Hotel** (230 South Main Street; 800–343–6562) is a Galena landmark. Recently renovated (at a cost of $8 million), the DeSoto was considered the largest hotel west of New York when it opened in the mid-1850s. Such notables as Abraham Lincoln (who once spoke from its balcony), Mark Twain, Susan B. Anthony, and Galena's most famous citizen, Ulysses S. Grant, were all guests here. The hotel features an elegant Victorian lobby, and rooms are decorated to reflect the period. Furthermore, its location is convenient, right in the heart of Galena's historic district. Parking (which is at a premium in downtown Galena) is also included. Rates: $89 (single) to $199 (two-room suite).

DAY 2

Morning

BREAKFAST: **Emmy Lou's Cafe** (200 North Main Street; 815–777–4752). Serves homemade breakfast specials such as gigantic pancakes and American fries. Sit on bar stools at the counter or mingle with the locals at the corner tables. Stop in any morning and you'll find the townfolk congregating over coffee to debate the day's news.

Needless to say, it's an excellent way to find out what to see and do in Galena. All the meals are good values for your money (that includes lunch, too). Hours are 5:30 A.M.–4:00 P.M.

Shopping is the first order of the day. Main Street, with its fancy storefronts and concentration of specialty stores, is a slice of heaven for the romantic at heart. Among the stores in its 6-block span are **The Store Next Door** (113 South Main Street), filled with lace curtains, china, and an assortment of memorabilia; **Lloyd George** (116 South Main Street), an emporium of American and European antiques and collectibles; **Follies** (205 South Main Street), an eclectic blend of contemporary fine crafts, imaginative giftware, and dazzling Christmas decor; **Churchill and Burns LTD** (301 South Main Street), a cigar aficionado's dream and an exceptional gift shop; **Galena River Wine and Cheese** (420 South Main Street), with an extensive collection of domestic and imported wines, beers, and cheeses, plus a Galena River gourmet line of specialty foods; the **Palette and Chisel Gallery** (421 South Main Street), a great spot for fine-art originals; and **Urban Gardener's Countryside** (110 South Main Street), selected by *Garden Design* magazine as one of the best garden shops in America.

Just a word or two about shopping in Galena: Don't expect to find any great bargains. Merchandise isn't overly inflated, but remember that this is a well-touristed area. Also, although we've devoted only a morning to this endeavor, you can easily fill an entire day perusing the place. And lastly, with more than one hundred shops on Galena's historic Main Street, you'll find enough to keep you busy. Some of the shops sell chic clothing, and there are a number of gift boutiques and art galleries. If all else fails, you can always treat yourself to some delicious homemade ice cream at **The American Old-Fashioned Ice Cream Parlor** (102 North Main Street).

LUNCH: **Jakel's Galena Backerei and Cafe** (200 South Main Street; 815–777–0400). This German bakery is the place to go for sandwiches on European breads. House specialties are cinnamon rolls, strudel, and cheesecake. It's worth remembering for continental breakfast or casual lunch (stews are served in a bread bowl).

Afternoon

The golf course is an excellent place to be for the balance of the afternoon. The **Eagle Ridge Inn & Resort** (Highway 20 East; 800–892–2269 or 815–777–2444) has four spectacular courses—all designed by Roger Packard and Andy North. The three eighteen-hole courses rank among *Golf Digest's* top resort courses in the U.S.A.

Tee time preferences are given to the inn's guests, but if you make a reservation seven days in advance, you won't have any problems on the weekends. Weekday tee times are easier to obtain. Greens fees range from $55 to $145 (including cart) depending on day, season, and course. Eagle Ridge does offer some "stay and play" packages, so check these out if you're interested.

This isn't a course where you'll be able to hit a quick round. Golfers of all skill levels are attracted to Eagle Ridge, so expect slow play, averaging five hours for the eighteen-hole courses.

DINNER: The **Eldorado Grill's** (219 North Main Street; 815–777–1224) imaginative Southwestern menu outshines most of the other local fare. Those with a discerning palate will taste and relish the difference. Homemade salsa, margaritas made from scratch, and delicious appetizers such as grilled wild mushroom quesadillas seasoned with red wine are early indications that your meal will be far from ordinary. Estofada, a spicy vegetable beef tenderloin stew made with four different types of chilies, and fresh trout in a lemon-almond sauce are among the most favored entrees and range in price from $10.95 to $19.95. Vegetarian dishes are also popular, especially the cassoulita, a hearty casserole of corn, white beans, a myriad of other vegetables, and white cheese in a delectable sauce. For dessert, try the Eldorado chocolate torte, a flourless chocolate cake, or the apple galleta, a razor-thin apple tart made of toasted tortilla served with goat's milk. Don't forget to make a reservation. At this restaurant, it's an absolute must! On weekends, dinner is served between 5:00 and 10:00 P.M. Moderate to expensive.

LODGING: The DeSoto House Hotel.

DAY 3

Morning

BREAKFAST: The Courtyard, located in a sunny plant-filled atrium in the center of the DeSoto House Hotel, is an inviting place to start the day. The charm factor here is multiplied by a number of quaint little shops that peer down from a balcony above. On Sundays a breakfast buffet is served between 8:00 A.M. and noon (adults $6.95; children $4.95), with most of the basics: scrambled eggs, bacon, sausage, hash browns, biscuits and gravy, sweet rolls, and a fresh fruit bowl. Coffee is included, but juice isn't. If you prefer something a little out of the ordinary, the menu has a few standouts, including the raspberry and chocolate chip pancakes (a little on the sweet side, $5.50); the Farmer's Skillet, made with home-style potatoes (diced potatoes with green peppers and onions), bacon, ham, and eggs and topped with melted cheddar cheese ($6.25); and a home-style breakfast full of favorite choices ($5.50).

After breakfast walk north to the far end of Main Street until you reach Diagonal Street. There you'll find the **Dowling House** (220 Diagonal Street; 815–777–1250). Once a trading post, this is the oldest stone house in Galena. A vernacular-style home, the house was built in 1826 and has been restored with period furnishings. Allow a half hour to tour. The Dowling House is open daily, 10:00 A.M.–3:30 P.M., Memorial Day through December; 10:00 A.M.–4:00 P.M. on weekends, January through Memorial Day. Admission is $3.50 for adults, $1.75 for children ages 12–18.

Much more elaborate than the Dowling House, the **Belvedere Mansion and Gardens** (1008 Park Avenue; 815–777–0747) has also been completely restored. Built in 1857 for steamboat magnate J. Russell Jones (an ambassador to Belgium), this twenty-two-room Italianate mansion is Galena's largest. The Belvedere is elegantly furnished with Victorian pieces, items from Liberace's estate, and the famous green drapes from the film *Gone with the Wind*. Allow a half hour to tour. Admission is $3.50 for adults, $2.00 for children. A combination ticket with the Dowling House is available for $6.00. Open 11:00 A.M. to 4:00 P.M., Sunday through Friday; 11:00 A.M.–5:00 P.M. Saturday; Memorial Day through October.

The final destination before returning to Chicago is the **Vinegar Hill Historic Lead Mine and Museum** (8885 North Three Pines Road; 815–777–0855). You'll need to drive 6 miles north, taking U.S. Highway 20 to Highway 84. The mine is typical of those operating during the early 1800s. The tour lasts a half hour, with the first portion aboveground in a museum where you can check out ore samples and mining tools and hear about various lighting techniques. The remaining time is spent underground taking a guided walk. This is a good way to end your trip since it illustrates so much of what you will have seen at the museums. Open daily June through August, 9:00 A.M.–5:00 P.M.; weekends in May, September, and October, 9:00 A.M.–5:00 P.M. Adults, $5.00; students first grade through high school, $2.50; children under 5, free.

LUNCH: Woodlands Restaurant (at the Eagle Ridge Inn & Resort, Highway 20 East; 815–777–2444). Take Highway 20 east 7 miles from downtown Galena. Located inside the resort's newly renovated main lodge, the Woodlands Restaurant offers diners a spectacular view of Lake Galena. Deli sandwiches and hamburgers as well as more creative entrees like shrimp stir-fry and aged steaks are the fare. Hours: Sunday through Thursday, 7:00 A.M.–10:00 P.M.; Friday and Saturday, 7:00 A.M.–11:00 P.M. (open later during the summer months). Lunch menu items average $10. Before heading home, stop next door at **Scoops,** Eagle Ridge's ice cream parlor (also located off the lobby), and treat yourself to a generously dipped waffle cone. If you're looking for a more relaxed atmosphere, check out **Spike's Bar and Grill** (in the General Clubhouse). Choose from traditional sandwiches and savory combinations; steaks, barbecue, and fresh fish spice up the menu. Seasonal hours.

Afternoon

Return to Chicago, taking U.S. Highway 20 east to I–90.

THERE'S MORE

Horseback riding. The Shenandoah Riding Center, Highway 20 East; (815) 777–2373. Part of the Eagle Ridge Inn & Resort, the center offers trail rides, lessons, hayrides, and sleigh rides. Open daily, weather permitting.

Downhill skiing. Chestnut Mountain Resort, 8700 West Chestnut Road; (800) 397–7320 or (815) 777–1320. Overlooking the Mississippi River 8 miles south of Galena, this ski resort has seventeen runs and a seven-acre terrain park with a vertical drop of 475 feet. Open 9:00 A.M.–10:00 P.M. daily, Thanksgiving through St. Patrick's Day.

Cross-country skiing. Eagle Ridge Inn & Resort, Highway 20 East; (800) 892–2269 or (815) 777–2444. Sixty-one kilometers of groomed trails winding through woods and around a lake. There's a snack bar where you can warm up with a hot drink. Open November through March.

Ice skating and sledding. Eagle Ridge Inn & Resort, Highway 20 East; (800) 892–2269 or (815) 777–2444. Open November through March.

Alpine Slide. Chestnut Mountain Resort, 8700 West Chestnut Road; (800) 397–1320 or (815) 777–1320. Toboggan-like track carries wheeled sleds 2,500 feet from a bluff down to the Mississippi. Open daily Memorial Day through Labor Day.

Riverboat gambling and sightseeing cruises. If gambling is your aim, head across the river to the *Dubuque Diamond Jo Casino* (20 miles west across the Mississippi River at Third Street and Ice Harbor; 800–LUCKY–JO), a restored 1864 steamboat. This vessel, which holds 667 passengers, departs only once per day at 7:30 A.M., Monday through Friday. (Boarding is free for the boat's two-hour gambling cruises.) More traditional, family-oriented sightseeing trips are offered by the *Spirit of Dubuque*, which also leaves from downtown Dubuque (Third Street and Ice Harbor; 319–583–8093 or 800–747–8093). A smaller riverboat (holding 377 passengers), this replica of a turn-of-the-century stern-wheeler has two decks that are perfect for exploring. Cruises last an hour and a half. Longer dinner and brunch excursions are also available.

Hiking. Eagle Ridge Inn & Resort (U.S. Highway 20 East; 800–892–2269 or 815–777–2444) and Apple River Canyon State Park (between U.S. Highway 20 and Stagecoach Trail on Canyon Park Road; 815–745–3302).

Camping. Area campsites in Galena include Palace Campground (U.S. Highway 20 West; 815–777–2466); and near Apple River, Apple River Canyon State Park (8763 East Canyon Road; 815–745–3302).

SPECIAL EVENTS

For detailed Calendar information, visit the Convention & Visitors Bureau Web site at www.galena.org.

January. Klondike Kapers. Slalom races, freestyle skiing, snow sculptures, fireworks, a torchlight parade, and skydivers. Chestnut Mountain Resort, 8700 West Chestnut Road, Galena.

March. Irish Heritage Festival. A variety of cultural events celebrating Galena's Irish heritage, culminating in a small-town family parade. Held in downtown Galena.

Mid-May–late fall. Farmer's Markets. Held on Saturdays from 7:30 A.M. to 10:00 A.M. at the Old Market House Square, Galena.

June. Annual Tour of Historic Homes. Guided tours of privately owned nineteenth-century homes in Galena.

June. Stagecoach Trail Festival. A celebration of Native American and pioneer history of a 30-mile stretch of the original stage route between Chicago and Galena.

June. Skills from the Hills. Turn-of-the-century open-air market with farmers' shacks and stands offering produce, flowers, crafts, breads, and pastries served by women in period costume. Held on the brick plaza surrounding the Old Market House State Historic Site.

July. Galena Arts Festival. Fine arts and crafts with continuous music, theater, storytelling, dance, a children's creative corner, and gustatory delights. Held in Grant City Park.

August. Willow Folk Festival. More than one hundred folksingers and musicians from throughout the Midwest perform from a hay wagon outside a country church, Stockton.

August. Civil War Encampment. Men and women in period dress re-create a typical campsite of the Civil War era. Held at Eagle Ridge Inn & Resort.

September. Historical Society's Ice Cream Social. Continuous band music, homemade pies, cakes, desserts, ice cream, and frozen yogurt. Held at Galena Middle School.

September. Dedicated to the pastimes and celebrations of women; entertainment, lectures, classes, teas, shopping, and prizes. In downtown Galena.

September. Annual Fall Tour of Homes. Guided tours of privately owned nineteenth-century homes in Galena.

September. Mallardfest. Duck and prime rib dinner, parade, fun runs, live music, food booths, adopt-a-duck program, duck-calling contest, beer garden, arts-and-crafts fair, Ducks Unlimited auction. Held in Hanover.

October. Galena Country Fair. Old-fashioned harvest festival with arts and crafts, food, games, continuous music, silent auction, face-painting, balloon release, and Galena generals and wives in period costume. Held in Grant City Park.

November. Nouveau Wine Release. Fall vintage is released with great festivity; horse-drawn wagon delivers first bottles to Main Street merchants and restaurants; limited poster signing. Held at Galena Cellars Winery.

November. Country Christmas. Artists and artisans demonstrate traditional skills in shops throughout Galena's Main Street historic district; includes themed weekend events and the magical Luminaria Extravaganza Evening. Continues through December.

OTHER RECOMMENDED RESTAURANTS AND LODGINGS

Galena

Aldrich Guest House, 900 Third Street; (815) 777–3323. An 1845 Greek Revival mansion with five guest rooms. The decor is a mix of antiques and reproductions. The innkeeper personally serves breakfast to guests individually. Not suggested for young children. Rates range from $86 to $160 per night; two-night weekend minimum.

Fried Green Tomatoes, 1301 North Irish Hollow Road; (815) 777–3938. Upscale country Italian in a historic brick farmstead. This new addition to Galena's dining scene is also highly praised for its Black Angus steaks, chops, and extensive wine list. Entertainment in piano bar on Saturday nights. Moderate.

John Henry Guest House, 812 South Bench Street; (812) 777–3595. 1996 National Trust Award–Winning turn-of-the-century four-square brick home with two guest suites, each with private bath, bedroom, and sitting room, with a view of the Galena River. Full breakfast. Just 3 blocks from downtown.

Chestnut Mountain Resort, 8700 West Chestnut Road; (800) 397–1320. A full-service, 119-unit resort located 8 miles southeast of Galena on a bluff overlooking the Mississippi River. Children are welcome. Special packages are available. Rates: $89 to $135 per night.

Eagle Ridge Inn & Resort, U.S. Highway 20 East; (800) 892–2269 or (815) 777–2444. A full-service resort complex on 6,800 wooded acres. Excellent golf facilities. Eagle Ridge was rebuilt and expanded after its original lodge went up in flames in January 1992 (only the indoor pool survived). Aside from 80 inn rooms, there are 325 condos, townhomes, and resort dwellings, with fireplaces and/or whirlpools, depending on the units. Children are welcome. Ask about special package deals. Peak season rates range between $195 and $255 per night for the inn rooms.

Hellman Guest House, 318 Hill Street; (815) 777–3638. A Queen Anne brick mansion built in 1898 with stained glass windows, fine oak paneling, a turret, and a wraparound front porch that offers spectacular views of Galena and the surrounding countryside. The guest rooms are Victorian in decor. Breakfast is included. Not suggested for young children. Rates: $119 to $159 per night, including a full breakfast; two-night weekend and holiday minimums.

Log Cabin Guest House, 11661 West Chetlain Lane; (815) 777–2845. Six country cabins located about 2 miles from downtown Galena. Five of the guest houses are early log cabins that were disassembled and rebuilt on the premises. The sixth is a former servant's quarters above a garage. The log cabins have double whirlpools and wood-burning fireplaces. Other modern touches such as microwave ovens, small refrigerators, and coffee makers have also been added. Rates: $175 to $225 per night.

Market House Tavern, 204 Perry Street; (815) 777–0690. Another good place for lunch. Try the Crab Louis or the Tavernburger. Open 11:00 A.M.–9:00 P.M. Moderate.

Vinny Vanucchi's "Little Italy," 201 South Main Street; (815) 777–8100. This popular family restaurant offers three levels of dining, plus an outdoor cappuccino garden. Imported artifacts will make you feel right at home in the "old neighborhood." Moderate.

Dubuque

Hancock House, 1105 Grove Terrace; (319) 557–8989. More than an ordinary antique-adorned Victorian B&B. With nine guest rooms, the house overlooks the bluff all the way to the river valley. The owner tries to make "fun breakfasts that you couldn't eat at home or in a restaurant" like apple-raisin walnut crepes and caramel French toast. Rates: $95 to $150.

Mario's, 1298 Main Street; (319) 582–0904. Serves up traditional Italian cuisine with flair in a comfy atmosphere. Diners' favorite is Mario's panzerotti, a pizza folded in half, deep-fried with the sauce on top. Indulge in entrees from hearty steaks and elegant shrimp to shells Florentine and fettucine a la lumberjack. Prices range from $7.50 to $17.50. It is not uncommon here to find customers who come for lunch and return for dinner. Reservations recommended.

Restone Inn, 504 Bluff Street; (319) 582–1894. This bed and breakfast's selling point is its location in the center of town. Guests can walk to downtown shops, trolley rides, and the waterfront. The breakfast highlight is an assortment of flavorful homemade breads. Rates: $75 to $175.

East Dubuque

Timmerman's Supper Club, 7777 Timmerman Drive; (815) 747–3316. If you're looking for a hearty meal before you park yourself at the blackjack table, this supper club (a fifteen-minute drive west on Highway 20; near the Silver Eagle) is a sure bet. The blufftop view overlooking the Mississippi River Valley is stunning, and the steaks are more than tasty. Rib eyes are the house specialty. Dinners range from $9.00 to $23.00. A buffet brunch ($7.95) is served on Sunday between 10:00 A.M. and 2:00 P.M. The restaurant is part of Timmerman's Lodge, a comfortable complex with seventy-four rooms.

Rockford

Paragon, 205 West State Street; (815) 963–1660. A lively and contemporary place just west of the Rock River. There's live jazz several days a week and a menu highlighted by smoked scallops and crab-salmon cakes. Moderate.

FOR MORE INFORMATION

Galena/Jo Daviess County Convention & Visitors Bureau, 101 Bouthillier Street, Galena, IL 61036; (800) 747–9377; www.galena.org.

Dubuque Chamber of Commerce/Convention and Visitors Bureau, 770 Town Clock Plaza, P.O. Box 705, Dubuque, IA 52004; (319) 557–9200; www.dubuquechamber.com.

Downtown Chicago
IN YOUR OWN BACKYARD

1 NIGHT

Architecture • *Museums* • *Boat rides* • *Zoo* • *Aquarium*

Sometimes, the best places are close to home. Chicago attracts tourists from all over the world. It would be silly not to take advantage of the wealth of attractions it has to offer—and without the ride.

In a city as large and diverse as Chicago, coming up with a single weekend is an exercise in decision making. Do you go for one big attraction (Great America), take in an ethnic festival, attend a professional sports event, or just soothe yourself with retail therapy? There are entire guidebooks devoted to Chicago, so it would be futile to try to duplicate their efforts.

Instead, here are two variations on the in-town getaway. The first is planned with families in mind; the second is more adult-oriented. (Of course, places like The Berghoff are perfectly appropriate for children; that isn't the problem. It's more like whether the Hard Rock Cafe is appropriate for adults—or at least adults who value their hearing.)

You'll find that these itineraries will also come in handy when you're playing tour guide for out-of-towners.

Since restaurants change owners as frequently as the Cubs change managers, we've tried to stay away from the overly trendy. Even so, recommendations can be obsolete before any book even rolls off the press. (Martial arts master Steven Seagal may hold the record here, with his ill-fated River North venture closing a mere week after it opened.) At any rate, do what Ma Bell tells us and phone first.

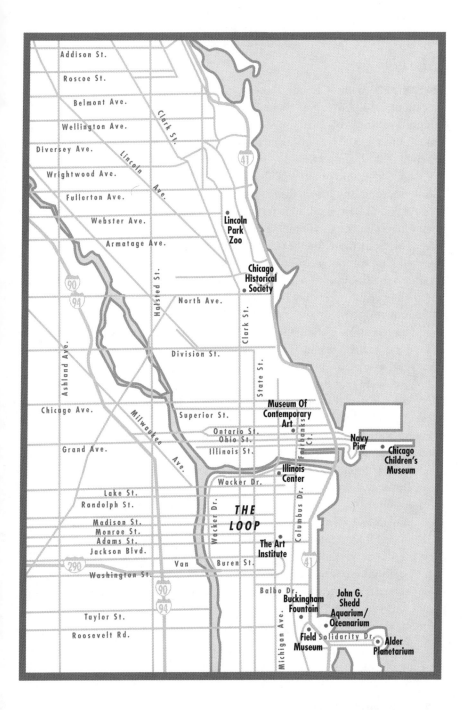

FAMILY DAY 1

Morning

BREAKFAST: At the **Corner Bakery** (63 Grand Avenue and five other Loop locations; 312–257–1956) there are enough breakfast options that the kids might even tell you that you're right (but don't hold your breath). With so much great bread, it is no surprise that this would be the source for a baked French toast that is sublime. So is the Southwest casserole, a spicy combination of eggs, chilies, and potatoes. There are also dozens of muffins to choose from, so if everyone isn't happy, they're just not trying. Inexpensive.

After breakfast, head over to **Navy Pier** (312–595–7437 or on the Web at www.navypier.com), where you can easily spend an entire day. Every inch of the pier, from the entrance at 600 East Grand Avenue to Lake Michigan, is packed with fun things to do. Here a lively fountain sends jets of water bursting into the sky. Just beyond, a carousel and a 150-foot Ferris wheel (modeled after the version from the 1893 World's Fair) offer a spectacular view of the lakefront.

The next stop is the **Chicago Children's Museum,** located in the new Navy Pier at the east end of Grand Avenue. This is a delightful place for kids— pretty amazing for adults, too.

It's the rare spot that can occupy a 2-year-old and a 10-year-old. Older kids love the water-play area, the fantasy vehicles (including a very popular ambulance), and the climbing apparatus. The art room (lower level) is staffed with terrific instructors and provides yet another opportunity for fun skillfully intertwined with education (but don't tell the kids). There are plenty of benches for mom and dad to take a breather. Open Tuesday, Wednesday, Friday, Saturday, Sunday 10:00 A.M.–5:00 P.M.; Thursday, 10:00 A.M.–6:00 P.M. Admission: $6.50; children under 1 year are free. Call (312) 527–1000.

Also in the Family Pavilion is the **IMAX Theater** (312–595–0090 or 312–444–FILM), featuring the almost-surround film experience with movies on the six-story-tall screen. Ticket prices vary with attractions.

The **Shakespeare Theater** and the **Skyline Stage Theater** offer excellent entertainment year-round. There are some matinees for families, but basically this is an evening out for parents. Call the general Navy Pier phone line for schedule of events and ticket prices.

LUNCH: There are the usual food court options at Navy Pier (and a futuristic McDonald's, if the kids wear you down). Three better choices would be **Charlie's Ale House,** where you can get some better-than-average pub food; **Joe's Be-Bop Cafe,** which has some fine barbecued ribs and a Memphis-style pulled-pork sandwich on the menu, and the popular **Bubba Gump Shrimp Co.,** featuring . . . shrimp and fish. Moderate.

Or, if it's too nice to be indoors, head over to the **Wacky Pirate Cruise,** a one-hour trip led by "Buccaneer Bob." The complimentary pirate hats and kazoos are always a big hit. Board at the Mercury Dock, at the southwest corner of the Michigan Avenue bridge, on any Friday, Saturday, or Sunday between July 1 and Labor Day. Call (312) 332–1368. Admission: $14.00 for adults; $7.00 for kids.

Afternoon

Another insider's tip: If you missed the Wacky Pirate Cruise, you can pick up a **Landmark Cruise** right at North Pier for a ninety-minute trip.

If you want to be a spectator to marine life, schedule a stop at the **Shedd Aquarium** (1200 South Lake Shore Drive; 312–939–2438), where you can still get that salt-and-sea feeling. If you're planning on seeing the Oceanarium, the home of beluga whales, dolphins, and penguins, remember to get your tickets in advance, and don't hype this to the kids as a Midwest version of Sea World. In truth, the emphasis is on education, not entertainment, and if they think they're going to see Flipper leaping through blazing hoops, they're going to be disappointed. If you didn't get Oceanarium tickets ahead of time, don't despair. The aquarium itself is still quite astounding. Open daily (closed Christmas and New Year's Day), 9:00 A.M.–6:00 P.M. Admission: adults, $11.00; kids 3 to 11 and senior citizens, $9.00. No charge for children under age 2. (For aquarium only, adult admission is $5.00; $4.00 for senior citizens.) To purchase Oceanarium tickets in advance, call Ticketmaster (312–559–0200). Monday is discount day, when tickets for the Oceanarium are available for $6.00; $5.00 for seniors and children 3–11 years old.

Your kids will love you for the rest of your life if you succumb to **Disney Quest** at the corner of Rush and Ohio Streets; (312) 222–1300. It's a five-story interactive theme park that combines Disney magic with cutting-edge game technology. There are retail stores and a **Cheesecake Factory**

Restaurant express for a quick refueling. (The wrap sandwiches are winners.) The $34 unlimited-play card is a bit pricey, but it'll last all day and is a much better deal than the $16 limited-play option, which runs out in about fifteen minutes. Hours 10:00 A.M. until midnight. This is a guaranteed winner.

In case you haven't had enough sensory overload, visit **ESPNZone,** a sports-theme restaurant/entertainment complex just a block from Disney Quest. Everything you need to know about this place can be summed up in one simple fact: there are TV sets in every bathroom stall.

DINNER: You will certainly be a hit if you are willing to queue up at the **Hard Rock Cafe** (63 West Ontario; 312–943–2252) or the **Rainforest Cafe** (605 North Clark; 312–787–1501). Actually, you'd have to be on another planet to not know that these places exist, but if the idea here is to be a visitor in your own city, these establishments are nothing if not touristy.

If you have more influence with your children than we have with ours (or yours are too young to have a vote), there are better places that will cater to a kid's palate without compromising yours, such as **Primavera** in the Fairmont Hotel (200 North Columbus; 312–565–6655), which also offers first-rate pasta. The children will be delighted by the singing costumed servers who will trill an aria at a moment's notice. Expensive.

After dinner, take your kids on a **carriage ride** on Michigan Avenue. Sure, it's meant to be romantic—but when that isn't possible, the next best thing is to go for fun, and a carriage ride fills the bill. The grand finale is a stop at **Buckingham Fountain,** the crown jewel of **Grant Park.** The color show is from 9:00 to 11:00 P.M. and runs from Memorial Day to October 1. Call (312) 294–4610.

LODGING: Fairmont Hotel, 200 North Columbus; (312) 565–8000. True, there are other, less expensive hotels that offer suites—a must for families—but for a little more you can stay at the Fairmont. Not only will you get a much larger suite and loads of luxury, you also will get the most sweeping views of any downtown hotel because the Fairmont sits closest to the lake. (Remember this for July fourth fireworks viewing.) Extras include access to the Athletic Club's, five floors of fitness, which includes a climbing wall that older kids will love. (Note that children are allowed in only on Sunday and there is an extra charge for use of the club.) The proximity to Navy Pier is also a big plus. Rates: $239 to $500 (for suites). Check the availability of package deals.

FAMILY DAY 2

Morning

BREAKFAST: Lou Mitchell's (563 West Jackson Boulevard; 312–939–3111) is a Chicago classic. Whether it's waffles (Belgian malted is the fave), omelets, or French toast, the portions are large, hot, and delicious.

Unlike humans, animals are friskier in the morning, so head over to **Lincoln Park Zoo** (2200 North Cannon Drive; 312–294–4660). Amazingly, the thirty-five-acre, 2,000-animal zoo still manages to open its doors totally free of charge. If you're at the park during the summer months, you can rent Rollerblades, bicycles, or a paddleboat at Cannon Drive.

LUNCH: If you're planning to stay in the Lincoln Park area, grab a quick sandwich at the beautifully restored **Cafe Brauer.** Or, if you are moving just a few blocks away to the Chicago Historical Society for the afternoon, eat first at the **Big Shoulders Cafe** (161 North Clark Street; 312–587–7766). The light, airy room, dominated by the original old Union Stock Yards arch, features sophisticated offerings (try the curried chicken salad) as well as usual kid stuff.

However, if Michigan Avenue is next on the agenda, travel south to one of the city's best-kept secrets: **The Signature Room** on the ninety-fifth floor of the John Hancock Center (875 North Michigan; 312–787–9596). The lunch buffet—a pleasing array of salads and pastas—is an inflation-busting $10.95, and the view is breathtaking from any direction. When you consider that admission to the observatory deck alone costs about $6.00, it's almost as if they're giving the food away. If you want something quick, hold off until you get to other spots on Michigan Avenue.

Afternoon

The **Chicago Historical Society,** at Clark Street and North Avenue, often gets overlooked in favor of larger, glitzier museums. But its small size and accessibility are precisely what make it a good choice for the afternoon, as energy levels wane. Kids can climb aboard Chicago's first locomotive or "experience" the Great Chicago Fire. Admission: adults, $5.00; seniors and teens, $3.00; children under 6, free. Monday is a free admission day. Open daily. Call (312) 642–4600.

Chicago's glittering skyline

If you've already moved on to Michigan Avenue, the pastime of choice is shopping—possible with kids only if you hit the stores that push their hot button, like **Niketown** (669 North Michigan; 312–642–6363) or **The American Girl Place** (111 East Chicago Avenue; 312–943–9400).

These are both retailing phenomena that have more to do with fun than shopping. Niketown is a shrine to sports and has the latest of everything, from baseball caps to sneakers.

The American Girl Place is the showcase store for the popular American Girl Dolls, clothing, and accessories. There's also a cafe that offers lunch and tea—and a theater that stages *The American Girl Revue.*

ADULT DAY 1

Morning

BREAKFAST: Continental breakfast, included in the tab, is served on board the **Chicago from the Lake Cruise,** sponsored by the Chicago Architecture

Foundation. This ninety-minute ride on the Chicago River highlights some of the glittering jewels of the city's skyline. From June through September 30, cruises depart at 10:00 A.M. and noon, Wednesday through Sunday; 10:00 A.M., noon, and 6:00 P.M. on Monday and Tuesday. Admission: $20.50 for adults; $18.50 for seniors and teens; reduced fares for children under ten. Call (312) 527–1977.

If you love architecture, but are a confirmed landlubber, sign up for one of two **walking tours of the Loop.** Have breakfast at Lou Mitchell's or the Corner Bakery (see Family itinerary) before the two-hour tour. Loop tours depart daily from the Chicago Architecture Foundation (224 South Michigan Avenue; 312–922–3432) at 10:00 A.M. and 1:30 P.M. The Architecture Foundation also has a tempting design shop and gallery, so leave yourself some browsing time when you return. Each tour costs $10.00; the cost of a combination of two tours is $15. For recorded schedule information on all tours, call the Foundation's general information number or visit its Web site at www.architecture.org.

LUNCH: The Berghoff, 17 West Adams; (312) 427–3170. How can you peruse Loop institutions and not stop at The Berghoff? Its modestly priced Chicago cuisine has been around since 1898 and continues to be one of the city's best values, even if the service gets sloppy at times. The weiner schnitzel, creamed spinach, and hearty rye bread, all washed down with The Berghoff's own private-label beer (or root beer), is the perfect meal. And do leave room for the strudel.

Afternoon

Walk off lunch by heading north toward **River North,** the heart of Chicago's art district. If you walk 4 blocks north on either Clark or Adams, you'll pass the **State of Illinois Center** at 100 West Randolph. This ultramodern glass-and-steel structure designed by Helmut Jahn is either a masterpiece or a travesty, depending on whom you talk to. Pop inside to visit the **State of Illinois Artisan Center,** which features quilts, carvings, textiles, and just about anything else made by the state's best artists.

At River North (Superior Street between Orleans and Franklin), you'll find dozens of galleries showcasing painting, sculpture, and the decorative arts. As you would expect, River North is the place to shop for that one-of-a-kind item or funky jewelry that you could never pick up at the mall. The people-watching is pretty good, too.

DINNER: How do you choose? The Near North Side is prime restaurant territory, with probably more fine dining per square mile than almost anywhere in the country, and it is virtually impossible to pick just one. Here are two very different favorites:

Kiki's Bistro, 900 North Franklin Avenue; (312) 335–5454. A wonderfully cozy atmosphere, with probably the best onion soup this side of the Left Bank. Steak and fries is also not to be missed, and the crème brûlée is a silky finale. The menu is authentic and the wine list is unpretentious, with prices to match.

Gibson's, 1028 North Rush Street; (312) 266–8999. When nothing but a steak and a dry martini will do, opt for Gibson's. The beef is prime and the portions must be seen to be believed. The sides are stellar: spicy onion rings and the most unbelievable double-baked potato in the city. Fish and seafood lovers are not overlooked, either. Expensive.

AFTER DINNER: The dance floor is rarely empty at **Yvette Wintergarden,** 311 South Wacker. In fact, diners get up and take a few spins between the soup and the salad—just as they did in the forties. Call (312) 408–1242.

Another option is **The Pump Room,** 1301 North State; (312) 266–0360. This place is so legendary that *it* is the show. Besides, you can spend an evening just perusing a half century of celebrity photos that line the wall, such as one of 11-year-old Liza Minelli, wearing lipstick for the first time, lunching with her mom, Judy Garland.

LODGING: Four Seasons Hotel, 900 North Michigan Avenue; (312) 280–8800. While Chicago has many world-class hotels, the Four Seasons is the only one with five-star and five-diamond rankings from the *Mobil Travel Guide* and AAA, respectively. The furnishings are beautiful, and the service is flawless. The health club is one of the most luxe in the city. And since it's tucked into Chicago's most upscale mall, you just have to ride the elevator to Bloomingdale's. (Surprisingly, the Four Seasons caters to a family clientele, too, albeit a wealthy one. There are plenty of kids' videos for the VCR in your room, and Fruit Loops are available for breakfast in bed.) Rates: $450 per night, but may vary early in the week depending on various travel discounts.

ADULT DAY 2

Morning

BREAKFAST: Have room service bring you up a tray stocked with flaky croissants and beautiful berries. If you are anxious to get out and about, you'll love the convivial Sunday morning atmosphere of the **Oak Tree** (312–751–1988), which is located in the adjoining 900 North Michigan mall. Everyone is weighed down by their Sunday papers and is doing the lox-bagel-omelet routine, although the eclectic menu goes way beyond the standard fare.

If you are on North Michigan Avenue and don't shop, you are probably without a pulse. It doesn't get any better than this. Marshall Field's, Bloomingdale's, Lord and Taylor, Neiman Marcus, and Saks Fifth Avenue are all no more than a couple of blocks from your hotel. (**Water Tower** is the oldest and best known of the Michigan Avenue malls.) Also, right out your door is **Oak Street** (between Michigan Avenue and State Street), where Gianni Versace, Sonia Rykiel, and Giorgio Armani are just a few of the names that put the "chic" in Chicago.

LUNCH: What to do about this meal depends on your time constraints. If you are at Water Tower and the idea is to eat quickly and get back to serious shopping, then Foodlife (on the mezzanine) is fine. The selection is far more cosmopolitan (and pricey) than the usual food court offerings; at peak hours, expect to fight for a table.

If you have time for a more civilized option and don't mind leaving Water Tower, consider **Bistro 110** (across the street at 110 East Pearson; 312–266–3110), where you can't go wrong with anything from the wood-burning oven. On Oak Street? Then walk a few blocks north to **Big Bowl Cafe** (on the corner of Rush and Cedar; 312–640–8888) for food that is both sensational and a terrific value. Don't miss the potstickers, barbecued chicken flatbread, or sesame chicken. Inexpensive to moderate.

If The Signature Room at the Hancock is the best deal (see Family Day 2), then the Mediterranean buffet at the **Seasons Lounge** (312–280–8800) is the second-best bargain and an unexpected one, considering it's at the high-end Four Seasons Hotel. The $13.50 spread includes two daily hot pastas, plus soup and salad and abundant baskets of fresh breads and seasonal fresh fruits.

Afternoon

There's not enough time to take on a mega-museum, so scale back with something magnificent, but manageable. The **Museum of Contemporary Art,** 220 East Chicago Avenue (312–280–2660; www.mcachicago.org), fills the bill quite nicely. The sculpture garden is especially nice for stealing some quiet moments. Admission: $7.00 ($5.00 for students and seniors). Members are free.

End the afternoon by doing something really special: Have a full British tea ($15). All the finest hotels serve one, but you'll find the scones at the **Drake,** Michigan at Lake Shore Drive (312–787–2200), the most delectable. Finger sandwiches, cakes, and pastries are also a part of the ritual.

THERE'S MORE

It is very difficult to sum up Chicago's cultural institutions without giving something short shrift. Also, there are numerous worthwhile destinations in the suburbs as well. Those apologies aside, here are seven that you don't want to miss:

Adler Planetarium, 1300 South Lake Shore Drive; (312) 922–STAR; www.adlerplanetarium.org. If it's been a while since you've been to the sky shows, you'll find many improvements, thanks to a major addition completed in 1999. A 77-foot escalator now carries visitors from the Universe Theater to the Sky Theater, and the fiber optics in between simulate a journey through the galaxies. Museum open 9:00 A.M.–5:00 P.M. Monday through Thursday; until 9:00 P.M. Friday; and until 6:00 P.M. Saturday and Sunday. Show times (June through Labor Day) are hourly between 11:00 A.M. and 4:00 P.M. Children under 6 are not admitted to the shows, but they have one of their own each Saturday and Sunday at 10:00 A.M. Admission: $5.00 for adults; $4.00 for seniors and teens; free for children under 6. Tuesdays free.

Art Institute of Chicago, Michigan Avenue at Adams Street; (312) 443–3600; www.artic.edu. You can easily spend a day at this museum, one of the world's finest, but if you're on a tight schedule, head for the French Impressionist paintings. And if the kids aren't impressed with Degas and Renoir, take them to the Thorne Miniature Rooms, which never fail to enchant. Admission: $8.00 ($5.00 for students and seniors). Tuesdays free. Open Monday, Tuesday, Wednesday, Friday, 10:30 A.M.–4:15 P.M.; Thursday until 8:00 P.M.; Saturday 10:00 A.M.–5:00 P.M.; Sunday noon–5:00 P.M.

Field Museum of Natural History, Roosevelt Road at Lake Shore Drive; (312) 922–9410; www.fmnh.org. The Field has made giant strides in recent years to transform itself from a dusty, traditional temple into a more hands-on type of place. The dinosaur skeletons and stuffed animals are always winners. Kids will love the sneakily educational play area on the second floor. On weekends there are family tours highlighting various exhibits. Admission: $7.00 for adults; $4.00 for seniors and teens; children free. Wednesdays free. Open 9:00 A.M.–5:00 P.M.

Michael Jordan statue. There's a new landmark in town, and this impressive statue of the legend draws crowds to the United Center, at 1901 West Madison Street, whether there is a Bulls game or not. The artists, Julie and Omri Rothhlatt-Amrany, have succeeded at making 2,000 pounds of bronze look airborne. Free.

Museum of Science and Industry, 57th Street and Lake Shore Drive; (773) 684–1414. Is there a kid who grew up in Chicago who doesn't have fond memories of the coal mine or the German submarine? While those old favorites are still there (the coal mine opened in 1933), The freshly remodeled and enhanced MSI is definitely poised for the twenty-first century. The Crown Space Center is a state-of-the-art approach to space exploration, with the Omnimax theater its crown jewel. If you have your heart set on whatever is being shown on the 76-foot domed screen, be sure to get your tickets in advance. A newly refurbished "Curiosity Place" for kids up to age 16 is a parent's dream, not only because it challenges the imagination but also because it offers such a comfortable place for grown-ups to sit and rest. Admission: $7.00 for adults; $3.50 for ages 3–11. A separate admission is charged for the Omnimax Theater. Thursdays free. Open 9:30 A.M.–4:00 P.M. Monday through Friday and until 5:30 P.M. on weekends. Parking is $5.00.

National Vietnam Veterans Art Museum, 1801 South Indiana Avenue (across the train tracks from the museum campus); 312–326–0270; www.nvvam.org. Home to many acclaimed works of art created exclusively by Vietnam veterans. Open 11:00 A.M.–6:00 P.M. Tuesday through Friday, 10:00 A.M.–5:00 P.M. Saturday, and noon–5:00 P.M. Sunday (when the Bears aren't at Soldier Field). Admission: $5.00, adults; $4.00, seniors, veterans, and children.

Peggy Notebaert Nature Museum, 2430 North Cannon Drive (773–755–5100 or www.chias.org), is the latest addition to Chicago's rich museum tradition. The 73,000-square-foot facility is part of the adjacent Chicago Academy of Science and makes learning frun with its innovative approach. (Any kids caught scampering through tunnels beneath prairie soil like ground squirrels will be highly praised.) Hours: 10:00 A.M.–5:00 P.M. daily; until 8:00 P.M. Wednesday. Admission: $6.00, adults; $4.00, seniors and students; $3.00, children under 17. Tuesday is free.

SPECIAL EVENTS

Where to start? There are more than forty ethnic festivals alone. Here's a selective look at some of the city's major events:

June. Gospel Fest. World's largest free gospel festival. Grant Park Petrillo Music Shell, Columbus Drive and Jackson Boulevard.

June. Blues Festival. National names and local favorites belt out the blues. Grant Park Petrillo Music Shell.

June–August. Grant Park concerts. Bring a blanket and listen to classical, pop, big band, and opera under the stars.

Late June–July 4. Taste of Chicago. Strap on the feed bag. More than eighty restaurants participate, and there's big-name entertainment, to boot. Grant Park.

July. Chicago Air and Water Show. Two days of daredevils in the air and in the water. On the lakefront.

August. Gold Coast Art Fair. The granddaddy of art fairs is spread out between Dearborn and Franklin Streets, along Huron and Ohio Streets.

September. Jazz Festival. National and local talent. Grant Park Petrillo Music Shell.

OTHER RECOMMENDED RESTAURANTS AND LODGINGS

Summing up Chicago's restaurant scene is next to impossible. Here are several restaurants that should fit almost any occasion.

Best choice when you've won the lottery:

Ambria, 2300 North Lincoln Park West; (312) 472–5959. Chef Gambino Satelino sets the standard of what a luxury restaurant should be. It's all like a dream, from the scallop appetizer with wild-mushroom stuffed cannoli to the airy soufflés.

Best choice when you want to look as if you've won the lottery, even though you have negative cash flow:

A tie between two places—Le Bouchon and Yoshi's—both of which will let you entertain guests like a Trump.

Le Bouchon, 1958 North Damen; (773) 862–6000, is a Bucktown storefront. It gets a little crowded and you should make reservations weeks in advance, but no one seems to mind when the bistro classics (French onion soup, steak fries, roast chicken) are this delectable and affordable.

Yoshi's, 3257 North Halsted; (773) 248–6160, overhauled its haute cuisine formula a few years ago and reinvented itself with contemporary dishes, from seafood terrine to baby lamb chops to decadent fruit tarts.

Best deli:

Manny's, 1141 South Jefferson Street; (312) 939–2857. So grab a tray and queue up for food like your bubbe would make: cabbage soup, brisket, prune tzimmis, potato pancakes. If there's a better corned beef sandwich served in Chicago, we haven't found it. Inexpensive.

Best place for seafood:

McCormick & Schmick's, 41 East Chestnut Street; (312) 397–9500. Sophisticated but not stuffy, M&S's could hold its own with any coastal restaurant. It serves great oysters, crab, and shrimp, as well as exotic specialities, such as Ecuador Stuffed Tilapia, New Zealand Blue Nose Sea Bass, and Hawaiin Moonfish Opah. Insider's tip: The "happy hour" is one of the best values in town. Expensive.

Best places to eat when you're visiting the Museum of Science and Industry:

Great museum, horrible food. Turn up your nose at the concessions and head directly across the street to Piccolo Mondo, 1642 East 56th Street; (773) 643–1106. In a corner of the Windemere, a vintage Hyde Park apartment building, is a casual spot that features robust Italian cooking. Pastas, eggplant parmigiana, fresh gelati, and a frothy cup of cappuccino will make you feel smug. Also worth noting in Hyde Park: Medici's, for great burgers and onion rings.

Best place to eat when you're visiting Shedd Aquarium, Field Museum, Adler Planetarium, or McCormick Place.

No other city in the country can boast so many museums on the same block, but while it's a cultural mother lode, it's a culinary wasteland. No matter. You're just minutes from Chinatown, where Emperor's Choice, 2238 South Wentworth (312–225–8800), does an equally fine job with nouvelle-style dishes as with Cantonese classics. (For dim sum, make it Three Happiness, 209 West Cermak.)

Best inexpensive place for a true Chicago dining experience:

Deep-dish pizza was born in Chicago, but now that you can get it at the Pizza Hut in Aberdeen, South Dakota, it hardly qualifies as distinctive. The Chicago hot dog is a better culinary calling card. Gold Coast Dogs, 418 North State (312–527–1222), serves an outstanding dog, loaded up with fresh toppings. The shakes make a perfect accompaniment. Two other city locations include 2100 North Clark and 325 South Franklin.

Best place if it absolutely has to be pizza:

Then at least choose the place where it all started: Pizzeria Uno, corner of Wabash and Ohio Streets (312–321–1000), is the birthplace of the deep-dish pizza, and Uno's still has a hold on natives and tourists alike. Inexpensive.

Best place when you've been dumped:

Ghiradelli Ice Cream, 118 East Pearson; (312) 337–9330. Is there a better way to mend a broken heart than with a hot fudge sundae?

Looking for some more suggestions? The list of top-notch eateries in Chicago alone could fill this book, but here are a dozen more spots that have proven to be winners year after year.

Wishbone, 1001 West Washington Street; (312) 850–2663. Specializes in Southern cuisine—drenched in hospitality, of course. This is a great breakfast spot. Later in the day try the North Carolina–style smoked pork or charbroiled chicken. Leave room for the corn muffins and key lime pie. Warm and satisfying food and moderately priced.

Blackbird, 619 West Randolph; (312) 715–0708. In the middle of the hot West Loop restaurant area. The cooking here is excellent, and *Food and Wine* magazine named Paul Kahan one of America's best new chefs. The braised veal and wood-grilled sturgeon are standouts that more than atone for the packed and noisy quarters. Moderate to expensive.

Cafe Iberico, 739 North LaSalle; (312) 573–1510. Authentic tapas that are worth the wait at this popular downtown spot. Again, be prepared for some noise. After a few sips of a sweet Spanish wine, you'll be glad you made the effort. Moderate, if you don't go overboard on the tapas selections.

Spago, 520 North Dearborn; (312) 527–3700. All right, it's from Southern California, but the Cal–Asian cooking is unique and heavenly, so please excuse us while we gush over this Wolfgang Puck import. The famous smoked salmon pizza has to take a backseat to the Chinese chicken salad, the perfect "ladies-who-lunch" entree. Moderate to expensive.

Frontera Grill and Topolobampo, 445 North Clark; (312) 661–1434. Casual, elegant, and graceful Mexican fare as you've never had it before. Chef Rick Bayless took cuisine relegated to storefront status and gave it panache. These two side-by-side restaurants have national reputations, so be prepared to wait. Topolobampo, the haute dining room, takes reservations and is higher-priced. There's brunch on Saturday at Frontera; both are closed on Sunday and Monday.

Cafe Absinthe, 1954 West North Avenue; (773) 278–4488. A comfortable French bistro in the Bucktown area, with the most unpretentious entry in town—through a back alley. The Pernod flows from beginning to dessert. An intelligent stop for all chocoholics. Moderate.

Mantuano Mediterranean Table, NBC Tower, 455 North Cityfront Center Plaza; (312) 832–2600. An interesting blend of Italian and Mediterranean cuisine. How about some Middle Eastern antipasto or Portuguese stew? The dessert platter of baklava and other treats will please your dentist and was voted one of the best desserts in the city. A very attractive and comfortable spot, 2 blocks east of Michigan Avenue and the river.

MK the Restaurant, 868 North Franklin; (312) 482–9179. A sophisticated and charming spot that has quickly earned a reputation as one of the city's best finds. The fresh fish of the day is always a welcome treat, and there's usually a Maine lobster treatment on the menu when in season. It's right down the street from Kiki's Bistro, by the way. Call way ahead for reservations.

Tru, 676 North St. Clair Street; (312) 202–0001. Quickly became one of the city's most popular restaurants—for several very tasty reasons. Everything is exquisite here—from the art on the walls to the tableware settings to the creative desserts. The service is polished, and you can experience one of America's great restaurants with either a prix fixe or a tasting menu. For dinner only. Expensive.

Printer's Row, 550 South Dearborn Street; (312) 461–0780. This is one of the pioneering establishments in the city in that it was primarily responsible for starting the regentrification of the entire South Loop area in the early 1980s. The Prairie-style interior is perfect for this city. There's a nightly venison special, along with an American nouvelle cuisine that could have you quickly scheduling a return visit.

Pegasus, 130 South Halsted Street; (312) 226–3377. No list would be complete without mention of one of the city's best in Greektown, just west of the Loop. In summer ask to be seated on the rooftop deck. The great views of the city will enhance the lamb chops as well as the broiled quail. The menu is extensive and creative; the service is polite and very efficient. Moderate.

Ritz-Carlton, Water Tower Place; (312) 266–1000. Everything a lavish hotel should be. The twelfth-floor lobby—complete with fountain—has a real presence. The rooms are beautifully furnished in quiet, understated tones. A number of rooms feature two bathrooms. The restaurant is top-notch, too. Weekend rates start at $180 and can go up to $800.

The Drake, Michigan at Lake Shore Drive; (312) 787–2200. For decades, the premier address in Chicago. Ask for a room that faces north to get an optimum view of "the Drive" (as the natives say) and Lake Michigan. The entire place oozes old money. Despite the formality, The Drake hosts a number of events geared for children, such as a puppet show in the lobby during the holidays. Weekend rates: $119 to $289.

Chicago Hilton and Towers, 720 South Michigan Avenue; (312) 922–4400. Massive, ornate, enormous. This magnificent property is the best place to stay near Grant Park. The lobby (part of a top-to-bottom renovation in 1989) is lovely. Its decor of cool mauves, grays, and marble is echoed in many of the rooms. The pool/health club is among the best in the city. Weekend rates vary depending on holidays and availability but generally start at about $159.

There are a few other lodging options downtown that are often more interesting than the usual chains, and less expensive. But be forewarned. Visitor taxes can boost the bill by as much as 20 percent.

The Hotel Burnham, 36 South State Street; (312) 782–1111. In the newly remodeled Reliance Building, a historically significant gem in the Loop. The 123-room hotel has standard rooms from $145 and suites from $250 to $350. Close to the Art Institute, Grant Park, and the downtown theater district.

Lenox Suites Hotel, corner of Rush and Ontario Streets; (800) 44–Lenox. It's easy to overlook the Lenox, but the combination of prime location (close to Disney Quest and ESPNZone) and good value (rates start at $159 and include an in-suite continental breakfast) makes this an excellent choice for families.

Hotel Monaco, 225 North Wabash Street; (312) 960–8500. Another new entry in Chicago's burgeoning hotel market. With 192 rooms, it is reminiscent of a European pensione. Not only welcomes pets but will give each guest a goldfish and food upon arrival. Check out the Massant Bistro, which has gone through some ups and downs—and currently is up again. Rates: $155–$450.

Swissotel, 323 East Wacker Drive; (312) 565–0565. A beautifully appointed hotel, located 3 blocks east of Michigan Avenue. Close enough to all the action but far enough away to guarantee peace and quiet. Also home to the world-famous Palm Restaurant and one of the most attractive lobby bars in the city. Rates: $189–$509.

FOR MORE INFORMATION

The Chicago Office of Tourism has two offices downtown. One is in the Cultural Center at 77 East Randolph; the other is across from Water Tower Place at 163 East Pearson Street. Call (312) 744–2400 or (800) 226–6632 for recorded information, or visit them on the Web: www.ci.chi.il.us/tourism.

WISCONSIN

ESCAPES

Milwaukee

BREWING UP OLD WORLD CHARM

2 NIGHTS

Architecture • *Brewery* • *Museums* • *Zoo* • *Historical sites*
Theater/Opera/Ballet • *Professional sports*
Ethnic dining • *Hiking/Fishing* • *Cross-country skiing*
Shopping • *Swimming*

Totally unpretentious and teeming with tradition, Milwaukee, Wisconsin's largest city, is just an hour's drive north of Chicago on Lake Michigan's shore. This is a metropolis with a small-town flair, a place where Old World European influences are striking, but blend harmoniously with the modern day.

Peaked roofs, rising church spires, copper gables, and conspicuous clock towers are the protruding landmarks of Milwaukee's beautifully preserved nineteenth- and early-twentieth-century Germanic heritage. While Milwaukee's breweries are what the city is best known for, it has plenty of other enticing features that give credence to its Indian-inspired name, "a gathering place by the waters." For starters, it has an elaborate spread of 137 parks, 60 miles of lakefront, ethnic restaurants, cultural attractions, big-league sports teams, and one of the nation's finest zoos.

The city's compactness is still another virtue. Milwaukee's central business district is only a mile long and a few blocks wide, so sightseeing is easy on foot. But have no fear, even if you do resort to driving, congestion as it's known to Chicagoans is a rare occurrence. Also note that the Milwaukee River divides the downtown area into east and west sections and the city's main east-west thoroughfare is Wisconsin Avenue.

Lastly, Milwaukee is a friendly place. Basically, it's just a cluster of folksy neighborhoods—perfect for a comfortable, easygoing weekend away.

DAY 1

Evening

Getting to Milwaukee is easy. Just head north on I–94 (Edens Expressway), following the signs to Milwaukee. As you approach the city, you'll see the shimmering (24-karat gold leaf) twin domes of St. Stanislaus, the mother church of all Polish-American urban parishes. Soon you'll be on I–43 and in the heart of the city.

DINNER: It depends on your mood. If it's casual, Friday nights and fish fries go hand in hand in Milwaukee. One of the local favorites is the **Historic Turner Restaurant** (1034 North Fourth Street; 414–273–5590). Not very fancy and located in a 137-year-old gymnastics club, this family-style, all-you-can-eat bargain is friendly, fun, and just plain good. Indulge in deep-fried perch and cod, cole slaw, hearty German potato salad, and fries.

If you're craving something more sophisticated, we suggest the **Sanford Restaurant,** 1547 North Jackson Street; (414) 276–9608. Tiny and elegant, this fifty-seat storefront restaurant has been newly redecorated and is a choice pick among critics. Reservations are a must! Cuisine is French–nouvelle American. Best buy is the $49 seasonal menu. Four courses of pure heaven, from the caramelized onion tart to the grilled lamb to the outrageous warm chocolate espresso cake with mocha custard. Expensive.

After dinner, head for **Zur Krone** (839 South Second Street; 414–647–1910), a typical German-style Milwaukee neighborhood bar, which stocks more than 200 brands of beer. Sipping from boot-shaped steins is a Zur Krone tradition. (By the way, you'll know you're in close proximity to Zur Krone when you see the famous **Allen Bradley four-faced clock,** which is located on the Bradley factory tower at 1201 South Second Street. It's the world's largest, and when you see its enormous faces illuminated at night, you'll swear you've just seen a close-up view of a full moon.)

If you'd like to hear a little jazz before turning in, treat yourself to some smooth and soothing piano sounds at the **BBC Lounge** at the Milwaukee Hilton (509 West Wisconsin Avenue; 414–271–7250).

LODGING: Soak up heady amounts of luxury at the **Pfister Hotel** (424 East Wisconsin Avenue; 414–273–8222 or 800–558–8222). Born in the final gilded decade of the nineteenth century, the Pfister has been restored to its former splendor. Its lavish lobby, ballroom, and 307 tasteful rooms earned it an international reputation. Rooms start at $159 a night and include every amenity—right down to a TV in the marble bathroom. Be sure to book a room in the older part of the hotel, which was redone a few years ago. The result is a perfect marriage of vintage architecture and nineties convenience.

DAY 2

Morning

BREAKFAST: The Cafe at the Pfister is the Pfister Hotel's coffee shop and is located on the lobby level. The French toast is nice and plump with powdered sugar dusted on top, and the sausage is something you can really sink your teeth into. The pancakes (both buttermilk and blueberry) are also rather tempting.

Begin your day by venturing about on foot. A variety of self-guided neighborhood walking tours is available at the **Greater Milwaukee Convention and Visitors Bureau** (510 West Kilbourn Avenue; 800–554–1448), but you may decide to be innovative and explore a few of the sites in your own fashion.

Try heading north on Jefferson Street, past **George Watts & Son,** an exceptional china shop with beautiful displays of china, crystal, silver, and oh-so-lovely art objects. A little farther up the street is Cathedral Square, a park, which aptly faces the **Cathedral of St. John the Evangelist** (802 North Jackson). On Thursday evenings in summer, outdoor jazz concerts add a festive note.

Turning toward the river on Kilbourn Avenue, saunter by **Old Saint Mary's Church,** Milwaukee's oldest Catholic church (built in 1846). Within seconds another head turner, **City Hall,** will appear. This copper-domed Flemish Renaissance gem was built in 1895. Free tours can be arranged on weekdays between 8:00 A.M. and 4:45 P.M., when City Hall's doors are open (200 East Wells; 414–286–2221). Once you gain access, even if you forgo the tour, note the ornately carved woodwork and stenciled ceilings in the Common Council chamber and anteroom.

Continue toward the Milwaukee River until you reach the **Marcus Center for the Performing Arts** at 929 North Water Street, which recently unveiled a $16.5 million renovation. Made from brilliant Italian travertine marble, this is the home of the Milwaukee Symphony Orchestra, the Milwaukee Ballet, the Florentine Opera, and the First Stage Theater group. Nearby stands the new red brick and slate-peaked **Milwaukee Center,** which encompasses the Milwaukee Repertory Theatre, the Wyndham Hotel, and the magnificently restored Pabst Theater (144 East Wells Street; 414–286–3665). Free tours of this late-nineteenth-century, Victorian-style theater are given on Saturdays at 11:30 A.M. (allow forty-five minutes).

While downtown, check out Milwaukee's bustling **Riverwalk,** which opened in 1996. Meandering through the heart of the city, the walk is located near fine restaurants and arts venues. Also included in the project are boat docks to help make the area more accessible by "sea" as well as by land. Gondolas and water taxis add an element of urban romance.

Next, head over the river and around Père Marquette Park before turning south down the cobbled streets of Old World Third Street. In the heart of this old German business district lie some historic 1880s architecture and a few quality delectables. One landmark, **Usinger's Famous Sausage,** is a great place to pick up some knockwurst, bratwurst, and liver sausage munchies for the trip home (1030 North Old World Third Street; 414–276–9100). Open 8:30 A.M.–5:00 P.M., Monday through Saturday. A few doors down is the **Wisconsin Cheese Mart** (215 West Highland Avenue; 414–272–3544). Open 9:00 A.M.–5:00 P.M., Monday through Saturday. Here you'll find an incredible selection of cheeses, some even shaped like the state of Wisconsin. The shop has lots of samples, so indulge. Also, if you're the collecting type, check out the second-floor gift shop at **Mader's** (1037 North Old World Third Street; 414–271–3377), one of Milwaukee's famous German cuisine hot spots. Don't worry if you haven't time to dine; you can still peruse the shop.

If it works out that you're here for mealtime, there are some new entries worth checking out: **Edelweiss** (1110 North Old World Third Street; 414–332–4194), a cruise through downtown and onto Lake Michigan, which offers a surprisingly good brunch (lunch and dinner are also available), and **Third Street Pier,** (1110 North Old World Third Street; 414–272–0330), downtown's most dramatic waterfront restaurant, especially good for steaks and seafood.

The next stop is the elegant, 4-block-long **Grand Avenue Mall** (275 West Wisconsin Avenue). From its facade, the Mall (a composite of five artfully preserved turn-of-the-century buildings) bears no resemblance to a newfangled shopping center. Yet sure enough, once you get inside you'll find loads of modern shops, including the Boston Store. The skylights, skywalks, and an exquisite circular stairway leading down to the lower level in the Plankington Arcade make this an experience you won't soon forget.

At this point you may want to return to pick up your car and take off for the **Marquette University** campus, straight west on Wisconsin Avenue. In the middle of the university is a real treasure—the **St. Joan of Arc Chapel** (14th Street and Wisconsin Avenue). Originally, this medieval French chapel was constructed in the fifteenth century near Lyon, France, where it stood for more than 500 years. Falling into disrepair after the French Revolution, the chapel was eventually transported to a Long Island estate in 1927, where American architect John Russell Pope reconstructed it stone by stone. In the mid-1960s, the chapel was moved and reassembled again at its present site. Near the altar you'll find the stone St. Joan supposedly kissed just before she was executed. Some say it's cooler to the touch than those surrounding it, but you'll have to decide for yourself.

Another campus jewel is the **Patrick and Beatrice Haggerty Museum of Art** (13th and Clybourn Streets on the east side of the university's square). Among the permanent exhibits in this intimate museum are Renaissance, Baroque, and modern paintings, as well as sculpture, prints, photography, and examples of decorative art. Call (414) 288–7290. Open Monday through Friday, 10:00 A.M.–4:30 P.M.; Thursday, 10:00 A.M.–8:00 P.M.; Sunday, noon–5:00 P.M. Free.

LUNCH: A west side favorite is **Saz's,** located in the Miller Valley, just minutes from the brewery (5539 West State Street; 414–453–2410). The house specialties are barbecued ribs and mozzarella marinara, hunks of mozzarella cheese wrapped as egg rolls.

Afternoon

No traditional tourist can visit Milwaukee without including a trip to a brewery. Tour options are available at several breweries, including the "beer city's" best: **Miller Brewing Company** (4251 West State Street; 414–931–BEER). The free tour (Monday through Saturday, 10:00 A.M.–3:30 P.M.) starts off with a video presentation on how the operation got started plus some tidbits about the beer-making process. Then it's off to see Miller's mammoth shipping center (the size of five football fields) and the huge copper-topped vats in the brewhouse. The finale, which most consider to be the best part, is a free sampling at the Miller Inn.

Plankington Arcade at the Grand Avenue Mall

To give some equal time to a competitor, journey over to the **Pabst Mansion** (2000 West Wisconsin Avenue; 414–931–0808). This lavish, thirty-seven-room Flemish Renaissance home was built in 1893 for the beer baron himself, Captain Frederick Pabst. Carved wood, stained glass, ornamental ironwork, and terra-cotta are among the handsome accents in this magnificent Victorian landmark. Allow about an hour. Open Monday through Saturday, 10:00 A.M.–3:30 P.M.; Sunday, noon–3:30 P.M. Admission: adults, $7.00; children ages 6–17, $3.00; seniors and students, $6.00.

Mitchell Park Conservatory, affectionately dubbed "the Domes," makes a great afternoon adventure. There's nothing quite like it anywhere, particularly not in Chicago, so make sure you put it on your weekend to-do list. The conservatory is housed in three gigantic domes, each 140 feet wide by 85 feet tall and each with a different climate. The first is a floral garden (the "show dome," where five themed shows are displayed annually), the second is an arid dome (filled with cacti and other desert plants), and the third is tropical. The conservatory is at 524 South Layton Boulevard. Call (414) 649–9800. Open daily, 9:00 A.M.–5:00 P.M. Admission: adults, $4.00; children ages 6–17, $2.50.

DINNER: Karl Ratzsch's Old World Restaurant (320 East Mason Street; 414–276–2720) is just a short walk from the Pfister Hotel. This is a Milwaukee classic with a sumptuous menu, impeccable service, and plush Germanic decor (antiques, steins, and hand-painted murals abound). Sauerbraten (marinated roast sirloin with spicy, sweet-sour gravy) and Swabian Schnitzel (veal prepared with sour cream, red wine, and onion) are just two of a long list of house specialties. Dinners are complete (though coffee and dessert are extra), and there's even a lighter menu for the after-theater crowd. A wonderful pianist plays nightly, and kids get a trip to the famous treasure chest for candy after they finish their meals. Even though the prices are on the high side, dress is casual.

To make your night complete, return to the **Pabst Theater** (144 East Wells Street; 414–286–3665) to enjoy a performance of dance or drama or a musical. The Pabst is listed on the National Register of Historic Places. It's a small theater with 1,400 seats and two balconies, so virtually every seat in the house is good. Tickets average around $36 for the prime seats.

LODGING: The Pfister Hotel.

DAY 3

Morning

BREAKFAST: Wake up with a stop at **Alterra Coffee Roaster,** 2211 North Prospect Avenue (414–273–3747) and witness a wholesale coffee-roasting facility in action. While sipping your brew you can see two enormous coffee roasters at work. For breakfast stop in at **Le Peep of Wisconsin,** 250 East Wisconsin Avenue (414–273–7337), for mouth-watering skillets and creative crepes. Specialty pancakes in varieties like cinnamon-pecan are a don't-miss.

Head west again for the **Milwaukee Public Museum** (800 West Wells Street; 414–278–2702). (It's a part of a complex that also houses the Humphrey IMAX Dome Theater, Discovery World, and the James Lovell Museum of Science, Economics and Technology.) This is one of the largest natural history museums in the country. It even has its own Costa Rican rain forest soaring 19 feet upward. The museum is also noted for its "Streets of Old Milwaukee" exhibit and a series of outstanding dioramas. Plan to spend at least an hour and a half here. Open 9:00 A.M.–5:00 P.M. daily (closed Christ-

mas, July fourth, and Thanksgiving). Admission: adults, $6.50; children ages 4–17, $3.50. The museum also has special rates on designated family days.

The **Humphrey IMAX Dome Theater,** 710 West Wells Street (414–391– 4629), is always a good time. The 275-seat theater is the first of its kind in Wisconsin. Open daily. Admission: adults, $6.50; children and seniors, $5.50.

Another first is **Discovery World Museum,** 712 West Wells Street (414–765–0311), the state's only science and technology museum. Explore the clouds, lift a robot or watch a lightning bolt; they're all among the more than 140 interactive exhibits. Open daily.

Next on the agenda is a trip to the **Milwaukee Art Museum** (750 North Lincoln Memorial Drive; 414–224–3200), overlooking Lake Michigan in the War Memorial Center, designed by Eero Saarinen. The Art Museum's new addition is scheduled for completion in the fall of 2000. Exhibits, which include more than 20,000 works of art, range from sculpture and paintings to decorative art and photography. The museum's permanent collection of nineteenth- and twentieth-century European and American art is strong. Don't miss the collection of Haitian art and the Mettlach steins, either. Open Tuesday, Wednesday, Friday, Saturday, 10:00 A.M.–5:00 P.M.; Thursday, noon–9:00 P.M.; Sunday, noon–5:00 P.M. Admission: adults, $5.00; seniors and students, $3.00; under age 12, free.

If you're with kids, a better choice that is also on the lakefront is the **Betty Brinn Children's Museum,** 929 East Wisconsin Avenue; (414) 291–0888. Admission: ages 2 and older, $4.00. The museum, which is chockablock with hands-on exhibits, was recently named one of the top ten children's museums in the United States.

LUNCH: Boulevard Inn, 925 East Wells; (414) 765–1166. Not far from the Art Museum in the Cudahy Towers is this pleasant dining room that overlooks the lake. During the summer months the patio, dressed with pretty flower boxes, is even nicer. The food is continental in flavor (fresh seafood, meat, and poultry) and a great value for its high quality at moderate-to-expensive prices. A family-owned establishment, this restaurant has years of history. Lunch menu ranges from $6.75 to $10.00.

Afternoon

Round out your day at the spectacular **Milwaukee County Zoo** (10001 West Blue Mound Road; 414–771–3040). Ranked among the world's finest, this zoo is really big, with more than 3,000 animals on display in five continental groupings. One of the nicest features of the zoo is its emphasis on natural settings. For example, in the center of the park is a series of predator/prey exhibits where species share nearby resources just as they would in the wild. And the aviary has a generous free-flight area where there are no barriers between the birds and the public. Plan to allot three hours at the very least. Open Monday through Saturday, 9:00 A.M.–5:00 P.M.; Sunday, 9:00 A.M.–6:00 P.M. Admission is $8.00 for adults, and $6.00 for children ages 3–12. Prices deflate slightly November through March. Parking is $5.00.

Before heading off for the highway, savor one last Milwaukee treat—frozen custard from **Kopp's**. The burgers are great here, too. Although you'll find a few tables, this is essentially an establishment designed for on-the-go types. The nearest Kopp's location is 76th and Layton; take Highway 894/45 south to 76th Street and follow it to Layton Street.

Note: Return home by picking up Highway 894 east (½ block from Kopp's) and turning south onto I–94.

THERE'S MORE

Antiques. If it's bargains you're after, Milwaukee's **Historic Third Ward** is a real boomtown. Not only will you find a fine selection of antiques and collectibles to rummage through (even the junk is better than comparable finds at the Kane County Flea Market), the absence of crowds, ease of parking, and reasonable prices are worth the trip. Interestingly enough, this antiques district is also conveniently located (off I–43/94; only 1 block south of downtown and 3 blocks west of the Summerfest Grounds at the lake).

The Third Ward, somewhat akin to Chicago's River North, is filled with renovated warehouses, produce markets, artsy shops, restaurants, and galleries. You'll find that the majority of dealers are grouped together in large antiques malls with three and four levels. These include the **Milwaukee Antique Center,** 341 North Milwaukee Street, (414) 276–0605, open daily; **Water Street Antique Market,** 318 North Water Street, (414) 278–7008, open daily; **Centuries Antiques,** 326 North Water Street, (414) 278–1111, open Friday through Monday; **Jacquelynn's China Matching Service,** 219 North Milwaukee Street, (414) 272–8880, closed Sunday.

Six blocks west of the Third Ward, across from the Amtrak station, is another mall worth visiting, **Fifth Avenue Antiques,** 422 North Fifth Street; (414) 271–3355. Likewise, a little farther south, near the Allen Bradley four-faced clock, is another, **Antique Center Walkers Point,** 1134 South First Street; (414) 383–0655. Also remember to make time for the miscellaneous shops and restaurants. As for scheduling, plan on allotting at least three hours for minimal exploration; however, you could easily make a day of this.

Broadway Theatre Center, 158 North Broadway (located in the Historic Third Ward); (414) 291–7800. From its facade, nothing about this performing arts complex (which consists of a renovated turn-of-the-century warehouse and an adjoining new building) hints at the lavish eighteenth-century baroque-style opera house inside. This is the center's main stage and the new home of the Skylight Opera Theatre, where the city's musical and operetta productions are performed. The 358-seat theater, modeled after the regional baroque theaters of eighteenth-century Italy, is quite a sight to behold. Its lyre-shaped balconies and hand-painted trompe l'oeil ceiling are stunning. Humorous artistic touches are worth noting, too. Take a good look at the winged, allegorical figures on the theater dome. Some are wearing eyeglasses; others sport tattoos. The center has two other resident companies: the Milwaukee Chamber Theatre, 158 North Broadway (414–276–8842), which performs literary plays and the country's only Shaw Festival; and Theatre X (414–278–0555), an experimental studio presenting avant-garde works. Free tours are given Fridays at noon or can be arranged by appointment; (414) 291–7811.

Milwaukee County Historical Center, 910 North Old World Third Street; (414) 273–8288. An architectural landmark with exhibits on the city's past and a genealogical research library. Open Monday through Friday, 9:30 A.M.–5:00 P.M.; Saturday, 10:00 A.M.–5:00 P.M.; Sunday, 1:00–5:00 P.M. Free.

Charles Allis Art Museum, 1801 North Prospect Avenue; (414) 278–8295. This elegant Tudor mansion, formerly the home of Charles Allis (the first president of the Allis-Chalmers Company), contains a number of collections, including the home's original antique furniture, Oriental art objects, French and American nineteenth-century paintings, and Renaissance bronzes. Open Wednesday through Sunday, 1:00–5:00 P.M.; Wednesday nights, 7:00–9:00 P.M. Admission is $4.00 for adults; children under 13 are free.

Boerner Botanical Gardens, 5879 South 92nd Street in Whitnall Park; (414) 425–1130. The gardens (both formal and informal) are a lovely respite during the warmer months. The rose garden alone has more than 3,000 plants of 300 varieties. Open mid-April through October, 8:00 A.M.–sunset. Parking is $3.50 and admission is free.

Whitnall Park (5879 South 92nd Street) is one of the nation's largest municipal parks (660 acres). It includes an eighteen-hole golf course, picnic areas, an environmental education center (the Wehr Nature Center), and botanical gardens. It's also a great spot for cross-country skiing during the winter.

Annunciation Greek Orthodox Church, 9400 West Congress Street, Wauwatosa; (414) 461–9400. The last major building from architect Frank Lloyd Wright's drawing board, this bright blue-domed masterpiece is a magnificent example of Byzantine architecture. Take I–94 west (Highway 894 bypass), which turns into Highway 45 as you head north. Exit at Capital Drive. Go east to 92nd Street, then north to the church. Group tours by appointment Monday through Friday. Admission is a donation.

Olson Planetarium, 1900 East Kenwood Boulevard on the University of Wisconsin campus; (414) 229–4961. Star show and informative lectures by members of the University of Wisconsin–Milwaukee Planetarium staff. A good time for astronomy buffs. Show times: Friday nights (during the school year) at 7:00 P.M. and 8:15 P.M. (Closed for the summer but open after Labor Day.)

Spectator sports. Watch the Milwaukee Brewers play baseball at the new Miller Park, which is projected to open in the summer of 2001. Although the new stadium has 10,000 fewer seats, the seating area is larger, including many skyboxes. Miller Park's selling point—a retractable dome roof.

The Milwaukee Bucks and the Marquette University Golden Eagles play basketball at the Bradley Center (1001 North Fourth Street; 414–227–0400).

Fishing. Lake Michigan can reward anglers with prize catches of salmon and trout (as big as thirty pounds). Full- and half-day charters are offered by numerous companies, including Jack's Charter Service (414–482–2336 or 800–858–5225) and Leisure Time Charters (414–781–1704).

Cross-country skiing. Several local parks provide rentals and lessons, including Brown Deer Park (7835 North Green Bay Avenue), Currie Park (3535 North Mayfair Road), Dretzka Park (12020 West Bradley Road), the Milwaukee County Zoo (10001 West Blue Mound Road), Whitnall Park (5879 South 92nd Street), and Lincoln Park (1301 West Hampton Avenue).

Old World Wisconsin, 1½ miles south of Eagle, Wisconsin, on Highway 67 (35 miles southwest of Milwaukee); (414) 594–6300. This 576-acre outdoor museum consists of more than fifty preserved and furnished buildings erected by nineteenth-century immigrants. Costumed interpreters explain the story of immigration to Wisconsin and each ethnic group's role. A 2½-mile tour is needed to see the entire museum. Bring your most comfortable walking shoes. Allow a minimum of five hours. Open daily, 10:00 A.M.–5:00 P.M. in July and August. Hours in May, June, September, and October: Monday through Friday, 10:00 A.M.–4:00 P.M.; Saturday and Sunday, 10:00 A.M.–5:00 P.M. Admission: adults, $11.00; seniors, $9.90; children ages 5–12, $5.50. Family rates available.

SPECIAL EVENTS

June. Polish Fest. Continuous polka music, dancing, international polka contest, beauty pageant, ethnic foods, and historical and cultural demonstrations. Held at Henry W. Maier Festival Park.

June. The Asian Moon Festival, Cajun Fest, at Henry W. Maier Festival Park.

June–July. Summerfest. The world's largest outdoor music festival with comedy, food, and sports activities. It includes eleven stages and booths from more than thirty area restaurants. Held at Henry W. Maier Festival Park.

July. Great Circus Parade. Bands, costumed units, animals, and a unique collection of horse-drawn wagons from the Circus World Museum (at Kilbourn and Wisconsin Avenues, the heart of the downtown area).

July. Festa Italiana. Four-day Italian festival with eight stages of entertainment, plenty of Italian delicacies, cultural exhibits, fireworks, and a traditional mass and procession. Held at Henry W. Maier Festival Park, 200 North Harbor Drive.

July. German Fest. Nonstop German music and entertainment, folk dancing, cultural presentations, souvenirs, fireworks, food, and beverages. Held at Henry W. Maier Festival Park.

August. Wisconsin State Fair. Entertainment on twenty stages, blue-ribbon livestock, 500 exhibits, 200 food concessions, 150 carnival rides and games.

Held at the State Fair Park in West Allis, a fifteen-minute drive from downtown.

August. Milwaukee a la Carte. Milwaukee's premiere food fest, with more than thirty restaurants serving sample-size gourmet portions. Held at the Milwaukee County Zoo.

September. Oktoberfest. Authentic fall festival featuring brass bands, Bavarian folk dancers, yodelers, music, dancing, German food, and beer. Held at Old Heidelberg Park in Glendale, a fifteen-minute drive north of downtown.

Late November. Christmas Parade. Bands, floats, live animals, clowns, radio and TV personalities, and Santa parade on Wisconsin Avenue near Grand Avenue shopping mall to the lakefront. Also, the Holiday Folk Fair at Wisconsin State Fair Park showcases the heritage and culture of more than fifty ethnic groups through informational exhibits, food, and dance performances.

OTHER RECOMMENDED RESTAURANTS AND LODGINGS

Milwaukee

Astor Hotel, 924 East Juneau Avenue; (414) 271–4220. One of the loveliest Milwaukee hotels. Designed in the grand tradition, the Astor is well located on a somewhat residential, tree-lined street. Accommodations are plush and full of amenities. All the suites have kitchens. Rates range from $87 to $113 per night.

Bartolotta's Lake Park Bistro, 3133 East Newberry Boulevard; (414) 962–6300. Bistro Classics (extraordinary French onion soup) in a casual, chic setting, atop a bluff overlooking Lake Michigan.

The Knick, 1030 East Juneau Avenue; (414) 272–0011. Without mincing words, the food here is excellent. You'll find a large assortment of wonderful menu items such as ahi tuna au poivre and grilled duck breast.

Conejitos Place, 539 West Virginia; (414) 278–9106. In a neighborhood packed with Hispanic and Latino restaurants, this is one of the best. The food (Mexican) is excellent and very cheap. The mood can be a little raucous, but it's all part of the fun. Try the chicken mole and the guacamole and chips. This is a lunch or early dinner choice.

Coquette Cafe, 316 North Milwaukee; (414) 291–2655. The owner of Sanford's, a seven-course dining extravaganza, opened this spin-off casual bistro
in 1999. The thin-crust pizza appetizers are a favorite, along with the char-
grilled filet of salmon. On weekends, reservations are a must. Moderate.

Elsa's on the Park, 833 North Jefferson Street; (414) 765–0615. Fancy hamburgers make this place special. The pork chop sandwiches and buffalo
wings also get two thumbs up. Atmosphere is casual. No credit cards. Inexpensive.

The English Room, 424 East Wisconsin Avenue, in the Pfister Hotel; (414)
273–8222. Known for its fine continental cuisine, The English Room is
considered one of Milwaukee's best restaurants. The atmosphere, which is
enhanced by an original nineteenth-century art collection, is elegant and
formal. Despite the name, the fare is very French. Expensive.

John Ernst Restaurant, 600 East Ogden Avenue; (414) 273–1878. One of the
city's finest purveyors of steaks and seafood. Family-owned and -operated
for three generations, the Ernst Restaurant is Milwaukee's oldest restaurant.
Music nightly. Expensive.

Hilton Milwaukee City Center, 509 West Wisconsin Avenue; (414) 271–7250.
Located away from the lake, this is Milwaukee's largest hotel, with 500
rooms. Built more than sixty-five years ago, the Hilton is noted for its comfort and service. Rates range from $109 to $179 per night and include a
full breakfast on the weekends.

Park East Hotel, 916 East State Street; (414) 276–8800 or (800) 328–7275.
Almost on the lakefront (across from Juneau Park), the Park East is another
choice pick for the traveler with discriminating taste. This hotel is contemporary in feel. Rates range from $88 to $200 per night per suites.

The Safe House, 779 North Front Street; (414) 271–2007. Don't be fooled by
the sign out front: INTERNATIONAL EXPORTS LIMITED. Yes, you've arrived at
the right place. The Safe House, a spy's hideout, is a Milwaukee favorite.
Secret doors, an ejection seat, a CIA phone booth, and a collection of spy
gear are a few clues to what you'll find inside. Inexpensive.

Watts Tea Shop, 761 Jefferson Street; (414) 291–5120. A delightful discovery
on the second floor of George Watts & Son's china shop. All of the food
on the three menus—breakfast, lunch, and afternoon tea—is delicious.
Recipes are original and very fresh. Allow yourself to be tempted by the
baked goods. They're worth it! This is a great place to take Mom. Inexpensive to moderate.

Wyndham Milwaukee Center, 139 East Kilbourn Avenue; (414) 276–8686. If you like theater, you can't get any closer. The Wyndham is part of the Milwaukee Center and the city's "theater district." Accommodations are luxurious, and you'll find lots of amenities, including a health club. Rates range from $149 to $259 per night.

Whitefish Bay

Pandl's Whitefish Bay Inn, 1319 East Henry Clay Street; (414) 964–3800. Another family-owned spot, this elegant supper club is located in a county landmark building. Food specialties include German pancake whitefish, walleye, and roast duck. The homemade soups are tasty, too. Whitefish Bay is north of downtown Milwaukee; take the scenic route—Lincoln Memorial Drive and Lake Drive North. Moderate.

FOR MORE INFORMATION

Greater Milwaukee Convention and Visitors Bureau, 510 West Kilbourn Avenue, Milwaukee, WI 53203; (800) 554–1448.

Metropolitan Milwaukee Association of Commerce, 756 North Milwaukee Street, Milwaukee, WI 53202; (414) 287–4100.

Lake Geneva

LUXURY AND THE LAKE

2 NIGHTS

Antiques • Boating • Fishing • Shopping • Skiing • Golf

If you're the kind of traveler who doesn't like to shave on the weekend, you may perceive Lake Geneva to be too tony for your tastes. But that elitist air is as much part of the area's history as the lake itself. As far back as the 1870s, Chicago's chewing-gum, meat-packing, and retailing barons turned this into a playground of the rich by practicing competitive mansion building.

Today a lot of the formality of Lake Geneva is gone. There are still a few places that require jackets and ties at dinner, but for the most part you'll find an equal mix of suburban families and stylish young professionals.

Lake Geneva is just one resort community situated on the 26 miles of shoreline that rim this picturesque, spring-fed lake. The two others are Fontana and Williams Bay, but visitors tend to refer to the entire area as "Lake Geneva."

You'll find a wealth of accommodations, from sprawling resorts to rustic cabins and cottages—but that doesn't mean you can count on a vacancy. With the lake's being the absolute center of activity, it should come as no surprise that the area is positively packed during summer weekends. The long lines and bumper-to-bumper traffic can really diminish the experience, so consider a midweek or post–Labor Day visit instead.

In the fall the lake positively shimmers against reds, oranges, and golds. Even in the dead of winter, Lake Geneva is warm and hospitable, thanks to a concentration of resorts that cater to skiers, snowmobilers, and sailors. That's right: During the last few years, ice sailing has become popular among the diehards who can't bear to put their boats in dry dock. Sailboats are mounted onto large skates and glide atop the frozen lake at speeds as high as 60 miles

per hour. Those brave enough to try it claim it is an invigorating experience; others may find that curling up with a good book near the hotel hearth provides all the activity one needs.

Best of all, Lake Geneva is just 75 miles away—and if traffic cooperates, you can leave the Loop by six and be sipping a glass of chablis by eight.

One last piece of advice: While there are some lovely B&Bs for couples, the pool of family-friendly lodging that is both modern and affordable is thin. Befriend someone with a summer home.

DAY 1

Evening

Bring your weekend bag to work, so you can make a quick getaway Friday evening. Take I–94 north to Highway 50 west, which takes you right into Lake Geneva.

DINNER: The **Grandview Restaurant,** Geneva Inn, North 2009 State Road 120; (414) 248–5680. The chef does a splendid job with fish, and the salmon is as good as anything you'll find in the Pacific Northwest. The service is polished, and the atmosphere is romantic, especially if you snare a table overlooking the lake or sit out on the terrace. Even if you don't want a full-blown meal, at least stop by for a nightcap. Ice cream drinks are the house specialty, and the piano bar adds just the right touch. Prices for entrees are in the $19 to $25 range.

LODGING: Go no farther than up the stairs to unwind from a rough week. While the **Geneva Inn,** North 2009 State Road 120, which opened in 1990, is expensive, it offers the charm of a country inn with the service of a luxury hotel. The rooms are beautifully furnished in an English country motif, and the lake views from your balcony are spectacular. Some rooms have whirlpools; all have VCRs. Rates range from $145 to $350 per night. Call (414) 248–5680 or (800) 441–5881.

DAY 2

Morning

BREAKFAST: Continental breakfast is included at the Geneva Inn. Or take a morning stroll to the Riviera Docks, where you'll find Le French Donut, which isn't a donut at all, but an authentic beignet, as good as any you'll find in New Orleans.

Do what everyone else does—enjoy the lake. The best way to do that is by being smack in the middle of it. The **Geneva Lake Cruise Line** offers sightseeing tours on restored turn-of-the-century paddle wheelers, the perfect vessels for viewing the elegant Victorian estates. Tours range from one to three hours, and some include lunch or dinner. Some also offer Sunday champagne brunches or feature Dixieland jazz.

Another interesting way to cruise the lake is aboard *Walworth II,* one of the last operating marine mail services in the United States. During the 2½-hour loop around the lake, the mail carrier periodically leaps off the moving boat, dashes to a mailbox, and jumps back into the boat without missing a beat. Besides agility, the carrier needs a sense of history as well. He or she points out landmarks and other local lore in between leaps. The mailboat operates between June 15 and September 15; other cruises, through the end of October. Prices: adults, $14.95; students ages 13–16, $11.50; children ages 4–12, $7.55; children under 4 ride free. Board at the Riviera Docks at the foot of Broad Street. Be sure to bring a camera. Call (414) 248–6206 or (800) 558–5911.

LUNCH: Right near the Riviera Docks is **Popeye's Galley,** 811 Wrigley Drive; (414) 248–4381. Its menu is a rather eclectic mix of sandwiches, salads, and Greek and Mexican fare. You can also dine outdoors—the best way to enjoy this casual restaurant's prime location.

Afternoon

Since you're so close, you can always return to the beach. The **Lake Geneva Municipal Beach** is right across the street. **Fontana** and **Williams Bay Municipal Beaches** also rate a recommendation. Fontana is on the west side of the lake, and Williams Bay is on the north. You can rent just about anything, from a yacht to a Jetski. If hipness is important, try boogie boarding, which is similar to waterskiing, except you're strapped to a small surfboard.

More serious, perhaps, but no less stimulating is a trip to **Yerkes Observatory** (373 West Geneva Street, Williams Bay, 5 miles west of Lake Geneva). This research outpost of the University of Chicago was built in 1897 and houses the world's largest refracting telescope. It is open only on Saturdays. Tours are offered year-round at 10:00 A.M. and noon. For more information, call (414) 245–5555. Free.

The lovely lake is still this resort town's number-one attraction.

If the only science you're interested in is the science of economics, then head over to the main shopping streets of Main and Broad. You'll find the usual souvenir and T-shirt emporiums, but there are some finds, as well. An off-price mini-mall, called **Fancy Fair Mall,** contains several quality stores with bona fide bargains.

Bibliophiles should check out the **Breadloaf Book Shop** (253 Broad Street; 414–248–9446), and **Allison Wonderland** has a terrific toy selection (720 Main Street; 414–248–6500). If you have time to see only one gallery, make it the **Geneva Lake Art Association Gallery** (647 West Main Street; 414–877–2744), which represents more than twenty-five artists. Those who believe you can never have too much jewelry should check out **Starfire** (159 Broad Street; 414–248–3878), or **Expressions** for great glass beads (829 Broad Street; 414–248–8134).

Grazers will note that the entire area is a minefield of bakeries, ice cream parlors, and candy stores. For chocolate, try **Kilwin's** at the corner of Main and Broad (414–248–4400), and for ice cream, try **Annie's** at 712 Main Street

(414–248–1933). In the summer, locals swear by the peppermint, but in the winter, the house specialty seems to be chili.

You will also find numerous antiques stores. Try the **Lake Geneva Antique Mall** (829 William Street; 414–248–6345) or the **Bungalow Antique Emporium** (721 Geneva Street; 414–348–0000). And on the other side of the lake in Walworth is the **Square Antique Mall,** located just west of the Village Square, which displays wares from fifty dealers (414–275–9858).

DINNER: The Red Geranium, Highway 50 East; (414) 248–3637. This restaurant is mentioned repeatedly as one of the area's best and most consistent. Seafood (especially fresh tuna, salmon, and lobster) and steaks dominate here. Everything is cooked on an open hearth, and it's fun to watch the chefs at work. Entrees, which come with soup, salad, potato, and vegetable, average about $20. Dress is casual, and there is also a children's menu. Try to get a table on the glass-enclosed porch.

After dinner watch the "world's fastest greyhounds" compete at the **Geneva Lakes Greyhound Track and Simulcast Center,** one of four dog tracks that opened in 1990 in Wisconsin. Races, which are held year-round, are fun even if you stay away from the win, place, and show windows. Weekend races start at 1:00 P.M. and 7:30 P.M., and it will cost you just a buck to get in and another buck to park. If you're unsure that this is an appropriate place to take children, rest assured that in terms of atmosphere these tracks more closely resemble a suburban shopping mall than anything Damon Runyon would have thought up. The tracks are located at the intersection of I–43 and Highway 50, in Delavan. Call (414) 728–8000.

LODGING: Geneva Inn.

DAY 3

Morning

BREAKFAST: Two choices, depending on how you like your Sunday mornings. Try **Millie's Restaurants and Shopping Village** (South Shore Drive and County Highway O, south of Delavan; 414–728–2434) for Swedish pancakes, caramel rolls, and other traditional breakfast favorites. Inexpensive.

For lighter fare—via foot or bicycle—check out the **Sweet Jemma Rae's,** 221 Broad Street; (414) 248–6607. Scrumptious muffins, scones, and espresso drinks are best enjoyed in the tiny outdoor garden. Inexpensive.

If you're staying in Lake Geneva and have had enough of sun and water, take a drive through the country. You'll soon discover that Walworth County is horse country, with more than a dozen stables and ranches in the area. You'll also find that horse-related activities take place the year-round, with fall's hayride becoming winter's sleigh ride.

LUNCH: Trying to squeeze in one more meal? Try **Kirsch's** at the French Country Inn (Highway 4, just off Highway 50 West; 414–245–5220). Kirsch's is a charming spot to have a lovely lunch while looking out over Lake Como. Try a basket of homemade corn muffins with the warm scallop salad—a first-rate combination of greens, vinaigrette, and large sea scallops. Moderate.

Afternoon

Start to wend your way back to Chicago, going south on Highway 12. Just over the Illinois–Wisconsin border is the tiny town of **Richmond,** which has more than two dozen antiques shops—in fact, as far as anyone can tell, Richmond is nothing but antiques shops. Depending on your schedule you can spend an hour or a day here. If it's just a quickie, don't miss **Anderson's Candy Shop**, 10301 Main Street; (815) 678–6000, a traditional stop for Chicagoans trekking to summer homes since 1919. The recipes for hand-dipped chocolates are the same ones from way back when—so are the marble slab and copper kettle.

THERE'S MORE

Ballooning and hang gliding. Sunbird Balloons Inc. offers a view of the entire area that would be hard to duplicate with more traditional transportation. You also travel in style; the balloon comes stocked with champagne, a throwback to the days when the balloonists made a peace offering to farmers for landing on their property. Fees are $135 to $175 for a 2½-hour experience, including a champagne breakfast. Call (414) 249–0660.

Boating. There are numerous marinas and boat rentals. Here are just a few: Marina Bay Boat Rentals, Lake Geneva (414–248–4477); Gordy's Lakefront Marina, Fontana (414–275–2163); and Jerry's, Fontana (414–275–5222).

Fishing. Lake Geneva provides primarily lake trout. Any of the aforementioned marinas will also rent fishing boats or help arrange fishing charters.

Golf. Since Lake Geneva has always been a playground for the rich, good golf courses abound. Geneva National Golf Club is a duffer's paradise, with three eighteen-hole courses by Arnold Palmer, Gary Player, and Lee Trevino. Grand Geneva Resort and Spa has thirty-six holes (800–558–3417). Other highly recommended courses include Abbey Springs Country Club in Fontana (414–275–6111) and Lake Lawn Resort (414–728–7950), Hillmoon Golf Club (414–248–4570), and Alpine Valley Resort (414–642–7374) in East Troy.

Hiking. The 26-mile path around the lake is a hiker's dream for all seasons. The fact that you are never more than 3 feet from the water accounts for its popularity. However, doing the whole circuit generally consumes nine or ten hours. Another alternative is to do a walk-and-cruise tour. Buy your boat ticket at the Riviera boat docks and take the 8-mile footpath to Williams Bay. Board the *Belle of the Lake* there and cruise back for the best of both worlds. For reservations call Geneva Lake Cruise Line, (414) 245–2628.

Skiing. It's not Aspen, but Lake Geneva is about the closest area to Chicago where ski bums at least have a few options. The vertical drops are on the smallish side, but you'll find an interesting mix of trails and decent amenities, such as restaurants, rentals, and repair.

Alpine Valley, 3 miles south of East Troy, has twelve runs, with a vertical drop of 388 feet (414–642–7374). Wilmot Mountain, 1 mile south of Wilmot, has twenty-five runs, with a vertical drop of 230 feet (414–862–2301). The Grand Geneva has twelve runs, with a vertical drop of 211 feet (414–248–8811).

Theater. The Eddie Cash Show/Belfry Music Theatre. Highways 50 and 67, Williams Bay, WI; (414) 245–0123. Eddie Cash, "America's Musical Storyteller," showing at the Historical Belfry Music Theatre. The only Branson-style music show in the area. So if this is your thing, don't look any farther. The tickets are a bargain ($8.00 to $20.00). For kids, check out the children's theater.

SPECIAL EVENTS

May. Chocolate Festival. Nestlé is the biggest employer in Burlington, so it stands to reason that people would want to celebrate its very existence with music, clowns, a petting zoo, and of course, chocolate concoctions of all kinds. Burlington.

August. Venetian Festival. Decorated boats, entertainment, food. Lake Geneva.

December. Children's Christmas Parade. Lake Geneva.

OTHER RECOMMENDED RESTAURANTS AND LODGINGS

Delavan

Lake Lawn Resort, Highway 50; (414) 728–7950. The Lake Lawn Resort can keep you busy in even the worst weather. Activities include miniature golf, horseback riding, ice skating, and just about anything else you can think of. A bonus for weary parents: A children's program (for ages 3–12) features games, hikes, crafts, and more, year-round. (The property, however, is badly in need of updating.) Rates range from $120 to $295 per night.

Fontana

The Abbey Resort & Fontana Spa, Highway 67; (414) 275–6811. The accommodations are a bit frayed and you won't catch anyone raving about the kitchen, but the Abbey can't be beat for recreational facilities—indoor and outdoor pools, bike rentals, tennis courts, golf course, and a location right on the beach. Each room has a VCR (nice to have on those rainy days), and there's a video arcade for the kids. Rates: $150 to $210.

For real indulgence, check out the day packages at the spa, where you can revel in massages, facials, loofah, the whole works.

Lake Geneva

Anthony's Steak House, Highway 50 just west of town; (414) 248–1818. Steaks may be in the title, but this is the best place to go for a real Wisconsin Friday night fish fry. It's all you can eat, with tasty side dishes of cole slaw and potato pancakes. Moderate.

Cafe Calamari, Highway 67 and Geneva Street, Williams Bay; (414) 245–9665. Pastas and seafood are the specialties at this relatively new restaurant on the lake. The ambience is that of an authentic Italian cafe, and the cuisine lives up to the billing. Homemade focaccia is baked daily on the premises, while cannoli and Italian ices will delight your sweet tooth. Moderate.

The Cove of Lake Geneva, 111 Center Street; (414) 249–9460. An all-suite hotel that offers a great location (across from the lake), indoor/outdoor

WISCONSIN

pool, and a small kitchen. Rates: $95 to $135.

Harbor Shores/Best Western, 300 Wrigley Drive; (414) 248–9181 or (888) 746–7371. On the shores of Geneva Lake, deluxe guest rooms with kitchenettes. Indoor and outdoor swimming pools, indoor Jacuzzi and sauna. Rates: $119 to $169.

French Country Inn, Highway 4 just off Highway 50 West; (414) 245–5220. Another popular spot for those who want privacy and luxury. Off the beaten track on smaller Lake Como (3 miles west of Lake Geneva), the French Country Inn is picturesque without being pretentious. The inlaid floor previously occupied the foyer of the Danish Pavilion at the 1893 World Columbian Exposition in Chicago. It was dismantled, board by board, and brought north—with spectacular results. Rooms have a country French motif. Rates range from $135 to $155 per night and include a full breakfast and afternoon tea (sherry and pastries).

Grand Geneva Resort and Spa, 7036 Grand Way, just off Highway 50 East; (800) 558–3417. A whopping $29 million went into renovating the old Playboy Club in 1994, and the Grand Geneva is a gem. The Grand Adventure Kids Club is a terrific solution if you want to bring the kids but still get some time to yourself. Counselors take the kids for half- or full-day programs. Other amenities include a spa, two swimming pools, racquetball, tennis, and two championship golf courses. Rates: $179 to $380.

Harpoon Willie's, right next door to Cafe Calamari (and owned by the same folks); (414) 245–6906. Sandwiches with homemade shakes and malts. Antique nautical decor, which you'd expect, given the big boating crowd. Open late. Inexpensive.

Interlaken Resort, Highway 50; (414) 248–9121. A full-service resort that offers all amenities, from exercise room to rental boats. This is a popular choice with families. Rates range from $99 to $245 per night.

St. Moritz, 327 Wrigley Drive; (414) 248–6680. A very popular restaurant, with a wonderful location, right in the heart of Lake Geneva. The Victorian mansion and the view of the water are as big a draw as the food is (try the salmon), but be advised: These are Chicago prices that hover in the $18 to $29 range.

Su Wing, 743 North State Street; (414) 248–1178). Better-than-average Cantonese cooking. The shrimp with cashews, in particular, is a winner. Inexpensive to moderate.

Tempura House, 306 Center Street; (414) 249–8822. Opened in 1997, the Tempura House brings a nice change of pace to the lake. Sushi bar, hibachi offerings (try the beef tenderloin) and more than thirty kinds of light, lacy tempura. Moderate.

FOR MORE INFORMATION

Geneva Lakes Area Chamber of Commerce, 201 Wrigley Drive, Lake Geneva, WI 53147; (414) 248–4416 or (800) 345–1020; www.lakegeneva.com.

Madison and Spring Green

A CAPITAL ADVENTURE

2 NIGHTS

Government seat • Museums (art and historic)
Prehistoric caves • Zoo • University of Wisconsin
Bicycling • Watersports • Arboretum • Shopping • Theater
Architecture • Botanical gardens

"Madtown," as some affectionately refer to Wisconsin's water-laden state capital, is set on four freshwater lakes spanning more than 18,000 acres combined. An 8-block-wide isthmus formed by the two larger lakes, Mendota and Monona, is the heart of the city. This is the home of Madison's most commanding feature: the Capitol, a splendorous sight during the day but even more so at night, when its 2,500-ton dome radiates the sky with a magnificent glow.

Madison is also the stomping ground for 40,000 students during the academic year. The University of Wisconsin's main campus stretches along the hilly south shore of Lake Mendota.

Always a bastion of liberalism, Madison was a front-row seat during the turbulence of the sixties and seventies. Even well into the eighties, pockets of hippies still found refuge in the campus environment. Today the rebelliousness has mellowed, and a warm, friendly, easygoing atmosphere pervades.

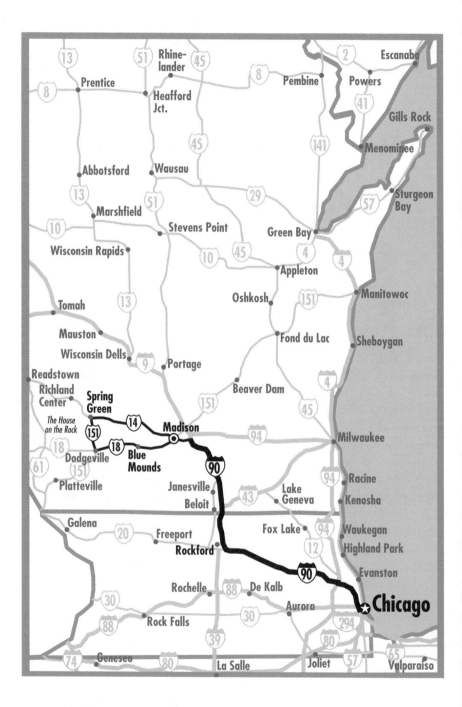

WISCONSIN

From an ethnic standpoint, the savvy-minded will delight at Madison's mix of cultures. Nowhere is this mélange more distinct than in the food department. Eating is an adventure, running the gamut from American cooking to foreign fare (Greek, Italian, Chinese, Mexican, German, and virtually any other cuisine your palate craves).

Don't be surprised by the magnitude of things to see and do in Madison and its surrounding area. Centrally located, Madison is a convenient base from which to travel to the Dairy State's calendar-art countryside and historic (and prehistoric) attractions. Furthermore, Madison is a recreational haven all year 'round. One word of caution, however: During football season, unless you're a Badger fan, stay away on Saturdays. Motels and restaurants are booked for miles around when the team is in town.

DAY 1

Morning

The drive to Madison can be a quick 2½-hour trip. From downtown Chicago take I–90 northwest to Madison; from the northern suburbs take I–94 north to Milwaukee, bypass the city on I–894 west, which will eventually feed back into I–94 for the remainder of the journey.

On the other hand, you can choose a more ambitious alternative and do some local sightseeing. If you opt for this version, an early start is highly recommended.

BREAKFAST: Heading northwest on I–90, make a brief stop in Rockford (one hour out of Chicago) at the **Pocketwatch Restaurant,** located in the Best Western Clock Tower Resort. Here, you'll find an ample menu with everything from waffles to omelets to Swedish pancakes served with lingonberries. The coffee shop is located at the junction of I–90 and U.S. Highway 20 (7801 East State Street; 815–398–6000).

Continue your drive on I–90, turning west on the Beltline Highway (U.S. Highways 12 and 18) just outside Madison. Stay on Highway 18, also known as U.S. Highway 151, to Blue Mounds (about a 1½-hour drive from Rockford). The first stop, the **Cave of the Mounds,** is a magical maze of underground caverns, considered the most significant caves in the upper Midwest. This geological jewel is a registered National Natural Landmark. Its colorful, iciclelike stalactites and stalagmites glisten so tantalizingly you'll be tempted to touch. But don't, or at least save your curiosity for the samples provided solely for that purpose. Your appreciation for the place will soar when you hear that the main cavern's earliest rock formations began more than a million years ago. You'll also develop an acute appreciation for light. The guides get a kick out of repeatedly extinguishing the lights and showing you the true definition of darkness.

Although a hot summer day is the ideal time to visit the Cave of the Mounds (the temperature remains at a cool fifty degrees, so bring a sweater), tours are given daily mid-March through mid-November and on Saturdays and Sundays during the winter. They last about an hour. Cost is $10.00 for adults; $5.00 for children (5–12); $9.00 for seniors. Call (608) 437–3038.

Not far (only a thirty-minute drive farther west on U.S. Highway 18 and north on Highway 23) is **The House on the Rock,** billed as Wisconsin's number-one tourist attraction. Some might argue that it's the most peculiar as well.

A monument to obsession, The House on the Rock was originally built in the 1940s as a country retreat by its now-deceased owner, Alex Jordan. The grottolike house, an architectural wonder built in and atop a 60-foot-high chimney of rock, is only a mere trifle compared with the labyrinth of bizarre collections that await in a series of adjoining, dimly lit museums. Prepare yourself for a brush with the twilight zone and slip into some comfortable shoes; you'll be doing a lot of walking.

Once you get past the first hour of your three-hour (self-guided) tour, you'll be doing a lot of marveling, too. This is a place of superlatives, including the world's largest carousel, the world's largest fireplace, the world's largest theater organ console, and the world's largest collection of Bauer and Koble stained-glass lamps.

Especially memorable is the Music of Yesterday Museum, which houses an extensive collection of animated, automated musical machines, as well as the gigantic carousel, illuminated with more than 20,000 lights. Also worthy of remaining in the deep recesses of your memory bank is the Organ Building. Some say Jordan considered this to be his pièce de résistance. Here lies the renowned theater organ console, which has fifteen manuals and hundreds of stops. Twenty-nine of The House on the Rock's fifty-two grand pianos are wired to the console. You'll feel as if you're in a dream (or perhaps a nightmare) when you enter this cavernous chamber, which gleams with copper (500,000 pounds are in the room). Catwalks zigzag, bridges that go nowhere abound, and spiral staircases will lead you to a photographer's deck. If you have an affinity for dolls, the Dollhouse Building is a must. A mammoth collection of dollhouses, ranging in architectural style from colonial to contemporary, is furnished in minute detail.

The best time to visit The House is in the morning. Crowds seem to triple in the afternoons. Also, because The House on the Rock relies heavily on natural lighting, an overcast, rainy day can greatly diminish your outing. Hours are 9:00 A.M. to dusk, April through October; tickets are sold until 2½ hours before closing. Admission is $15.40 for adults; $9.25 for children ages 7–12, $3.75 for children ages 4–6. Call (608) 935–3639.

LUNCH: Riverview Terrace (a twenty-minute drive north from The House on the Rock at Highway 23 and County C). During the summer of 1994, this Madison dining institution opened a locale inside the new Frank Lloyd Wright Visitors Center, the former home of the Spring Green Restaurant, the only restaurant Wright designed. Nestled among the trees and overlooking the Wisconsin River, the building's earth-red roof and spire are conspicuous. Interior furnishings are also Wright-inspired. The views are splendid, and fortunately, so is the food. Lunch is served between 9:00 A.M. and 4:00 P.M. Prices range from $1.25 to $6.95. Call (608) 588–7937. Open April through October.

Afternoon

Don't linger too long over a late lunch, because 4:00 P.M. is the last tour of the day at **Frank Lloyd Wright's Hillside Home School** at Taliesin. Tours begin at the visitors center, starting at 10:00 A.M. daily, May through October, and are given every hour on the hour. Wright was born just 30 miles from Spring Green and spent much of his childhood in the area working on his uncle's farm. He chose this community as the site for his home, Taliesin (pronounced "Tally-es-in," accent on the second syllable; the name means "shining brow" in Welsh), and for his architectural school. Also located on the grounds of Taliesin are several other Wright structures: the Hillside Home School, Midway Farms, Romeo and Juliet Windmill, and a house called Tan-y-deri, which he built for his sister Jane. Today Taliesin is the summer and fall headquarters of the Frank Lloyd Wright Foundation. Architects trained in the Wright tradition still practice here.

Allow at least an hour for the tour, which includes the school, a small theater, living and dining rooms, drafting studios, and a gallery containing Wright-designed furniture, artwork from his extensive Oriental collection, and models of Wright buildings. Admission is $10.00 for adults and $5.00 for children under 12. Pricier walking tours of the grounds ($15.00 for adults and $5.00 kids) are given daily. Call (608) 588–7900.

One of many badgers in the Wisconsin State Capitol

On the other side of the Taliesin estate, you can take a tour of Wright's home. There are two tour versions; a two-hour house tour and a four-hour estate tour. Both will take you through Wright's living room, garden room, study, studio, sitting room, and courtyard gardens. The estate tour begins with a lengthy talk and slide presentation. The guides are quite knowledgeable, and you'll feel that your time (if not your money) has been well spent. Two-hour tours cost $40. Four-hour estate tours cost $60. Tours do not allow children and require reservations.

You might also want to take a quick peek at **Unity Chapel** (go south on Highway 23 and east on County Road T). Designed by Chicago architect Joseph Silsbee in 1886, the chapel was built by Wright's mother's family. You'll be able to get a glimpse of Wright's former grave in the family cemetery, but that's all that remains. Although Wright was originally buried here in 1959, his third wife, Olgivanna, who hated Wisconsin, moved him to his final resting place in Arizona in 1985.

Also in the vicinity is the open-air **American Players Theatre,** set on seventy-one acres of the beautiful pastoral environs. The APT, which performs only Shakespeare and other classics, is recognized for having one of the nation's finest professional repertory companies. Matinee and evening shows (with more than one hundred performances per season) run from mid-June to early October. Attire is casual, so don't dress up. If you do call ahead and order tickets, arrive a little early so you can stroll the amphitheater. And don't forget the insect repellent. Tickets range from $15 to $32. Call (608) 588–2361.

DINNER: Head for **David W. Heiney's Dining & Spirits** in Black Earth. Go north on Highway 23 to Highway 14 and head east to Highway 78 South (1221 Mills Street; 608–767–2501). This restaurant was a meat market (bearing the same name) in earlier days (1888–1967), and many of the accoutrements are still in place, such as antique meat hooks that hang from the ceiling. Take a look at the bar; it was converted from the market's meat locker. As you might suspect, Heiney's serves some pretty choice steaks, ranging from $10.95 to $18.95. But don't let the carnivorous past fool you; you'll also find plenty of fresh fish and poultry specialties. Desserts, which include Bourbon Street pecan pie and white chocolate macadamia nut cheesecake, make a delicious finishing touch.

LODGING: After dinner, go east to downtown Madison to **Canterbury Inn,** (315 West Gorham; 608–258–8899). Actually this is a combination inn/bookstore/coffeehouse. Each of the six rooms is painted with a lush mural from a different Canterbury tale; some come with kitchenettes and whirlpools. Of course, as befitting an inn located over a bookstore, you'll find some wonderful reading on the shelves. Rates: $130–$260.

DAY 2

Morning

BREAKFAST: A continental breakfast can be taken in your room, the parlor, or the cafe in the Canterbury Inn.

Begin your morning at the **Henry Vilas Park Zoo,** on the banks of Lake Wingra and the Wingra Lagoon (702 South Randall Avenue; 608–258–1460). Admission is free and so is parking. As zoos go, this one is relatively small, but still very enjoyable. You can watch the animals, stroll to the beach, and if you've brought the kids along, you'll welcome the nearby playground. On Sundays, you can indulge them in free camel rides, too (10:30 A.M., June through Labor Day). The zoo's primates are a favorite among the locals, as are the felines. If you happen to still be hanging around at 3:45 P.M. (any day except Friday), you can also check out the lions at feeding time. The zoo is open from 9:30 A.M. to 8:00 P.M., May through August; 9:30 A.M. to 5:00 P.M., the remainder of the year.

Next take a walk, just 5 blocks away, to **Budget Bicycle Center** (1230 Regent Street; 608–251–8413) to rent some wheels. A reconditioned five- or ten-speed rents for $7.00 a day. If you prefer a mountain bike ($15) or a racing tandem ($30), try **Yellow Jersey** (419 State Street; 608–257–4737). First, take a quick spin to the **University Arboretum** (1207 Seminole Highway near Budget Bicycle Center) to see its impressive collection of the area's natural flora and fauna. Free nature lectures and walking tours are also given most weekends at the arboretum's McKay Center.

After spending a short time cycling around, you won't be surprised that Madison was voted one of the ten best bicycling cities in the country. Stay within the city limits to cycle around **Lake Monona,** a 12-mile ride. Just a note of local history: Rock-and-roller Otis Redding died when his plane crashed into Lake Monona on December 10, 1967, only three days after he recorded his biggest hit, "Dock of the Bay." A memorial to Redding is located on the lake's shore in Law Park off John Nolen Drive.

At the north end of Lake Monona, pedal into the **Olbrich Gardens** (3330 Atwood Avenue) to see its all-American rose garden. During the summer months, it's not uncommon to see a wedding in this romantic spot.

LUNCH: Before returning your bikes, ride back to campus and relax at one of the university favorites—the **Rathskeller,** located inside the Memorial Union (800 Langdon Street). Although the Rathskeller is nothing the students write home about, its fare of hamburgers, bratwurst, and beer (served cafeteria style) is inexpensive and transportable to the union's popular outdoor terrace overlooking Lake Mendota. This is one of Madison's best spots to find discussions on politics or philosophy, or just to do some serious people-watching.

While you're at the union, you can almost always join in a game of pool or table tennis, and the collection of video games rivals that of the best arcade.

Note: Free walking tours of the university depart from the Campus Assistance and Visitors center in the Old Red Gym (716 Langdon Street; (608) 265–9500) at 3:00 P.M. Monday and Friday; noon on Saturday and Sunday. Reservations are recommended, but walk-ins are also welcome.

Afternoon

Visiting the **State Historical Museum** (30 North Carroll Street on Capitol Square; 608–264–6555) is a good way to spend a Sunday afternoon. Closed on Mondays, museum hours are Tuesday through Saturday, 10:00 A.M.–5:00 P.M., and Sunday, noon–5:00 P.M. Admission is free. You'll be pleasantly surprised that there's nothing musty about this museum. It won't take you more than an hour to meander through the exhibits on Wisconsin history (from the prehistoric Indian culture to contemporary social issues). But remember to save some time for the gift shop. It is better than most and has some exceptionally designed Indian crafts.

DINNER: **Quivey's Grove** is a twenty-minute drive southwest from downtown Madison (6261 Nesbitt Road; 608–273–4900). Consisting of a stone farmhouse and stable built in 1855, this site is listed on the National Register of Historic Places. Dining is intimate, as you'll find each room of the house contains no more than five tables. Cheese, butter, and other dairy products are used generously, and all baking and cooking are done the old-fashioned way— from scratch. The menu is seasonal, but if your timing is right, try the stuffed tenderloin steak, oozing with Gorgonzola cheese and served on a bed of wild rice; polish it off with turtle pie. Dinner entrees range from $14 to $24, including soup or salad.

LODGING: The Canterbury Inn.

DAY 3

Morning

BREAKFAST: **Ovens of Brittany,** 3244 University Avenue; (608) 231–6858. This is the original bakery that grew into a restaurant. Ovens of Brittany is best known for the Brittany bun, a huge cinnamon roll sans the frosting. In deference to those trying to be trim, the bakery has also come up with a smaller version. Muffins, scones, and breads of all varieties are other specialties of the house. This is a Madison tradition that should not be missed.

A trip to the **State Capitol,** just down the street on Capitol Square, is a must. Free tours are given daily on the hour (except at noon): Monday through Saturday, 9:00 A.M.–3:00 P.M.; Sunday, 1:00–3:00 P.M. (608–266–0382); they begin at the ground-floor information desk. Allow one hour to tour the rotunda, the governor's conference room, the Wisconsin Supreme Court, and the senate and assembly chambers. You'll also hear a commentary on the artwork in the various rooms. Don't forget to look up at the Capitol's ornate ceiling or, when outside, to catch the glint of gold perched atop its white granite dome. That bit of gold (actually gold leaf) is a sculpture that's topped the Capitol since 1914.

State Street is really a great street in Madison. You'll enjoy roaming this 8-block pedestrian mall. The Capitol sits at one end and the University of Wisconsin campus is at the other. This is the emotional heart of Madison, and you'll find everything from ethnic restaurants, campus bars, and T-shirt emporiums to museums, coffee shops, art galleries, and bookstores.

The **Madison Civic Center** (211 State Street; 608–266–6550) is a restored movie theater that houses the 2,200-seat Oscar Mayer Theatre and the smaller, more intimate Isthmus Playhouse (330 seats). Tours of the theater spaces and facilities must be scheduled two to three weeks in advance. The **Madison Art Center** is also located at the same address. Its galleries contain changing exhibits of modern and contemporary art. Open Tuesday through Thursday, 11:00 A.M.–5:00 P.M.; Friday, 11:00 A.M.–9:00 P.M.; Saturday, 10:00 A.M.–5:00 P.M.; Sunday, 1:00–5:00 P.M. Closed Mondays. Admission free. Call (608) 257–0158.

LUNCH: Bluephie's, 2701 Monroe Street; (608) 284–8466. This is one of Madison's most popular spots, whether it's for breakfast, lunch, or dinner. Slide into one of the roomy booths and order something homey—such as an omelet with fried potatoes—or haute—like the chicken strudel. Moderate.

Afternoon

Time for dessert and another Madison tradition—ice cream from **Babcock Hall** (1605 Linden Drive; 608–262–3046). This is the campus dairy plant, where ice cream, yogurt, and cheese are manufactured. The milk is produced on a working dairy farm around the corner. If you walk upstairs to Babcock's second-floor viewing window, you'll be able to watch all the action. Babcock's scoops are generous. Flavors (about a dozen) are changed daily. Hours are Monday through Friday, 9:30 A.M.–5:00 P.M.; Saturday, 9:30 A.M.–noon.

One last stop before heading home—the **Elvehjem Museum of Art** (800 University Avenue; 608–263–2246). Designed by architect Harry Weese, the Elvehjem is said to be one of the largest university art museums in the country. The permanent collection includes more than 14,000 artworks, dating from 2300 B.C. to the present. Egyptian tomb sculpture, Russian icons,

American and European paintings, sculpture, prints, and drawings, as well as Asian art, are some of the highlights. Admission is free. Tours are offered if you call between two and six weeks ahead. Open daily, 9:00 A.M.–5:00 P.M.

THERE'S MORE

Farmer's Market. One of the Midwest's finest, this is held at Capitol Square in conjunction with other festivities on Saturday mornings, 6:00 A.M.–2:00 P.M., late April through early November. Get there early!

Capital Brewery Gift Haus & Beer Garden (7734 Terrace Avenue, Middleton; 608–836–7100). This traditional small German-style brewery opened in 1986 and specializes in lager beers. To get to Middleton from downtown Madison, go west on Highway 14 (University Avenue) and north on Highway 12. It's a fifteen-minute drive. Forty-five-minute tours of the working microbrewery (a very small brewery) are offered year-round. Call for tour times. During the summer season, the Beer Garden is open from noon to 8:00 P.M.

Watersports. To rent canoes, paddleboats, aqua cycles, kayaks, sailboats, sailboards, and waterbikes, try Rutabaga (220 West Broadway; 608–223–9300) or Wingra Canoe and Sailing Center (824 Knickerbocker Street; 608–233–5332).

Fishing. Picnic Point on Lake Mendota is a preferred spot on campus grounds to fish and picnic.

Ice skating. During winter months, the lagoons at Henry Vilas Park, 1400 Drake Street, and Tenney Park, 1440 East Johnson Street, offer skating. Both have warming houses. Call (608) 266–4711.

Cross-country skiing. The UW Arboretum (1207 Seminole Highway; 608–263–7888) is one of the most popular places. Other good trails can be found at Blue Mound State Park at Blue Mounds (608–437–5711) and Governor Nelson State Park, located on the northwest side of Lake Mendota, 5140 County Highway M (608–831–3005).

Golf. Two of the area's championship courses are the Springs Golf Course, which offers a total of twenty-seven holes (3 miles south of Spring Green at Highway C and Golf Course Road; 608–588–7707), and University Ridge, an eighteen-hole course rated one of the top three in Wisconsin by *Golf Digest* (at the intersection of Highways M and PD; 608–845–7700).

Madison Art Center (211 State Street, in the Madison Civic Center; 608–257–0158). Galleries contain changing exhibits of modern and contemporary art. Open Tuesday through Thursday 11:00 A.M.–5:00 P.M.; Friday 11:00 A.M.–9:00 P.M.; Saturday 10:00 A.M.–5:00 P.M.; Sunday 1:00–5:00 P.M. Free.

Madison Children's Museum, near Capitol Square at 100 State Street; (608) 256–6445. A real hands-on experience for the younger set (ages 1–13) and a real lifesaver on a rainy day. Open Tuesday through Saturday, 10:00 A.M.–5:00 P.M.; Sunday, 1:00–5:00 P.M. Admission is $3.00 (children under 2 free).

Geology Museum, 1215 West Dayton Street; (608) 262–2399 (first floor of UW's Weeks Hall). Rocks, fossils, a giant mastodon, and a 33-foot-long dinosaur skeleton, the trademark of this museum, can be seen Monday through Friday, 8:30 A.M.–4:30 P.M., and Saturday, 9:00 A.M.–1:00 P.M. Free.

U.S. Forest Products Laboratory, Gifford Pinchot Drive and North Walnut Street; (608) 231–9200. Established in 1910 by the U.S. Department of Agriculture and the university, this institution, which investigates the efficient use of forest products, was the first of its kind in the world. Tours Monday through Thursday, 2:00 P.M. Free.

Token Creek Balloons. Sunset rides spring to fall. Reservations required at least eight weeks in advance. Departures from Highways 190 and 151. Rides cost $145 to $175. Call (608) 241–4000 or (877) WE DO FLY.

Monona Terrace Community and Convention Center, 1 John Nolen Drive; (608) 261–4000. Almost sixty years after its original conception, Monona Terrace brings to life one of Frank Lloyd Wright's final creative visions. Visitors can stop by and peruse the building and rooftop gardens, which opened in 1997, either on their own or by guided tour (offered at 11:00 A.M. and 1:00 P.M.). This is also home to *Whad'ya Know,* the popular Saturday morning comedy/quiz show hosted by Michael Feldman. (See following information.)

Whad'ya Know Radio Show. Saturday morning comedy/quiz radio show with host Michael Feldman. Tickets are $5.00 for adults and $2.50 for children. Children under 12 get in free. Last-minute tickets are often available. Lines start early for seats; doors open promptly at 8:30 A.M. for the 10:00 A.M. show. Call (608–262–2201).

SPECIAL EVENTS

Late April. Capitol City Jazz Fest. Jazz jam attracting bands from throughout the United States. Held at Holiday Inn Southeast, intersection I–90 and Highways 12 and 18; (608) 233–2702.

July. Song of Norway. Musical production *Song of Norway* performed outdoors under the stars at Cave of the Mounds, in Blue Mounds.

July. Art Fair On the Square and Art Fair Off the Square. Hundreds of artists show works at Capitol Square and surrounding area.

July. Dane County Fair. Livestock judging, carnival, entertainment, and sampling of the area's best cream puffs. Dane County Exposition Center (Highways 12 and 18 and John Nolen Drive).

August. Middleton Good Neighbor Festival. Carnival, parade, art show, entertainment, and a classic German beer garden. Fireman's Park, Clark and Lee Streets, Middleton.

September. Taste of Madison. Madison's finest fare, plus entertainment. Capitol Square.

November. Holiday Parade. Santa and bands march at Capitol Square.

OTHER RECOMMENDED RESTAURANTS AND LODGINGS

Madison

Annie's Hill House, 2117 Sheridan Drive; (608) 244–2224. A small, traditional bed and breakfast; $124 per night, with a two-night minimum stay. No restaurant.

The Edgewater Hotel (666 Wisconsin Avenue; 608–256–9071), is everything its name suggests and more. Just a few short blocks from Memorial Union and Capitol Square (where the Capitol is situated), this hotel has 116 rooms and is within walking distance of all downtown Madison activity. Lakefront rooms (to $165), which are a bit more pricey than the lake view rooms (starting at $79), give a breathtaking panoramic view of Lake Mendota.

Blue Marlin, 101 North Hamilton Street (just off Capitol Square); (608) 255–2255. Informal and affordable. Seafood is the specialty of the house; try the grilled yellowfin tuna or the namesake blue marlin.

The Concourse and Governor's Club, 1 West Dayton Street; (608) 257–6000. Just steps from Capitol Square and the State Street Mall, this dual hotel offers luxurious executive suites at the Governor's Club and better-than-average accommodations at The Concourse. Rates range from $99 and up per night.

Dotty Dumplin's Dowry, 116 North Fairchild; (608) 255–3175. Don't miss the hamburgers voted number one in the state. Inexpensive.

Gino's, 540 State Street; (608) 257–9022. Specializes in veal, pasta, and stuffed pizza. Inexpensive.

Husnu's, 547 State Street; (608) 256–0900. Wonderful Mediterranean and Turkish cuisine. Soups, salads, and sandwiches for a casual lunch or dinner. Inexpensive to moderate.

Inn on the Park Hotel, 22 South Carroll Street; (608) 257–8811. Some of the city's best views of the Capitol. (Rates range from $96, double occupancy.) Indoor pool.

Kosta's Restaurant, 117 State Street; (608) 255–6671. Supper club with traditional Greek food and magnificent fish and seafood. The daily special is usually a splendidly creative Atlantic salmon dish. Diners rave about the leg of lamb and the filo chicken stuffed with feta cheese and spinach. Reservations recommended, especially on weekends, when live jazz fills the restaurant. Moderate to expensive.

La Paella, 2784 Fish Hatchery Road; (608) 273–2666. A gourmet's delight. Intimate Spanish restaurant, applauded by the critics.

L'Étoile, 25 North Pinckney; (608) 251–0500. Airy loft dining room with breathtaking view of Capitol Square. Named one of the top U.S. restaurants by Food Arts magazine. Expensive.

Mansion Hill, 424 North Pinckney Street; (608) 255–3999. Enchanting but pricey historic bed and breakfast renovated from a magnificent twenty-one-room mansion. Rates range from $90 to $290 per night. No restaurant.

Mariner's Inn, 5339 Lighthouse Bay Drive (off Highway M); (608) 244–8418. On the waterfront. Specialties of this Madison favorite are steaks, red snapper, whitefish, and lobster. Moderate to expensive.

Monte's Blue Plate Diner, 2089 Atwood Avenue; (608) 244–8505. This hot spot serves up good food any time of day. The meat loaf and garlic mashed potatoes will make you swoon. About half the menu is devoted to vegetarian dishes. The 1950s diner decor just adds to the experience. Inexpensive.

Sand Hill Inn, 170 East Main Street (Highway 78), Merrimac (30 miles north of Madison); (608) 493–2203. Take the free ferry from Madison to Merrimac, which takes about a dozen cars and runs from spring through fall. Three dining rooms in this 1907 Victorian home offer very cosmopolitan cuisine: beef tournedos, salmon en croute, duck with two sauces (ligonberry on the breast, peppercorn on the leg). Dinner only and Sunday brunch. Expensive.

Sheraton Madison Hotel, 706 John Nolen Drive; (608) 251–2300. Although not as well located as other accommodations, this hotel is quite comfortable and reasonably priced ($79 to $149 per night). For an extra $10 per night, you can get a room upgrade that is well worth the money. Indoor pool.

Spring Green

The Springs Golf Club Resort, 400 Springs Drive; (800) 822–7774. Not surprisingly, this 1,800-acre resort is Wright-inspired. Designed by an associate of the Frank Lloyd Wright Foundation at Taliesin, the Springs' long, low buildings blend beautifully with the surrounding trees and hills of the Jones Valley. True to the theme, all of the eighty two-room suites have fabrics and furnishings that reflect Wright. They also feature private balconies or patios that overlook the resort's two golf courses and the woods beyond. A European-style breakfast is included in your stay, as well as full use of the fitness center. There are two terrific indoor pools, racquetball and tennis courts, and a great masseuse to soothe stressed muscles. Rates start at $199 per night. All accommodations are two-room suites. The Springs also has packages, which include tours of Taliesin and plays at the American Players Theatre.

FOR MORE INFORMATION

Greater Madison Convention and Visitors Bureau, 615 East Washington, Madison, WI 53703; (608) 25–LAKES or 800–373–6376.

Madison Chamber of Commerce, 615 East Washington, P.O. Box 71, Madison, WI 53701-0071; (608) 256–8348.

Middleton Chamber of Commerce, 7507 Hubbard Avenue, P.O. Box 553, Middleton, WI 53562; (608) 831–5696.

Spring Green Area Chamber of Commerce, Box 3, Spring Green, WI 53588; (800) 588–2042.

Wisconsin Dells

CARNIVAL ALONG THE CLIFFS

2 NIGHTS

Theme parks • Boat tours • Miniature golf • Circus museum
Watershows • Indian ceremonials • Railway museum
Watersports • Horseback riding • Fishing • Golfing
Camping • Natural formations

The Wisconsin Dells is for the young and the young at heart. This is magnificent country, where natural formations of carved sandstone cliffs climb for miles along a serpentine channel cut by the Wisconsin River. A scenic beauty it is, but make no mistake: The Dells is also the land of cotton candy, go-carts, haunted houses, gigantic water parks, moccasins, and miniature golf. In short, the Wisconsin Dells is a rambunctious carnival beckoning tourists to try its wares and have a wonderfully good time.

Although the Dells, both Upper and Lower, are literally the well-springs of activity in this children's paradise, most of the area's eighty-plus attractions spill over into nearby Lake Delton and along the town's two main strips: Broadway (downtown Dells) and Highway 12. A seasonal spot (May through mid-October), the Wisconsin Dells doesn't really get rolling until mid-June when the crowds start pouring in. And they do. Summer in the Dells is somewhat akin to bees swarming a honeycomb.

The winter months may seem pretty sparse in comparison, but in recent years, tourism folks have tried to remedy that by attracting some new hotels with indoor water parks—just the thing for families who can't swing the Caribbean, but have cabin fever nonetheless. In addition, snowmobiling and cross-country and downhill skiing are all for the taking at Devil's Lake and Mirror Lake State Parks.

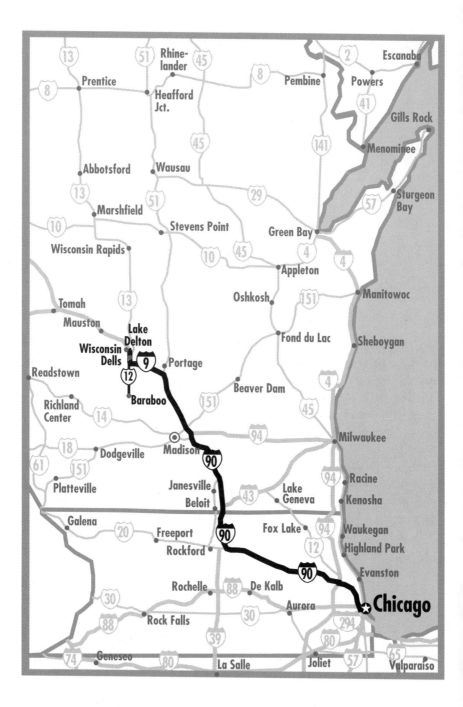

While picturesque scenery and hokey entertainment are Dells staples, don't expect much in the way of fancy cuisine. American fare served in "all you can eat" style is the norm, as are kiddie menus (which can be found in abundance). Oh, and one last pointer about this amusement haven: The Dells can be pricey. Discount tickets to various attractions or package deals are available, but when you come right down to it, there's no getting away cheap on this getaway weekend. The Wisconsin Dells—about a 200-mile drive from Chicago—can be a heck-of-a-lot-of-fun, but it will cost you.

DAY 1

Afternoon

DINNER: The first stop for anyone interested in getting beyond the pizza/burgers/fries repertoire should be the **Cheese Factory** (521 Wisconsin Dells Parkway; 608–253–6065). Since it opened in 1992, the restaurant has developed a loyal clientele grateful for a sun-dried tomato or balsamic vinaigrette. The emphasis is on vegetarian cuisine, which means the little ones can get pizza or grilled cheese while you order from the grown-up side of the menu, where pastas and stir-frys are all first-rate. Save room for the crème caramel or hazelnut torte.

Upstairs, on weekend nights, there's even live entertainment in a no-alcohol, smoke-free environment where kids are always welcome. Order a cappuccino (or ice-cream soda) and mellow out to the music. Inexpensive to moderate.

After dinner you can try out the "Tommy Bartlett Thrill Show" (U.S. Highway 12 at 560 Wisconsin Dells Parkway; 608–254–2525).

Bartlett, a veritable Dells institution, was a 1930s radio prodigy in Milwaukee and Chicago before becoming the vacation town's aquatic and air show impresario in the 1950s. The show, which is performed rain or shine, plays three times daily (1:00 P.M., 4:30 P.M., and 8:30 P.M.) at an outdoor amphitheater on the shores of Lake Delton. The best seats tend to be in the middle, but if you enjoy being part of the action, try the front-row seats.

Waterskiing, an acrobatic act atop a six-story spinning wheel, a trapeze artist who hangs from a helicopter, and a pair of juggling jokers are among the entertaining entourage. Although the night show can almost be a bit too long for children, this performance does have a colorful Laser-Rama light finale. If you have a hankering to participate, miniflashlights will do the trick.

Even though the theater is quite large (4,500 seats), you should order tickets in advance (especially if you drive up for the night show). Tickets range from $10.00 to $15.65. Children under 5 years old (who sit on your lap) are free. The show runs Memorial Day through the end of September.

LODGING: Black Wolf Lodge, 1400 Black Wolf Drive; (800) 559–WOLF. This hotel quickly made a splash when it opened in 1997, mainly because it boasts one of the nation's largest indoor water parks, with six slides (two for adults), a lazy river, and waterfalls. Not only can it save a rainy summer weekend, but it makes a wonderful off-season family destination, as well. The ambience is that of a North Woods lodge, and the furniture is all made by an Amish community in Wisconsin. Rates: $119 to $200.

DAY 2

Morning

BREAKFAST: Travel into downtown Baraboo—about a twenty-minute drive—for a stop at a local favorite, **Kristina's** (113 Third Street; 608–356–3430). Take U.S. Highway 12 south and Highway 33 east. **Baraboo,** which is built around a square, is the county seat as well as the original winter home of the Ringling Brothers' Circus (from 1884 to 1918). The Sauk County Court House, other municipal and civic buildings, a few historic circus sites, retail shops, and Kristina's are all easily identifiable. Kristina's serves a big breakfast, and at nearly half the price of a comparable early-morning eye-opener in the Dells. Belgian waffles, ham and eggs, omelets, and American fried potatoes (which are simply fabulous) are a sampling of the selection.

Just 3 blocks southeast of Kristina's (take Third Street east, turning south on Ash Street, and east again on Water Street) is the renowned **Circus World Museum** (426 Water Street; 608–356–0800 or 608–356–8341). For anyone who has even the slightest curiosity about the circus, the museum is a rewarding adventure into the realm of the big-top.

Live performances (two or three times daily), magic shows, circus parades, demonstrations of historic circus operations, concerts, and exhibits will absorb you. Plan on spending at least four hours here, and don't be surprised if you wind up hanging around for the entire day. In fact, you might find this museum to be the highlight of your weekend trip.

Make sure to catch one of the live shows. You'll see all the typicals: animal acts, high-wire walks, and a few flying-trapeze artists. All performances take place in a single ring, so there's no competition for your attention. The elaborate collection of circus wagons is also impressive. Ornate with three-dimensional statues and characters, some of these gaudy antique wagons are real works of art. It's not hard to imagine how they captivated the crowds while traveling from town to town.

The Circus World Museum is open from the first weekend in May to Labor Day from 9:00 A.M. to 6:00 P.M. Hours are extended to a 10:00 P.M. closing from July 23 to August 20, but exhibit facilities are open year-round. Admission is $11.95 for adults, $10.95 for seniors, and $5.95 for children ages 3 to 12.

LUNCH: The Circus World Museum. Children will enjoy the ever-popular circus fare: hot dogs, hamburgers, pizza. Eat outdoors picnic-style.

Afternoon

Head for the **Mid-Continent Railroad Museum,** 5 miles west in North Freedom (take Highway 12 to Highway 136, then head 2¼ miles southwest on County PF). A 9-mile ride on an early-twentieth-century train pulled by a vintage steam locomotive is the highlight here. What better way to get a glimpse of the countryside? The ride is exceptionally beautiful when the autumn colors are at their height, during the first two weekends of October.

The museum, run by volunteers who have restored dozens of antique engines and railcars, also includes an 1894 depot, a wooden water tower, locomotives, railroad cars, and equipment displays. Allow two hours for your visit.

Museum hours are 9:30 A.M. to 5:00 P.M. daily. Train rides depart at 10:30 A.M., 12:30, 2:00, and 3:30 P.M., mid-May to early September. Only weekend rides are given during September and October. A winter ride also runs the third weekend in February. Tickets cost $9.00 for adults, $8.00 for seniors, and $5.50 for children ages 3–15. Call (608) 522–4261.

DINNER: Retrace your steps back to Highway 12 and return to the Dells. Once there, head downtown to **Monk's Bar & Grill** (220 Broadway; 608–254–2955) for hamburgers, the house specialty. Part of the fun is watching the burgers fry in the front window. The other part is knowing that your bill won't punch too big a hole in your pocket. Don't forget to order the fresh-cut fries.

No trip to the Dells would be complete without a boat ride. After arriving at that conclusion, you'll need to decide which direction you want to take—namely, Upper or Lower. The Upper Dells tour (above the dam) lasts

2½ hours (adults $14.90; half-price for kids ages 6–11). It features two shore landings and an opportunity to see the famous Dells dog (the trademark of the place) leap over a rocky cliff to Stand Rock, a historic meeting ground of the Midwestern Indian tribes. The last Upper Dells boat ride of the night (7:45 P.M.) is a sunset cruise, complete with wine and cheese and a stroll through the tiki torch–lit paths of **Witches Gulch** ($22.50 per person). Boats leave the Upper Dells Landing in downtown Dells (11 Broadway; 608–254–8555 and 608–253–1561).

Lower Dells tours (below the dam) cost a little less than those to the Upper Dells (adults $10.90; same deal for the kids), but last only one hour, are non-stop, and less scenic. Combination tours are also available.

LODGING: Black Wolf Lodge.

DAY 3

Morning

BREAKFAST: In the mood for a hearty breakfast? Begin your day at **Paul Bunyan's Lumberjack Meals** (411 Highway 13; 608–254–8717). The place looks like an 1890s logging camp in a humongous log cabin. The menu (which is fixed) includes everything from sugar doughnuts and pancakes to eggs, sausage links, and hash brown potatoes. The food is unlimited, so don't be shy about asking the servers (earnest college students) for more. Lumberjack-style tables with old-fashioned wood benches add to the Bunyan ambience, as do the logging camp artifacts on the walls. The wait is never more than ten minutes. Breakfast is served 7:00 A.M. to noon, mid-April through mid-October. Cost for adults is $7.50; for children, 58 cents times their age.

OK, today you hit the attraction that everyone has been waiting for: This is the water park capital of the world, a title that Dells folks do not take lightly. One civic-minded gentleman told me that if you lined up all the water slides in the Dells from end to end, you could travel from Chicago to St. Louis on your butt. We've never crunched the numbers, but suffice it to say: Bring your swimsuit.

There are two major water parks and each has its fans: **Noah's Ark,** which claims to be America's largest water park, and **Family Land,** which is a little smaller. Both are open from late May through early September and feature wave pools, bumper boats, water-play areas for the preschool set, and just about any other aqua-attraction imaginable, as well as go-karts and miniature golf.

Hidden pockets of tranquility in the Dells

Noah's Ark is at 1410 Wisconsin Dells Parkway (608–254–6351) and Family Land is at 1701 Wisconsin Dells Parkway (608–254–7766), but you can't miss either; the billboards come fast and furious almost as soon as you cross the state line.

Know upfront that this is going to be an expensive outing, especially for large families. Noah's Ark admission: $24 adult or child; under age 3, free. (Family Land is a few bucks less.) At these prices, plan on spending the entire day. Insider's tip: To cut down on expensive concessions, pack your own snacks and make use of the picnic areas.

Believe it or not, there are other Dells diversions.

Doing the Ducks is considered an absolute must at the Dells. It's hard to tell who enjoys these amphibious World War II assault crafts more, adults or children. Basically, this is another boat ride (8½ miles on the Wisconsin River, Dell Creek, and Lake Delton). Yet these transports will also take you roaring through the woods. Remember not to wear nice shoes when you do the

Ducks and be wary of putting purses or other parcels on the floor (they'll get wet!). Start the ride at 1890 Wisconsin Dells Parkway (608–254–8751) or at 1550 Wisconsin Dells Parkway (608–254–6080). One-hour rides cost $14.50 for adults and $8.75 for kids ages 6–11. Open daily 8:00 A.M.–7:00 P.M., May through mid-October.

Next stop is **Pirates' Cove Adventure Golf** for a few rounds of miniature golf (at the intersection of Highways 12-13-16-23, exit 87, I–90/94; 608–254–7500). All in all, there are ninety holes on the numerous courses, which seem to go on endlessly. The park overlooks the Wisconsin River, and you'll find ponds and cascading waterfalls spread generously throughout.

LUNCH: Upper Crust, 232 Broadway; (608) 253–6001. Situated on the second floor with a big glass window, this restaurant will give you a good view of the goings-on along the downtown strip. Pan pizza is the main meal here, so sink your teeth in and enjoy. Open April through October.

Afternoon

Big Chief Go-Kart World bills itself as the nation's largest go-cart complex, and it very well may be. All ages will find a track to match their skills. You'll find lots of curves and multiple levels of track at Big Chief. The complex is located on Highway A off Highway 12. Admission: day pass (10:00 A.M.–5:00 P.M.) or night pass (3:00 P.M.–10:00 P.M.), $32 per person. Call (608) 254–2490.

A leisurely stroll in the downtown Dells along Broadway is another must. It won't take you long before you begin wondering whether the term "tourist trap" was coined here. Nonetheless, it's all part of the Dells experience. Besides, you'll find plenty to stick your nose into: game arcades, a wax museum, a haunted mansion, and shops that sell cotton candy, taffy, fudge, cheese, moccasins, old-time photos, blown glass, T-shirts, Indian mementos, and more.

DINNER: Ishnala Supper Club (Ishnala Road in Lake Delton) is one of the most serene and secluded spots in the area. The natural setting, overlooking Mirror Lake, is so tranquil and so beautiful that it makes the perfect ending to a weekend in the Dells. The hubbub is left behind; reservations aren't taken, and the wait can at times be long (1½ hours on Saturday nights). Nevertheless, the menu matches the scenery, and you'll be glad you decided to stay. Steaks, prime rib, fresh seafood, and lobster tail are the suggested choices. This isn't inexpensive dining, but your meal here will be most memorable. Call (608) 253–1771.

THERE'S MORE

Country music. It doesn't exactly rival Branson, Missouri, but country music certainly has surged in popularity at the Dells. The newest and largest of three theaters, the Crystal Grand Music Theatre (which seats 1,500), is open year-round and snares the newest country stars (Highway 23, near Lake Delton; 800–696–7999). Shows last 2½ hours, beginning at 8:00 P.M. Ticket costs vary with the performers. The Wisconsin Opry, the granddaddy of the Dells country music theaters (open since 1978), is part of an 80-acre working farm. Local and national professional talent performs nightly at 8:00 P.M., but dinner (which can be included in the price of your ticket) is served at 6:00 P.M. (Highway 12 at I–90, exit 92; 608–254–7951 or 800–453–2593). Tickets for the show only are: adults, $12.50, children ages 6–12, $5.00; ages 5 and under, free. With dinner: adult tickets, $24.50; children ages 6–12, $10.00; 5 and under, $3.00. Ticket prices include tax and gratuity.

Timber Falls, Highway 23 at the Wisconsin River Bridge; (608) 254–8414. If you like splashy water rides, then you'll love the new Timber Mountain Log Flume, one of the five longest water rides in the United States. About $2.3 million was soaked into this amusement, which carries passengers in little log boats up a 40-foot lift, then plunges them into total darkness and a landing pool down below. You'll also find a ninety-hole miniature golf course on the grounds. Open Memorial Day through mid-September.

Air Boingo Bungee Jump, 1455 Parkway Road, Lake Delton; (608) 253–5867. Not surprisingly, this absurd form of entertainment has found its way to the Dells. A 75-foot jump from the bungee tower will cost you $25. If you prefer being catapulted with a partner, try sitting in an ejection seat made for two, which Air Boingo shoots 150 feet into the air. It costs $60 per pair; $40 for solo launches.

Ripley's Believe It or Not, downtown at 115 Broadway; (608) 253–7556. Displays of the bizarre and unusual including a genuine shrunken head from the Amazon region and videos of other strange Ripley discoveries. Open May through October.

Nanchas Elk Ranch, County Road H, 9 miles west of the Dells and 5 miles beyond Christmas Mountain. You wouldn't expect to find a working elk ranch in the Dells (unless, of course, the elk had a water slide). Get an up-close look on a wagon tour. Open Memorial Day through October 31. Admission: $7.95 adults; $5.95 children 6–12.

Storybook Gardens, 1500 Wisconsin Dells Parkway; (608) 253–2391. Animated and live fairy-tale characters, a petting zoo, Ugh's Prehistoric Pals stage show, merry-go-round rides, and guided tours of the gardens aboard a miniature train. Open late May through Labor Day, 10:00 A.M. to 5:00 P.M. Admission: $8.99 ages 12 or older; $7.99 ages 2–11.

Lost Canyon Tours, 720 Canyon Road, Lake Delton; (608) 253–2781 or (608) 254–8757. Horse-drawn carriage rides down a mile of cliff-walled gorges. Tours operate mid-May through September. Admission: $5.75 for adults; $3.25 for children.

International Crane Foundation, Shady Lane Road, Baraboo; (608) 356–9462. (Take Highway 12 to Baraboo, then go 1¼ miles east on Shady Lane Road.) Another Dells anomaly: a center for the study, propagation, and preservation of endangered cranes. Open May through October, 9:00 A.M.–5:00 P.M. Admission for adults is $7.00; children 5–11 and seniors, $3.50; children 4 and under, free.

Sauk County Historical Museum, 531 Fourth Avenue, Baraboo; (608) 356–1001. Displays of American Indian and pioneer relics, Civil War equipment, household furnishings, toys, textiles, and memorabilia inside a 1906 mansion. Open mid-May through mid-September.

Museum of Norman Rockwell Art, 227 South Park Street, Reedsburg; (608) 524–2123. One of the nation's largest collections of Norman Rockwell art. Late May through early September, open daily 10:00 A.M.–6:00 P.M.; by appointment only for the remainder of the year. Admission: $5.00 for adults, $4.00 for seniors; $2.50 for children ages 6–17.

Devil's Lake State Park, Highway 123, Baraboo; (608) 356–8301. Devil's Lake is bounded on three sides by the quartzite cliffs of the Baraboo Range. Sailboard, rowboat, snorkel, and fishing equipment rentals are available. This is also the site of ancient Indian mounds. Naturalist programs and exhibits explaining the glacial phenomena of the area are provided. Open daily from 6:00 A.M. to 11:00 P.M.

Fishing. Beaver Springs Trout Farm on Trout Road (608–254–2735) and B & H Trout Farm at 3640 Highway 13 (608–254–7280). Catch rainbow trout from spring-fed ponds. Fish sold by the inch.

Gambling. Ho-Chunk Casino. Highway 12 between Wisconsin Dells and Baraboo (3 miles south of exit 92 off I–94); 608–356–6210.

Watersports. Lake Delton: Lake Delton Water Sports on Highway 12 (608–254–8702); Lake Delton Water Sports at Port Vista (608–253–7696). Wisconsin Dells: Holiday Shores Campground and Resort at 3900 River Road (608–254–2717); Point Bluff Resort at 3199 County Z (608–253 –6181); River's Edge Resort at 1196 Highway A (608–254–7707); Yogi Bear's Jellystone Camp Resort on Mirror Lake (608–254–2568). All have canoe, pontoon boat, paddleboat, shuttle, sailboat, sailboard, skiboat, waverunner, and parasailing rentals.

Horseback riding. Wisconsin Dells: OK Corral Riding Stable, Highway 16 (608–254–2811); Beaver Springs Riding Stable, 615 Trout Road (608–254–2707); and Canyon Creek Riding Stable, Highway 12 and Hillman Road (608–253–6942).

Golf. Coldwater Canyon Golf Course (4065 River Road, Wisconsin Dells; 608–254–8489). Nine-hole facility; lessons including package plans offered by the International Golf Academy (608–254–6361). Or try one of two eighteen-hole courses: Trappers Turn Golf Course (Highways 12 and 16, Wisconsin Dells; 608–253–7000) or Wilderness Woods Golf Course (511 East Adams Street, Wisconsin Dells; 608–253–4653). Christmas Mountain, Highway H, (S944 Christmas Mountain Road, Wisconsin Dells; 608–254–3971). Family golf resort (ski resort during the winter months) with twenty-seven new holes.

Theater of Illusion, 1666 Wisconsin Dells Parkway; (877) 254–5511. World-renowned master illusionist Rick Wilcox brought his skills to the Dells in 1999. Spend an evening watching grand-scale illusion such as the Spiker and Magic Elevator. Beware: Every night an audience member is cut in two! Rates: $20 for adults, $15 for children.

SPECIAL EVENTS

January. Flake Out Festival. Wisconsin's only state-sanctioned snow sculpting competition. Snowmobile races, ice skating, horse-drawn sleigh rides, snow volleyball, and hot-air balloon glows. Call (800) 223–3557 for details.

February. Wisconsin Sled Dog Championships and Christmas Mountain Winter Carnival. Sled-dog racing, weight-pulling championships, sleigh rides, entertainment, chili-cooking contest, cross-country and downhill skiing. Five miles west of Wisconsin Dells on Highway H, Christmas Mountain Village.

May. Auto Show. Car showcase for auto buffs includes antiques, street machines, and classics. Also features antiques flea market, swap meet, and "Parade of Cars." Held at Bowman's Park in downtown Wisconsin Dells.

May. Dells Balloon Rally. Hot-air balloon weekend competition at I–90/94 and Highway 12 (exit 92).

June. Heritage Days Celebration. Arts-and-crafts fair, ice cream social, tours of historic Jonathon Bowman Home at Bowman Park in downtown Dells.

September. Wo-Zha-Wa Days Fall Festival. Autumn celebration with arts-and-crafts fair, antiques flea market, street carnival, food, entertainment, and parade. Downtown Dells.

October. Autumn Color Tours. Authentic steam train tours amid brilliant hues of autumn. Held the first two weekends in October at the Mid-Continent Railway Museum, North Freedom.

October. Autumn Harvest Fest. This new festival features fall color tours, "Ghouls and Fools" parade, Taste of the Dells, and a craft fair. The more competative visitor can try the scarecrow stuffing contest or the fudge eating contest.

November. Dells Polka Fest. Polka music bash featuring ethnic food specialties and live polka bands. Holiday Inn, Highway 13, Wisconsin Dells.

OTHER RECOMMENDED RESTAURANTS AND LODGINGS

Wisconsin Dells

Chula Vista Resort, 4031 North River Road; (800) 38–VISTA. One of the more luxurious accommodations in the area. Lush suites with Jacuzzis, two-person bathtubs, and big-screen TVs. Indoor/outdoor pools, including a 40-foot-long water slide, health club, and tennis courts. Secluded on fifty-five pine-studded acres along the Wisconsin River. During peak season, rates range from $105 to $165 per night.

Ella's Kosher Deli & Ice Cream Parlor, 3 miles west of I–90/94 on Highway 151, 2902 East Washington Avenue; (608) 241–5291. Make a quick stop along the way at Ella's, an oversized ice cream parlor and perfect place for the kids. The menu is kosher, and the deli sandwiches are divine. Ice cream cones and milk shakes are another must. Make sure to look up—a fascinating menagerie of mechanized characters, ranging from Bart Simpson to Batman, perform amazing feats overhead. Don't forget to take a ride on the giant carousel out front, which operates May through October. Prices run from $3.75 to $8.00.

Field's Steak 'N Stein, Highway 13; (608) 254–4841. A local favorite that serves prime rib, steaks, and seafood. Moderate to expensive.

Meadowbrook Resort, 1533 River Road; (608) 253–3201. If you're trying to avoid sensory overload, this lodging will have a happy psychological effect. Only 8 blocks from downtown, this resort is a welcome respite from the relentless carnival atmosphere so pervasive in the Dells. The rooms are clean and spacious with kitchenettes. Six two-bedroom cabins (with fireplaces) were added in 1996. A small pool (with a nice slide) and barbecue grills are also on the premises. Peak season rates range from $99 to $219 per night.

The Monte Carlo Resort Motel on Lake Delton, 350 East Hiawatha Drive; (608) 254–8761. Within walking distance of Tommy Bartlett's. Kitchenettes are available. A heated swimming pool, tennis courts, and a small beach are other motel amenities. Just in case you were thinking of bringing Fido, don't. No pets allowed. Motel room rates range from $88 to $135 a night. Cottages and apartments can be rented on a weekly basis for about $750 (depending on summer dates).

The Polynesian Suite Hotel, Highway 13 at exit 87; (608) 254–2883. With its Polynesian theme, this hotel is geared more for the kids. A great water slide, a lazy river, a hidden cave, and kiddie play areas can be found, as can nice indoor and outdoor pools for the adults. Peak season rates range from $135 to $265 per night.

Sand County Service Co., 116 West Munroe Street; (608) 254–6551. Condominium, cottage, and other vacation rentals along the Wisconsin River. All have kitchens and provide towel/linen service.

Raintree Resort, 1435 Wisconsin Dells Parkway; (608) 253–4386. Another new addition designed to boost the Dells' off-season business, with its rainforestlike indoor water park. (The post–Labor Day rates drop by about 40 percent, providing another incentive.) Rooms are oversized and comfortable. Rates: $80 to $215.

Thunder Valley Inn, W15344 Waubeek Road; (608) 254–4145. This B&B is so quaint, you'll be surprised to find it in the Dells. Although this charming 130-year-old homestead, run by descendants of Norwegian immigrants, is one of the area's last bastions of tranquility, probably the best reason to stay here is the food. It's delicious, made from scratch, and one of the few Wisconsin Dells menus that appeals to an adult palate. Ann Sather–like cinnamon rolls, pancakes, whole-grain breads, and fresh fruit are just a sampling of the house specialties that are served at the inn's restaurant, a converted machine shed. Entertainment (a fiddler and sing-alongs) is also part of the fare. There's also a barn filled with animals to fascinate the kids. B&B rooms in the farmhouse (seven in total) include breakfast and range from $45 to $80 a night. Guest house rooms (there are six) cost less, $40 to $80, because dining is a la carte. A small cottage can also be rented.

Lake Delton

Wally's House of Embers, Highway 12, (608) 253–6411. A family-owned restaurant with classic American cuisine, especially known for hickory-smoked ribs. For intimate dining ask for the Omar Sharif room (a private booth for two). Moderate to expensive.

Del-Bar, Highway 12; (608) 253–1861. Seafood and steaks are the specialties here. Atmosphere is casual. Reservations aren't taken, but call ahead and ask to be placed on the priority seating list. Desserts are homemade and include tantalizing chocolate torte, pecan pie, key lime pie, and cheesecake. Moderate to expensive.

FOR MORE INFORMATION

Baraboo Chamber of Commerce, 124 Second Street, Baraboo, WI 53913; (608) 356–8333 or (800) BARABOO.

Wisconsin Dells Visitor and Convention Bureau, 701 Superior Street, P.O. Box 390, Wisconsin Dells, WI 53965–0390; (800) 22–DELLS or (608) 254–8088; www.wisdells.com.

Platteville and Mineral Point

BEAR HUNTING IN WISCONSIN
WITH A SIDE OF SWISS

2 NIGHTS

*Football summer camp • Antiques • Arts and crafts • Camping
Hiking • Museums • Festivals • Cheese tours*

Every year from about the end of July through mid–August, the favorite sport in Platteville is Bear watching.

For rabid fans, Platteville is sheer heaven. Here, on the University of Wisconsin's Platteville campus, is where the Chicago Bears have trained since 1984. Theirs is one of a handful of NFL training camps that make up "the Cheese League."

The primary objective of the hordes of fans is to catch the twice-daily scrimmages. That's easy. Just pull up a lawn chair or a blanket. The hard part used to be getting accommodations, but with the team's having fallen on hard times in recent years, lodging is easier to come by.

Still, the best advice is to book ahead. It used to be that a Platteville visit could be delightfully spontaneous, but no more. If you're aced out, consider a midweek getaway, use a more distant town as your base of operations, or consider the camping alternative.

Even if you're not a Bears fan, you don't have to spend the weekend hibernating. There are some other diversions in Platteville, where the entire downtown is a designated historic district. Or even better, you can parlay a Bears weekend into something more.

Platteville is situated amid the hills and valleys of southern Wisconsin, and you can take side trips to Mineral Point, which has some top-notch crafts

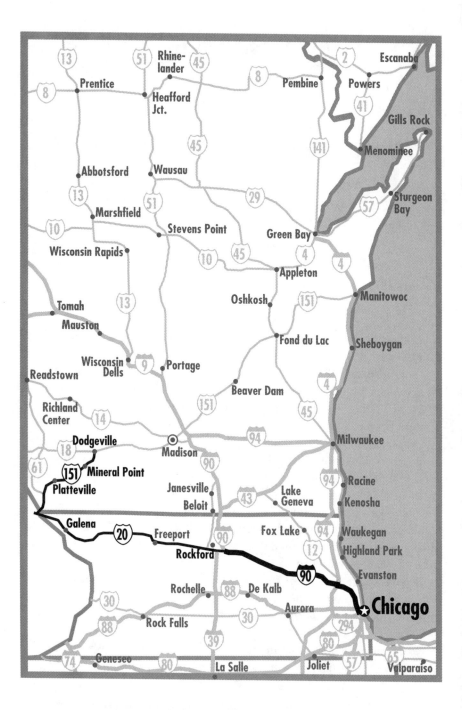

shopping; New Glarus, known as America's Little Switzerland; and Monroe, cheese capital of the Dairy State. All are easy drives from one another. The area bleeds into Madison and its environs (Wisconsin Escape Three), and Platteville's location makes even out-of-state forays accessible. (Galena and Dubuque are a mere thirty minutes away; see Illinois Escape Five.)

One cautionary note: If you're leaving Platteville with the Bears, be advised that the state troopers are out in force, just waiting to nab speeders. Former gridiron great Walter Payton got so many tickets that he finally gave up and hired a helicopter to bring him back to Chicago. Unless you plan to do the same, watch your speedometer.

DAY 1

Morning

Take I–90 west to Rockford and hook up with U.S. Highway 20 west to Galena.

LUNCH: Benjamin's Pub, 103 North Main Street in Galena; (815) 777–0467. Serves just about everything, but is best known for its toasted pitas and half-pound hamburgers. Inexpensive.

Afternoon

Take Highway 151 north to Platteville, about a half-hour's drive. Head right to the stadium, where afternoon scrimmage starts at about 2:00 P.M. Hang around after all the knees and ankles have been unwrapped and you may even get an autograph.

DINNER: Timbers Supper Club, Highways 151 and 80–81; (608) 348–2406. Known for its sprawling sirloins, it has surprisingly good seafood as well. Baking done on premises. Like everywhere else, the lines can get long during Bears camp. Eat early or late to avoid the crunch. Moderate.

There are two primary ways to occupy your evening hours in Platteville, and they could not be at more extreme ends of the entertainment spectrum.

The first is hanging out at one of the many drinking establishments on Mineral Street. Places like Freddie's Bar, Jobie's Tap, and the Patio Lounge not only give you a ready forum for your own preseason analysis, but you also have a pretty good chance of catching the players downing a few beers.

The second option is the **Wisconsin Shakespeare Festival,** which runs from early July to early August. Said one Shakespeare fan: "The quality is equal to that of Spring Green (home of the highly acclaimed American Players Theatre). The only difference is that you're seated in an indoor theater with cushions and air-conditioning." Call the university box office for the schedule: (608) 342–1298.

Actually, you can also catch a movie, thanks to a recent community drive to restore the **Avalon Cinema** downtown. First-run movies in an old-fashioned theater are an unbeatable combination. Follow with ice cream and you have one of life's great pleasures. Walk across the street to **Things of Importance** (100 East Main Street; 608–348–2233). Gourmet coffees, sandwiches, and pastries round out the menu.

LODGING: The **Governor Dodge/Best Western Motor Inn,** Highway 151 near junction with Highway 80; (608) 348–2301. The amenities include an indoor pool, a sauna, and cable TV. The Bears' practice field is 5 blocks away. Rates range from $67 to $87 per night.

DAY 2

Morning

BREAKFAST: Governor Dodge Coffee Shop.

No doubt those who are interested in football are already queuing up for the morning scrimmage. But if you have kids whose fascination with linebackers is dwindling, try the **Mining Museum** and the **Rollo Jamison Museum,** 405 East Main Street. The big hit here is descending the ninety or so steps into the Bevans Lead Mine, circa 1845, and riding the iron-ore cars around the museum grounds. At the Rollo Jamison Museum, you can view carriages, farm implements and other turn-of-the-century artifacts. Admission to both: adults, $6.00; seniors, $5.00; children, $2.50. Open daily, May through October 31, 9:00 A.M.–5:00 P.M. Check hours during the rest of the year. Call (608) 348–3301.

After all that mining stuff, get the lead out with an afternoon in Mineral Point, just about twenty minutes north on Highway 151. This region is known as the Uplands, because it was the only area not covered by glaciers. Like Platteville, Mineral Point's history is tied to mining, but today it is known as a center for arts and crafts.

LUNCH: If you'd like to experience a real small-town diner, save your midday meal for the **Red Rooster,** 158 High Street; (608) 987–9936. This is Mineral Point's main street. Don't miss an opportunity to try a Cornish pasty (rhymes with "nasty," but it's really quite a delicious turnover, stuffed with meat and potatoes). The homemade pies are blue-ribbon quality, and the prices are equally old-fashioned.

Afternoon

Check out **Pendarvis,** 114 Shake Rag Street; (608) 987–2122. This group of six carefully restored stone and log houses were originally built by Cornish miners in the 1840s. Winding footpaths connect quaint stone cottages. The complex is now owned by the State Historical Society, and costumed interpreters offer guided tours, recalling the days when this was a rough-and-tumble mining camp. Open daily May through October. Admission: adults, $6.00; children, $2.50; children under 6, free.

DINNER: Chesterfield Inn, 20 Commerce Street, Mineral Point; (608) 987–3682. This 1834 Cornish stone stagecoach-house-turned-restaurant features Cornish specialties, as well as standard American fare. In the summer, it's delightful to dine on the patio. Entrees cost $12 to $20; serving May through October.

After dinner, return to your base at the Governor Dodge Motor Inn in Platteville.

DAY 3

Morning

BREAKFAST: If you return to Mineral Point, the Red Rooster is a very popular gathering spot for breakfast, and it's open every day.

Travel another twenty minutes north from Mineral Point and see Spring Green, site of The House on the Rock, Wisconsin's number-one tourist attraction (described in greater detail in Wisconsin Escape Three).

Bargain-hunter's alert: **Land's End** (men's and women's wear) is headquartered in Dodgeville, just north of Mineral Point.

Head to **New Glarus** in time for lunch, which is fortuitous because New Glarus is the perfect town for people who love to eat. Known as "America's Little Switzerland," the town lives up to its culinary heritage, from cheese to chocolate. Indeed, many of the residents still speak their old-world tongue.

LUNCH: New Glarus Hotel, 100 Sixth Avenue, looks like a gingerbread castle with flowers overflowing from every balcony and window box. Don't miss the veal with roesti (hash browns swimming in cheese and butter). Other traditional fare includes fondue, which really hits the spot when there's a chill in the air. If you're here on a weekend night, you can also work up quite a sweat dancing to the lively polka band. Call (608) 527–5244. Rates for lodging: $54–$65.

Afternoon

After lunch, browse some of the shops that specialize in old-world goods. Snatch up sausages from **Ruef's Meat Market,** European imports from **Roberts,** and music boxes and clocks from just about everywhere.

No matter that you just ate lunch. If you have time for only one stop, make it the **New Glarus Bakery & Tea Room,** 534 First Street; (608) 527–2916. If the nut horns aren't illegal, they should be. These go so quickly that travelers who know they are going to be in the area order them in advance. During the holiday season there are people who come all the way from Chicago just to buy the stollen—a moist, dense bread studded with almonds and raisins. Baking begins in November and continues until Christmas.

A more touristlike experience can be had at the **Swiss Historic Village,** 612 Seventh Avenue; (608) 527–2317. The Swiss immigrant experience is retold by friendly guides who lead you through original and replica buildings. Admission: $6.00 for adults, $2.00 for children. Open May through October.

The **Chalet of the Golden Fleece,** an authentic mountain-style chalet, is the other significant museum. The chalet contains Swiss antiques and collectibles. It is located at 618 Second Street. Open 10:00 A.M.– 4:30 P.M. May through October. Call (608) 527–2614. Admission: adults, $3.00; children, $1.00.

En route home, continue south on Highway 69 to Monroe, which has a town square that looks like a Hollywood set. The focal point is the 1891 Green County courthouse and clock tower.

Monroe is also prime cheesehead territory. In this small town alone, four factories offer tours. The biggest is **Alp and Dell** (657 Second Street; 608–328–3555). Free tours are offered between 8:00 A.M. and noon (other times by prearranged request). Even if you don't hook up with a tour, you'll certainly have a good time stocking up on all varieties at the retail store. If it's just a quick sandwich, you can do no better than **Baumgartner's,** right on the square.

THERE'S MORE

Camping. Closest site to the Bears is Mound View Park, Platteville's city campground (with electricity and shower facilities). Also, check out the two state parks, Blue Mound (outside Mt. Horeb) and Governor Dodge (near Dodgeville, about 15 miles south of Spring Green).

Cycling. Military Ridge State Trail, which goes between Dodgeville and Verona, is particularly scenic. The 39-mile trail, developed on an abandoned Northwestern Railroad line, has a gentle grade of only 2 percent. For a guide, call (608) 935–2315. In New Glarus, try the 23-mile Sugar River State Trail, which runs to Brodhead; call (608) 527–2334.

Cross-country skiing. Military Ridge or Governor Dodge State Park, which is the second-largest state park and has exceptionally well-groomed trails. (But be on the lookout for wild turkeys.)

Downhill skiing. Tyrol Ski Basin, 5 miles west of Mt. Horeb. Ten runs. Longest run: 1,700 feet; vertical drop: 386 feet. Rentals, instruction, lodge. Call (608) 437–4135.

Fishing. Blackhawk Lake (crappie, blue gill). Also small streams in the area are known for bass and trout. Best spot is Locoma in East Dubuque, about twenty minutes away.

Fly-fishing. Orvis Midwest Fly-Fishing School. Five two-day courses a year held at Otter Creek, where pupils learn the tradition and craft of fly-fishing. Rates: $350 per pupil. Call (312) 440–0662.

Golf. Edelweiss Chalet Golf Course, Edelweiss Road. This lush course is Green County's only public eighteen-hole course. Call (608) 527–2315.

Hiking. Military Ridge State Trail, Governor Dodge State Park, and Sugar River State Trail.

Horseback riding. Governor Dodge State Park offers extensive bridle paths.

SPECIAL EVENTS

June. Heidi Days. The annual play with other festivities, such as yodeling. New Glarus.

August. Flavors of Old Cornwall. Demonstrations by costumed guides as they cook old-world favorites. Mineral Point.

September. Wilhelm Tell Drama and Festival. English version of the famous drama in outdoor setting. New Glarus. Call (608) 527–2095.

September. Monroe Cheese Days (held in even-numbered years). Farm and factory tours. Cow-milking contests. Dances, food, parade. Monroe.

OTHER RECOMMENDED RESTAURANTS AND LODGINGS

Hazel Green

Wisconsin House Stagecoach Inn, 2105 East Main Street; (608) 854–2233. This 1846 stagecoach inn has a stellar reputation that goes far beyond southwestern Wisconsin. It's furnished in country antiques, and most rooms have private baths. The breakfasts are consistently mentioned, especially the applesauce pancakes. Rates are $55 to $115. About twenty minutes from Platteville, ten minutes from Galena.

Mineral Point

The Duke House, 618 Maiden Street; (608) 987–2821. This Colonial house has three rooms furnished with antique beds and other collectibles. Tea and wine are served in the afternoon. The $55 rate includes homemade coffee cake for breakfast. Shared bath.

New Glarus

Chalet Landhaus, 801 Highway 69; (608) 527–5234. A comfortable but Spartan hotel. Some rooms with whirlpool baths. Good for cyclists because of proximity to Sugar River State Trail. Rates: $74 to $140.

Platteville

Cunningham House, 110 Market Street; (608) 348–5532. A lovingly restored 1906 home. The full breakfast may include such specialties as crunchy French toast, banana muffins, and fresh orange juice. Rates: $55 per room, which includes breakfast for two. Three guest rooms share two baths, but there are sinks in each room.

Mound View Inn, 1755 East U.S. Highway 151; (608) 348–9518. Downscale from the Governor Dodge, but clean and convenient. Rates: $45 to $55.

FOR MORE INFORMATION

Mineral Point Chamber of Commerce, 237 High Street, Mineral Point, WI 53565; (608) 987–3201.

New Glarus Tourism, P.O. Box 713, New Glarus, WI 53574; (608) 527–2095 or (800) 527–6838.

Platteville Chamber of Commerce, 275 Highway 151 West, Platteville, WI 53818; (608) 348–8888.

WISCONSIN

Oshkosh, Horicon Marsh, and Fond du Lac

COME FLY WITH ME

2 NIGHTS

Aviation • *Fishing* • *Hiking* • *Outlet shops*
Museums • *Geese migration*

For one week every year, this quiet community—otherwise known for overalls—has the busiest airport in the world. That fact may not sound too appealing to travelers weary of O'Hare, but if you love aviation and it's late July, you don't want to be anywhere but Oshkosh.

Air Venture Oshkosh is the world's largest aviation event, attracting more than 800,000 people and 15,000 planes. Visitors peruse row upon row of aircraft, ranging from antique classics to warbirds to NASA's latest technology.

If talking "wingspan" and "cruising altitude" isn't your idea of a good time, stick around. A highlight of each day's activity is the air show, when various sizes and configurations of aircraft make flybys over Wittman Field. Thousands of spectators crane their necks to get a better view of wing-walkers and daredevil pilots performing aerial stunts on aircraft such as Hawker Hurricanes and deHaviland Mosquitos. The show starts at 3:30 P.M. every day during the Fly-In except the last day, when it starts at 2:00 P.M.

Less awesome but just as important to aviation junkies are the forums and workshops, which have brought in name speakers such as Chuck Yeager and Wally Schirra.

Even if you can't schedule a visit during the Fly-In, it's possible to experience some of the city's aviation fever anytime at the EAA Air Venture Museum.

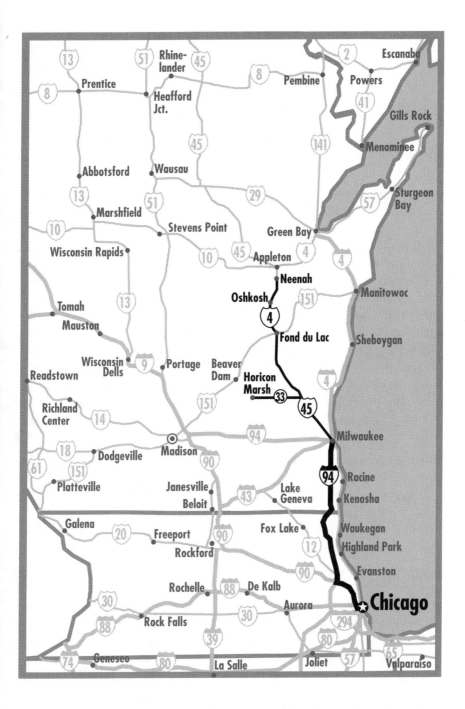

If you're not into aviation, you won't be grounded. Oshkosh is also home to two other exceptional attractions: the Oshkosh Public Museum and the Paine Art Center and Arboretum. Add some excellent fishing and off-price shopping, and you have a weekend that offers something for everybody.

DAY 1

Morning

Plan on a three-hour drive to Oshkosh. Head north on I–94 to Highway 41. About 40 miles outside Milwaukee, go west on Highway 33. This route will take you through **Horicon Marsh,** where 31,000 federally protected acres serve as a wildlife refuge—the largest in the United States. Each fall, tourists flock here, too, eager to breathe in the crisp, cool air and to enjoy the fiery hues of red and gold. But mostly they come to listen to the call of geese overhead.

Starting in late September and through October, tens of thousands of migrating Canada geese use the marsh as a layover on their way south. There are so many that the sky will actually blacken. (Be prepared to stop; everybody rubbernecks.) For a really good look, take a pontoon ride with **Blue Heron Tours,** on Highway 33, right near the bridge. Or, if you'd rather be your own captain, you can rent a canoe. Tours are daily from Memorial Day to Labor Day and on weekends only during September and October; (920) 485–2942.

If this sounds way too close to *Wild Kingdom* for you (or it's a month that doesn't end in an "r"), skip Horicon Marsh and stay on Highway 41 for another twenty minutes or so until you get to Fond du Lac.

LUNCH: Schreiner's, 168 North Pioneer Road (the intersection of Highways 41 and 23); (920) 922–0590. This restaurant in Fond du Lac has been a local institution for more than sixty years. Nothing fancy—the menu is long on beef, chicken, and sandwiches—but all the baking is done on the premises. Schreiner's gained fame with its clam chowder and pecan rolls. It's also a good bet for breakfast and dinner. Moderate.

Afternoon

After lunch, take the slightly kitschy "Talking Houses" tour. Two dozen Victorians are on the circuit, but by tuning in your car radio, you can hear about fifteen of them in detail. Stop by the Fond du Lac Area Convention and Visitors Bureau (19 West Scott Street) or any local motel for a tour map.

Exact replica of Lindbergh's Spirit of St. Louis *at the EAA Air Venture Museum*

If your architectural appetite has not yet been satisfied, head over to **Galloway House** (336 Old Pioneer Road; 920–922–6390), a thirty-room Italianate-style home purchased in 1869 by local banker-lumberman Edwin H. Galloway. This wedding cake of a mansion boasts many original furnishings, hand-stenciled ceilings, and intricately carved pine woodwork. Surrounding the home is a re-created village of almost two dozen buildings—grist mill, print shop, general store—many of which have been moved here from other locales in the county.

If, on the other hand, you're looking for someplace to let the kids run wild, then skip the history and go to **Lakeside Park** at the north end of Main Street. The deer park, minitrain, and carousel, as well as a lighthouse that's just great for climbing, will help relieve backseat bickering.

One more Fond du Lac note: The **Khristmas Kringle Shop** (1330 South Main Street; 920–922–3900) features ornaments from all over the world and other Yuletide trinkets—that is, if you can force yourself to think about winter.

In Fond du Lac, Highway 23 hooks up with Highway 41; then it's smooth sailing for another 17 miles or so to Oshkosh.

After you arrive in Oshkosh, you might want to spend the rest of the afternoon bargain hunting in the town's outlet stores. Check out **Prime Outlets–Oshkosh,** 3001 Washburn (off Highway 41), located just across from the Air Venture Museum. Brand-name outlet stores include Royal Doulton, Dansk, Oshkosh B'Gosh, and J.H. Collectibles. Elsewhere, there is additional off-price shopping at **CCA Candle Outlet** (1122 South Koeller Road), the factory outlet for Lenox candles, soaps, and accessories. **The Company Store** (901 South Main Street) is an outlet for down comforters, outerwear, and pillows.

DINNER: The Bellevue. House specialty is the smoky barbecued ribs at this lovely dining room at the Pioneer Inn. Entrees range from $15 to $20. Reservations are recommended.

LODGING: Pioneer Resort and Marina, 1000 Pioneer Drive (on Kini Island); (920) 233–1980 or (800) 683–1980. The Pioneer is situated on Lake Winnebago, which puts it a little farther away from the center of things, but gives it an edge in atmosphere. Extras include indoor and outdoor pools, whirlpool, tennis courts, miniature golf, and marina facilities. Rooms are well furnished, and some suites are available. Prices range from $115 to $139 per night.

DAY 2

Morning

BREAKFAST: The Pioneer Bellevue Dining Room for the obligatory Wisconsin sausage to go with an omelet.

Start your day at the **EAA Air Venture Museum** (3000 Poberezny Road, just off Highway 41 at Highway 44; 920–426–4818). It houses more than ninety planes—the largest private collection of aircraft in the world. In addition, there are several minitheaters throughout the museum, including one designed especially for future flyers under 12 years old, and a gift shop that the kids will go crazy for. Open daily (closed New Year's Day, Easter, Thanksgiving, and Christmas), 8:30 A.M.–5:00 P.M.; Sunday, 11:00 A.M.–5:00 P.M. Admission: adults, $7.00; kids under 8, $5.50; seniors, $6.00.

LUNCH: Right across the highway from the museum is **Wisconsin Farms Restaurant,** 2450 South Washburn Street (920–233–7555), which specializes in cuisine from the Dairy State. Not surprisingly, specialties are Wisconsin cheese soup and cheesecake. There's a good sampling of vegetarian dishes, but organically fed beef is a staple, too. Open for breakfast, lunch, or dinner, so it can plug into your itinerary almost any time. Inexpensive.

Or, if you prefer, combine food with fun and hop aboard the *Pioneer Princess* passenger yacht at the Pioneer Inn Marina. There are lunch cruises along Lake Winnebago, or later in the afternoon, hit the Cookies and Cruise (homebaked cookies and milk, iced tea, or lemonade). Couples should consider the Moonlight Cruise. Most trips are about ninety minutes in length, and prices range from about $10 to $26, depending on the meal. (800) 683–1980.

Afternoon

Take in the **Paine Art Center and Arboretum** (1410 Algoma Boulevard; 920–235–6903). A truly lovely Tudor Revival, the Paine Art Center and Arboretum was designed in the 1920s as the baronial residence of Oshkosh lumber mogul Nathan Paine. Construction was halted during the Depression but was resumed in the 1940s. Finally, in 1946, the Paines donated the home to the city, without ever having lived there themselves.

Today the public can enjoy the magnificent paintings, beautiful tapestries, and decorative arts (including one of the most magnificent collections of Tiffany silver), all displayed in period rooms representing the sixteenth through the nineteenth centuries. The five-acre arboretum changes with the seasons. Open Tuesday through Sunday, 11:00 A.M.–4:00 P.M.; weekends, 1:00–4:30 P.M. Admission: adults, $3.00; students with I.D., $3.00; seniors, $2.50; children under 12 accompanied by an adult, free.

DINNER: The **Granary Restaurant,** 50 West Sixth Avenue (920–233–3929), is a historic (1883) stone mill that has been converted into a very amiable restaurant. Prime rib is the specialty of the house, but there are always some seafood selections on the menu. The restaurant also has a children's menu, as well as a decent wine list. Moderate.

LODGING: Pioneer Inn.

DAY 3

Morning

BREAKFAST: Bellevue Pioneer Dining Room.

Complete your visit to the trio of museums with the **Oshkosh Public Museum,** just a stone's throw from the Paine (1331 Algoma Boulevard; 920–424–4731). The most popular attraction is easily the Apostles Clock, which sends twelve figures rotating every hour on the hour. Another favorite is the exhibit of stuffed animals (as in taxidermy, not toys). Its woodland settings are amazingly lifelike.

On the grounds adjacent to the museum are a replica train depot and fire station. Historians take note: The museum's reference library and archives, consisting of an impressive collection of manuscripts, photographs, maps, and other material, are available to the public by appointment. The museum is open Tuesday through Saturday, 9:00 A.M.–5:00 P.M.; Sunday, 1:00–5:00 P.M. Donations accepted.

To remember your trip to Oshkosh, stop at **Hugh's Homaid Chocolate** and pick up a box of crawlers. These pecan-chocolate confections (similar to turtles) are to die for. But call first—this family business is in operation only from mid-September to late May, and even then, hours can be irregular— (920) 231–7232.

Before returning home, take a slight detour and head north on Highway 44 for about twenty minutes to **Neenah** to fit in the **Bergstrom Mahler Museum** (165 North Park Avenue; 920–722–4658). The museum's collection of 1,700 glass paperweights is considered by some to be even more encompassing than the Art Institute of Chicago's. Donation. Open Tuesday through Friday, 10:00 A.M.–4:30 P.M.; weekends, 1:00–4:30 P.M. Downtown Neenah also has some cute shops that are worth browsing.

THERE'S MORE

Grand Opera House, 100 High Avenue; (920) 424–2355. This was the place for entertainment between Minneapolis and Chicago. Built in 1883, the Grand attracted some great touring stars, including Will Rogers and Sarah Bernhardt. It prospered through the early twentieth century, but in the 1940s it was converted to a movie theater and began to deteriorate. Thanks to some civic-minded folks, it has been restored to its original elegance and is now a fully functional center for the performing arts. Private tours last about sixty to ninety minutes; call for an appointment.

Camping. Circle R Campground, 5703 Knapp Street; (920) 235–8909. Also features free shuttle service during Fly-In.

High Cliff State Park, High Cliff Road, Menasha; (920) 989–1106. About thirty minutes north of Oshkosh (on Highway 55), near Neenah, is High Cliff, long a favorite for its stone bluffs. Besides camping, the park has facilities for horseback riding, hiking, cross-country skiing, and snowmobiling.

Fishing. Oshkosh is situated on Lake Winnebago, the largest inland lake in the state, and fishing is a big part of life in the city. While fishing is a year-round activity, peak season is May 5 through June 3. Good for walleye, perch, and white bass. Licenses may be obtained at local sporting goods stores and many bars. Also, with an abundance of marinas, boat rentals are easy and affordable.

Boating/Marinas. Fox River Marina (501 South Main Street; 920–236–4220), Gehrke's Marine Supply (1102 North Main Street; 920–235–3337).

Golf. Oshkosh has four eighteen-hole courses: Far-Vu (4985 Van Dyne Road; 920–231–2631); Lakeshore Municipal (2175 Punhoqua Road; 920–235–6200); Utica (3350 Knott Road; 920–233–4446); and Westhaven (1400 Westhaven Drive; 920–233–4640).

Larson's Famous Clydesdales. If you are willing to take a slight detour, visit Judy Larson and her stable full of Clydesdales—those huge horses made famous by Budweiser commercials. Visitors get an hour-long tour. (920) 748–5466.

SPECIAL EVENTS

June (second weekend). Walleye Weekend toasts Lake Winnebago's favorite fish. Fishing tournament and what is billed as the world's largest fish fry. Lakeside Park in Fond du Lac. Call (920) 923–3010.

Late July–early August. Air Venture Oshkosh. Wittman Regional Airport, 20th Avenue at Oregon Street. Call (920) 426–4800.

OTHER RECOMMENDED RESTAURANTS AND LODGINGS

Oshkosh

Ardy & Ed's Drive-In, 2413 South Main Street. A legitimate 1950s drive-in, complete with roller-skating carhops, burger baskets, and rootbeer floats. Open for lunch and dinner, March through mid-October. Inexpensive.

Ramada Inn, U.S. Highway 41 at Ninth Avenue; (920) 233–1511. This is an upscale property with lots of amenities, including pool, whirlpool, and sauna. Rates: $59 to $99 per night.

Lara's Tortilla Flats, 715 North Main Street; (920) 233–4440. Very good tacos, enchiladas, and burritos. Large selection of Mexican beers. Moderate.

Gardenview, 2605 Jackson Drive; (920) 303–0698. Straightforward Italian food, served in a garden atmosphere. Moderate.

Park Plaza Hotel, One Main Street; (920) 231–5000. Located in the heart of downtown near the Fox River. Request a room overlooking the water. Pool, whirlpool, gameroom. Rates: $77 to $97 per night.

FOR MORE INFORMATION

Fond du Lac Convention and Visitors Bureau, 207 North Main Street, Fond du Lac, WI 54935; (920) 923–3010.

Horicon Chamber of Commerce, Box 23, Horicon, WI 53032; (920) 485–3200.

Oshkosh Convention and Visitors Bureau, 525 West 20th Avenue, Oshkosh, WI 54902; (920) 303–9200; www.oshkoshcvb.org.

Kohler

PLUMBING AND PAMPERING

2 NIGHTS

Spa • Hiking • Hunting • Fishing • Golf • Wildlife refuge
Art galleries • Antiques • Crafts

Kohler—known for bathroom fixtures—doesn't sound as if it would be a particularly sumptuous place to spend a weekend. But most people leap at the chance to spend even a single night at The American Club, recognized as one of the finest hotels in the country and the primary reason people make the trek to this small town near Sheboygan. Since 1986 The American Club has earned the prestigious AAA five-diamond award, a claim that can be made by no other resort hotel in the Midwest. It also is one of the highest-rated resorts in the country, according to the readers of *Golf* magazine.

Kohler is less than a three-hour drive from Chicago, but it feels as if it's a world away. Built in 1918 to provide housing for the European immigrants who came to Kohler to work, the club was listed on the National Register of Historic Places in 1978. Two years later, it was completely renovated into a luxury resort.

Since this is the town that bills itself as the plumbing capital of the United States, you'd expect your room to have a nice bathroom. But are you ready for one with a greenhouse and a whirlpool? When you've reached the point of "prune," slip into the fluffy terrycloth robes that are provided for your stay. (They're also available for purchase.) Also impressive is the quality of other furnishings, from the crystal chandeliers and Oriental rugs to the down comforters.

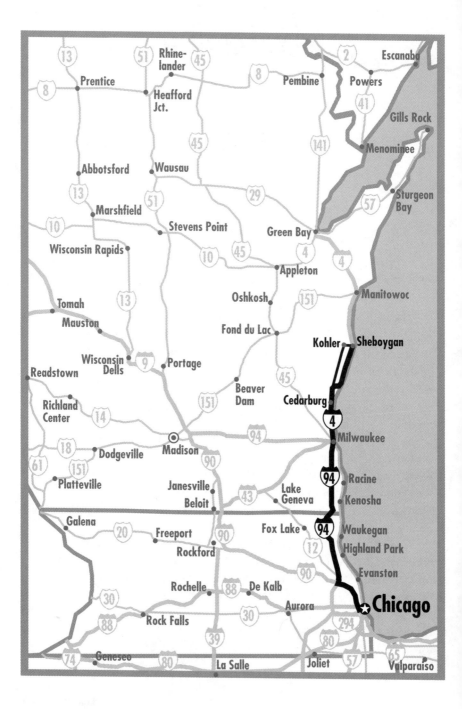

· DAY 1

Morning

The trip to Kohler is an easy one along I–94 to I–43. A stop in picturesque **Cedarburg,** about 17 miles north of Milwaukee, is an excellent idea, because check-in time at The American Club is not until 4:00 P.M.

The attraction in Cedarburg is the town itself, which has been designated a National Historic District. The venerable limestone-clad mill, the church spires, and the horse-drawn carriages that clip-clop through the streets in the summer all make this a charming destination, but it almost didn't happen. Some twenty years ago, Cedarburg Woolen Mill, built circa 1864, was scheduled for demolition. A visionary city council saved it from the wrecking ball, and it now is known as the **Cedar Creek Settlement,** a collection of thirty shops, boutiques, restaurants, and galleries. One of the tenants, the **Cedar Creek Winery** (N70 W6340 Bridge Road; 414–377–8020), offers a forty-five–minute free tour that includes sampling. Don't miss the upstairs, where you'll find more artisans. The pottery is especially attractive.

You'll find a thriving business district, dominated by antiques shops. **Washington Avenue Antiques** (china, jewelry, furniture) and **Grandpa's Barn Antiques** (where merchandise is displayed in roomlike settings) are among the best. You don't need to be a rock hound to enjoy **The Gem House,** which has more than 100,000 pounds of rocks for sale. We didn't have the time, but you can really get a feel for the district by taking a self-guided walking tour. (Maps are available from the Cedarburg Visitors Information Center in City Hall, W6 N645 Washington Avenue; 414–377–9620.)

LUNCH: Barth's at the Bridge, 194 Columbia Drive; (414) 377–0660. Regional American cooking (homemade soups, ribs, delectable desserts) served in an Early American setting of candlelit rooms and antique clocks. Children's menu. Moderate to expensive.

Or, consider stopping at **Covered Bridge Park** (junction of I–43 and Highway 60 at Five Corners). Not only are there excellent picnic facilities at water's edge, but the park also is the site of the last covered bridge in Wisconsin.

Afternoon

Continue traveling north on I–43. Take exit 126 to **The American Club** in Kohler.

Attention to detail is what gives The American Club an international reputation, which comes at a price—even by Chicago standards. All rooms have whirlpool baths, and are appointed with handcrafted woodwork and furniture. But rooms starting at the "Superior" level are more spacious, with amenities such as sitting areas, wet bars, and oversized whirlpools. Presidential suites are the most deluxe, with a separate living room with fireplace and a whirlpool for two.

If those extras are important to you, splurge on a more expensive room. If you won't spend that much time in your room but are eager to try everything from the game preserve to the racquet club, save the money. (All guests have the same access to the facilities, regardless of their accommodations.) Room rates range from $245 to $845 per night (slightly less November through April). Special weekend packages for two start at about $539, with varying meals and services included. Call (920) 457–8000 or (800) 344–2838.

DINNER: If you're feeling flush, dine at the **Immigrant,** which is the resort's most elegant restaurant. Prices start at about $25 and go up from there—and it's strictly a la carte. Again, the extras, which include monogrammed silver, palate cleansers of lemon sorbet served in crystal flutes, and impeccable service (two servers per table), help justify the freight. This is beef country, and the pan-seared filet of beef is excellent (as is the rack of lamb). Baby coho salmon is also a winner. If you still have some room left on the credit card, tell 'em to roll the pastry cart your way. Jacket and reservations required. In fact, this is such a popular spot, if you have your heart set on dining here, book a table as soon as you arrive at the resort.

DAY 2

Morning

BREAKFAST: In the **Wisconsin Room,** the hotel's classic dining room, start your day with such entrees as cardamom French toast or poached eggs Benedict.

You'll need the fortification for the 2½-mile tour of the **Kohler Company,** 101 Upper Road; (920) 457–3699. How often do you get to see how toilets are made?

The free tour takes a little more than two hours. You must be at least 14 years old, and reservations are required. Tours leave from the Kohler Design Center at 8:30 A.M. weekdays.

If you're more interested in the finished product rather than the process, head over to the **Kohler Design Center,** where you can see many room vignettes featuring state-of-the-art kitchens and baths. Settings in the 36,000-square-foot exhibition hall range from the traditional to the futuristic. The center is open daily and admission is free. Call (920) 457–3699.

Across the street from the Design Center is **The Shops at Woodlake,** an inviting shopping complex. Worth seeking out is **Artspace,** which is a gallery of the John Michael Kohler Art Center. You'll find a very well-edited selection of porcelain, earthenware, jewelry, and glass. (The hotel provides complimentary transportation for guests.)

LUNCH: Ready to eat? Depending on your mood, the shopping center offers two good dining options: **Cucina** and **Woodlake Market.** Cucina features moderately priced Italian cuisine. Enjoy alfresco lakeside dining in season and carryout service year-round. Call (920) 452–3888. Woodlake is a New York–style deli, with a very impressive selection of meats, cheeses, and gourmet foods. With a few tables and a dessert shop, this is just right for an impromptu snack. Call (920) 457–6570. Moderate.

Afternoon

Depending on the season, hike (or cross-country ski) the 30 miles of wilderness trails at **River Wildlife,** a private game preserve available to hotel guests with payment of a separate daily fee. Fishing (salmon or trout is usually the catch of the day), canoeing, trap-shooting, and hunting (pheasant) are also available for the outdoor enthusiast. In balmy weather this is an ideal spot for a picnic, or stop at River Wildlife's log cabin lodge for lunch daily or dinner on weekends. Here you can glimpse deer strolling right up to the dining room windows.

Speaking of fairways, the two PGA championship eighteen-hole golf courses at **Blackwolf Run,** 111 West Riverside Drive, are considered a real challenge. The River Course was ranked third among public golf courses by *Golf* magazine and was one of just eight public courses to receive five stars in *Golf Digest's* readers' poll. Obviously, golf is a very big deal here.

You could always move your fitness indoors and schedule a visit to **Sports Core** (a short distance from The American Club), where you can play a few sets of tennis, join in an aerobics class, or swim laps. The 2-mile jogging trail meanders through wildflowers (walkers welcome, too). Follow your regimen with some much-needed pampering at the spa salon. You'll be greeted with a cup of herbal tea, which is just the beginning of a hedonistic experience that may include facials, manicures, massages, and a hairstyling. Don't worry if you have kids in tow; a child-care center is right on the premises.

DINNER: If you want to try a more casual restaurant in the complex, the **Horse & Plow** is a glorified tavern, with pub fare such as hamburgers. Inexpensive.

After dinner, stop by the **Greenhouse,** a stained glass solarium that serves desserts, ice cream, and liqueurs.

DAY 3

Morning

BREAKFAST: Wisconsin Room.

The American Club may be the most famous place in the area, but it's certainly not the only one on the map.

Take Highway 23 about 15 miles west to the town of Greenbush and the **Old Wade House and Wesley Jung Carriage Museum.** Built in 1853 as a stagecoach inn, the Old Wade House was a stop on the trail between Sheboygan and Fond du Lac. The home is completely furnished in period antiques and open for tours, which also take in a smokehouse, blacksmith shop, and maple-sugaring cabin. The adjacent carriage museum features more than one hundred carriages, wagons, and sleighs from the nineteenth and early twentieth centuries. Open daily, 9:00 A.M.–5:00 P.M.; May through October. Admission: adults $7.25; children $3.25. Ticket sales end one hour before closing. Call (920) 526–3271.

Return east on Highway 23, past Kohler, and into Sheboygan, home of the **John Michael Kohler Arts Center** (608 New York Avenue; 920–458–6144). This former family mansion has been transformed into a gallery of contemporary American arts. Call for hours.

The **Sheboygan County Historical Museum** is at 3110 Erie Avenue; (920) 458–1103. Built in 1848, it is another home-turned-museum. Each room has a theme, such as children's toys or antique farm machinery. And, this being Wisconsin, there's a fitting homage to a nineteenth-century cheese factory. Open April through October, Tuesday through Saturday, 10:00 A.M.–5:00 P.M.; Sunday 1:00–5:00 P.M. Closed Monday. Admission: adults, $3.00; children, $1.00.

You can't leave Sheboygan without having a "brat." Try the **Hoffbrau Supper Club,** 1132 North Eighth Street (920–458–4153), for award-winning brats served every which way. If you ask for sauerkraut, you'll be marked as a tourist.

THERE'S MORE

Ecole de Cuisine, 765 H Woodlake Road (920–451–9151), offers weekend or weeklong professional cooking classes for the home chef, taught by head chef Jill Prescott. All classes have a specialized topic, from vegetarian entrees to Italian trattoria. Call ahead to reserve a place in class. Rates: $350 to $895.

Sheboygan Indian Mound Park, 5000 South Ninth Street, Sheboygan. This park contains eighteen of the original thirty-four effigy burial mounds of early Woodland Indians, circa A.D. 500–1000. The park has a self-guided mound and trail tour.

Kohler-Andrae State Park, 1520 Old Park Road (off City Road KK), 7 miles south of Sheboygan; (920) 452–3457. A lovely stretch of dunes and beach, as well as the **Sanderling Nature Center.** Camping and riding trails are also available.

Waelderhaus, West Riverside Drive, Kohler; (920) 452–4079. A reproduction of a home in Bregenzerwald, Austria, where the Kohler family originated, is open for tours at 2:00, 3:00, and 4:00 P.M. daily, except holidays.

SPECIAL EVENTS

March. Antique Weekend features fine antiques on display, as well as clinics and forums conducted by experts in various fields. At The American Club.

March. Ice Bowling. Could we make this up? The rules are the same as they are indoors: Bowlers can't wear spikes to improve their footing. Kohler. Call (920) 452–6443.

April. Spring Garden Market showcases plants and collectibles with informative presentations by experts. At The American Club.

June. Strawberry Festival. Strawberry desserts, contest, and all-you-can-eat strawberry pancake breakfast. Cedarburg.

July. Sousa Concert. Annual concert features the Kiel Municipal Band in Ravina Park, the same location used when John Philip Sousa and his band performed in 1919 and 1925.

July. Outdoor Arts Festival. The John Michael Kohler Arts Center holds a juried arts-and-crafts show, featuring 125 artists. Sheboygan.

August. Bratwurst Day. Sheboygan sets aside the first Saturday to pay homage to its favorite sausage.

Early November. Wisconsin Holiday Market includes arts and crafts to kick off the holiday season. At The American Club.

November. In Celebration of Chocolate presents an extravagant all-chocolate buffet, with dozens of cakes, tortes, and delicacies and thousands of imported and domestic chocolates. At The American Club.

OTHER RECOMMENDED RESTAURANTS AND LODGINGS

Cedarburg

Stagecoach Inn, W61 N520 Washington Avenue; (920) 375–0208. These twelve rooms are not as luxe as those at the Washington House (mentioned below), but they're filled with the same charm and graciousness. Some rooms have whirlpools. The inn also features a pub, a chocolate shop, and a bookstore. Continental breakfast features warm, flaky croissants. Rates: $70 to $130 per night.

Washington House Inn, W62 N573 Washington Avenue; (920) 375–3550. Lovers of Victoriana should put this B&B on their "must" list. The 1886 "cream city brick" building right in the heart of the historic district is terrifically cozy. Some of the twenty-nine rooms have fireplaces, some have whirlpool baths; all have antiques, down-filled comforters, and fresh flowers. Rates range from $69 to $189 and include an afternoon wine-and-cheese social hour and breakfast.

Kohler

Inn on Woodlake, 705 Woodlake Road; (920) 452–7800. A charming lakeside inn adjacent to The Shops at Woodlake, which opened in 1994 to offer more moderately priced lodging with access to many of The American Club's facilities. Rates: $155 to $265, which includes continental breakfast.

Plymouth

52 Stafford, 52 Stafford Street; (920) 893–0552. This is one of those inns that

make it onto everybody's "best" lists, so as long as you're so close (about 15 miles west of Sheboygan), you may want to add an extra night to your weekend just to see what all the fuss is about. The imported brass chandeliers, cherry hardwoods, and leaded glass make this Irish guest house a place to behold. There are twenty rooms, but the real center of activity is the bar, where Guinness stout flows freely. The rate of $80 to $120 per night includes continental breakfast.

FOR MORE INFORMATION

Cedarburg Visitors Information Center, W63 N645 Washington Avenue, Cedarburg, WI 53012; (920) 377–9620.

Kohler Visitor Information Center, Orchard at Highland Drive, Kohler, WI 53044; (920) 458–3450.

Sheboygan Area Convention and Visitors Bureau, 631 New York Avenue, Sheboygan, WI 53081; (920) 457–9495.

ESCAPE EIGHT

Door County

CAPE COD OF THE MIDWEST

3 NIGHTS

Biking • Boating • Hiking • Galleries/shopping
Theater/concerts • Fishing • Artists colony

You can easily spend a month in Door County, the finger of land that juts out from Wisconsin into Lake Michigan and Green Bay, so trying to distill the experience into a weekend is a formidable task.

With some 250 miles of shoreline (ranging from smooth beaches to rugged limestone), five state parks, and more antiques shops and gift boutiques than you could ever visit, it's no surprise that this has been one of the most popular spots in the Midwest for more than a century. After all, how many counties have not one maritime museum, but two? That's but one indication of just how strongly Door County has always depended on water for its livelihood—from fishing to shipbuilding.

Such geography has always been a magnet for artists, eager to capture its serene beauty on canvas. Then came the galleries and vacationers, and before you knew it, traffic was bumper-to-bumper on Highway 42 every weekend from June until Labor Day. Yet Door County has somehow managed to retain its small-town charm.

From Chicago, it's a lot of driving (about 250 miles), so if you don't want to spend your entire weekend behind the wheel, save this trip for a three-day weekend. One good way to pick up an extra day at no additional cost is to come during the off-season, when bargains abound. Door County has a wealth of wonderful little inns that seem especially cozy when the weather turns chilly. Nordic skiers can take advantage of more than 100 miles of cross-country ski and snowmobile trails.

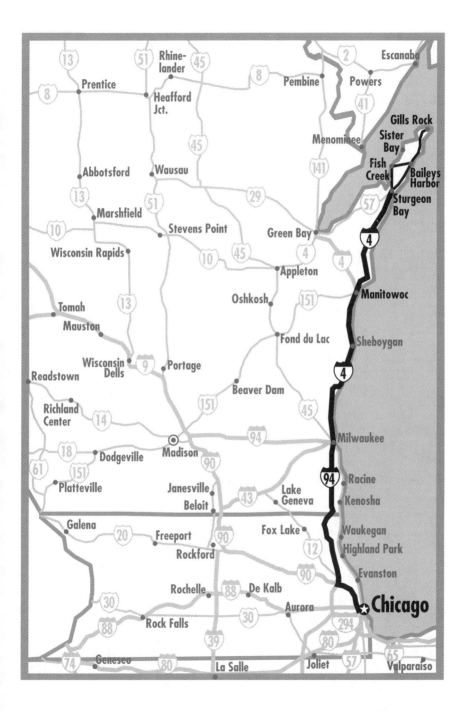

While there is a lot to see and do, the peninsula is only 18 miles across at its widest point, which makes getting around easy. (Highway 42 goes up the Green Bay side; Highway 57 goes up the Lake Michigan side.) The string of towns that run along the thumb each has its own personality, from Sturgeon Bay, the entry point for the county, to Washington Island, America's first permanent Icelandic settlement, accessible only by ferry.

DAY 1

Morning

Start your drive north on I–94, which turns into I–43, and take exit 76 into Manitowoc, about a three-hour drive from Chicago.

LUNCH: Head over to **Beerntsen's,** 108 North Eighth Street, which has been a fixture in downtown Manitowoc since 1932. Soups and sandwiches are available, but the real business here is superb homemade candies and ice cream. If you long for an old-time soda fountain experience, then this is a must.

You can travel even farther back in time at the **Wisconsin Maritime Museum** (75 Maritime Drive; 920–684–0218), which celebrates a century of nautical life. The highlight is the **USS *Cobia,*** a full-scale World War II submarine, which is moored outside the museum. The 311-foot-long vessel had a distinguished war record, sinking thirteen Japanese ships. Admission is $5.95. The submarine is open year-round.

Get back on Highway 43, which turns into Highway 42 around Sturgeon Bay. Continue on Highway 42 until you reach **Fish Creek.** Stop at **Ray's Cherry Hut,** Door County's oldest farm market, to stock up on goodies to take back to the room. What started as a humble produce stand is now a gourmet emporium stocked with cheeses, honey, jams, smoked fish, and homemade pies, along with twenty-three varieties of apples. During cherry season you can pick your own. Call (920) 868–3406.

While you're in Fish Creek, check out some of the stores. (Everything is on Highway 42 unless otherwise noted.) The more unusual offerings include the **Fish Creek Kite Company** (920–868–3769), just north of town, which offers a kaleidoscope of kites. **Spielman's Wood Works** is owned by Pat Spielman, the author of about twenty-five how-to books. At his shop you'll find everything from mailboxes to outdoor furniture. The **Edgewood Orchard Gallery** features two- and three-dimensional art (920–868–3579) and is a must for any true gallery hopper. Also stop by **Murray's Irish House** (920–868–3528) for beautiful sweaters, jewelry, and other gifts from the Emerald Isle.

DINNER: Inn at Kristopher's, 734 Bay Shore Drive, Sister Bay; (920) 854–9419. Owner Chris Milligan describes the cuisine as Midwestern eclectic, but patrons call it phenomenal. Enjoy drinks (or dessert) in the Aviary, a cupola just made for watching the sun dip into the bay. Signature dishes include: spice rub filet mignon and sautéed quail with Door County cherry sauce. Desserts include a to-die-for bumbleberry pie (a mixture of cherries and blueberries in a homemade crust). Dinner only. Expensive.

LODGING: Helms 4 Seasons Motel, just off Highway 42 in Sister Bay; (920) 854–2356. Located right on the water. Cable TV; some units have fireplaces. A room with a screened porch—where you can watch the sun dip into Green Bay—will add greatly to your enjoyment. So will the indoor pool. Rates: $74 to $89 per night.

DAY 2

Morning

BREAKFAST: Al Johnson's (Highway 42 in Sister Bay; (920) 854–2626) is a tradition in Door County. The history stretches back to the 1940s, when Johnson first opened a small lunch counter. Today it's a large complex that includes a boutique, a duck pond, and the trademark goats, grazing on the roof. Al Johnson's is busy all day long, but at breakfast you can sink your fork into some Swedish pancakes and lingonberries.

After breakfast you'll be ready for some physical activity. There are dozens of companies that will rent anything from a paddleboat to a 38-foot yacht. If you'd rather just relax, hit any of the public beaches on the bay side.

Afternoon

Pack up a picnic lunch (**Elquist's Market** in Ephraim, 920–854–2552, will do it for you) and explore **Peninsula State Park.** The 3,700-plus acres located between Fish Creek and Ephraim extend northward into the waters of Green Bay. A large percentage of the park is untamed, so you can almost count on seeing a deer or two, especially from the 10 miles of bicycle paths (bikes can be rented at the park entrance) or 20 miles of hiking trails. There are 467 campsites

Door County's exhilarating lakeshore

and a lush eighteen-hole golf course, as well. For great photographs and a spectacular view, climb the one hundred steps to the top of Eagle Tower.

DINNER: Trio, 42 and County Road E, Egg Harbor; (920) 868–2090. Another fine example of how Door County's restaurant scene has grown up. The menu is a melding of French and Italian, with a few American touches (such as horseradish mashed potatoes) thrown in for good measure. Entrees are as varied as lamb cassoulet and tuna steak. Also, you won't go wrong with any of the half dozen pasta dishes. Attention-grabbing desserts include cappuccino torte, key lime pie with raspberry sauce, and cobblers bursting with whatever produce is at its peak. Excellent wine list. No reservations. Open seasonally, so call first. Moderate.

If you're visiting between late June through mid-October, don't miss the **Peninsula Players** in Fish Creek, the oldest professional resident summer theater in the country. The repertoire runs toward Broadway classics, and the casts—professionals culled from New York, Los Angeles, and Chicago—are almost always first-rate. That it plays in a lovely setting, just steps from the Green Bay shoreline, merely makes a good experience even better. Sellouts are not uncommon, so if you have your heart set on theater, it's best to get your tickets in advance. Call (920) 868–3287.

LODGING: Helms 4 Seasons Motel.

DAY 3

Morning

BREAKFAST: The **White Gull Inn** in Fish Creek for fresh coffee cake, French toast stuffed with cream cheese and fruit, or the best corned beef hash you've ever had. Call (920) 868–3517. If you're staying farther south, check out the restaurant at the Inn at Cedar Crossing. (See "Other Recommended Restaurants and Lodgings.")

If you still feel like getting close to nature, there are four more state parks to explore. **Newport State Park** (920–854–2500), near Ellison Bay, is the second largest, with 2,200 acres and 13 miles of coastline. **Potawatomi,** named after the Indian tribe that populated the peninsula, is known for its "Ancient Shores" Nature Trail. This trail follows the edge of glacial Lakes Algonquin and Nipissing, which cut shorelines still visible 60 feet above the present level of Green Bay. Here, you'll find the county's only downhill skiing (920–746–2890).

Whitefish Dunes is the smallest of the county's parks (686 acres) and the only one that does not allow camping (920–823–2400). **Rock Island State Park** (920–847–2235) is the most primitive of the bunch. It may be reached by ferry from Gills Rock or Washington Island. The waves can be choppy and the winds can be wicked, so all but the most experienced sailors should leave the transportation to somebody else. Campers, however, love it because the entire 905-acre island is off-limits to motor vehicles, making for a blessedly tranquil experience.

LUNCH: Sister Bay Cafe, 611 Bay Shore Drive, Sister Bay; (920) 854–2429. Scandinavian-accented cooking from breakfast (heart-shaped pancakes with cardamom) to dinner (Norwegian salmon and dill sauce). Nice lunch stop, with a selection of open-faced sandwiches. Children's menu. Inexpensive to moderate.

Afternoon

Some people are die-hard shoppers who don't consider it a real vacation unless they return home with an armload of packages. Others would rather get a root canal than be dragged around from store to store on vacation. Even if you fall into the second camp, there are a few more shops that you really should squeeze in.

The juxtaposition of fine English collectibles and an eighty-year-old barn is just part of the cachet at **Chelsea Antiques,** located 2 miles south of Sister Bay on Highway 57. The names of various rooms (Chicken Coop, Country Loft, Milking Room) are as colorful as the merchandise. There's a huge variety here, from silver sugar tongs to a pine armoire. It's next door to **Tannenbaum** (10002 Highway 57; 920–854–5004). For people who truly want Christmas in July, this is the place to be. The shop stocks a huge selection of ornaments, wreaths, and other seasonal decorations. In December, St. Nick himself pays a visit.

DINNER: If you're a first-time visitor to Door County, you must attend a fish boil. A fish boil is to Door County what a luau is to Hawaii. It may not be the best food you've ever had, but it's part of the experience. Whitefish, potatoes, and onions are thrown into a big pot and boiled outside over an open fire (bring your camera). The dessert is always cherry or apple pie a la mode. There are several places that "do" fish boils. The **White Gull Inn** in Fish Creek serves it on Wednesday, Friday, Saturday, and Sunday evenings. Reservations are essential (920–868–3517). The **Viking Restaurant,** which has Door County's longest-running fish boil, serves nightly from mid-May through October (920–854–2998). Prices at each range from $10 to $18.

If you've already done the fish boil, then consider another excellent dining option on the Lake Michigan side of the peninsula.

Common House, 8041 Highway 57, Baileys Harbor; (920) 839–2708. Trissa Crowley and Patrick O'Boyle have been getting raves for turning out some of the most sophisticated cooking in Door County. Pasta and veal dishes change on a daily basis. Among main courses, don't miss the pork tenderloin with fruit, walnuts, and shallots in an apple cider sauce; and chicken dredged in cinnamon and cayenne, sauteed in olive oil, blanketed with goat cheese and garlic, and served with basil gnocchi. Extensive wine list. Chicago prices. Open May to October. Reservations highly recommended.

THERE'S MORE

Birch Creek Music Center, 3 miles east of Egg Harbor on County Road E; (920) 868–3763. This dairy-farm-turned-performing-arts-center sponsors an annual summer concert series. From mid-June through mid-August the center offers a wide variety of music—Strauss to Sousa, Big Band to Steel Band.

The Clearing, Ellison Bay; (920) 854–4088. Established in 1935 by noted Chicago landscaper Jens Jensen, The Clearing is an art school, but it's also for seekers of solitude. Even if you don't have an artistic bone in your body, stop by for the sheer peace.

Peninsula Art School, just off Highway 42 on County Road F, Fish Creek; (920) 868–3455. The Peninsula Art School has attracted serious and amateur artists ever since it opened its doors in the early 1950s. Anyone can sign up for a class, but perhaps the most accessible forum is the Saturday morning sketch sessions. It's open to anyone who wants to draw from a model and likes the camaraderie of artists.

Door County Maritime Museum, Gills Rock; (920) 854–1844. Full-size fish tug, which visitors may board, is the highlight; other nautical memorabilia. Open daily, July and August. Weekend-only hours in May, June, September, and October.

Door County Maritime Museum, 120 North Madison Avenue, Sturgeon Bay. More tribute to fishing and shipbuilding, including several ship sections and a sea captain's office. Open daily year-round. See the museum's Web page at www.dcmm.org.

Chief Oshkosh Museum, 7631 Egg Harbor Road, Egg Harbor; (920) 868–3240. Dedicated to the memory of Chief Roy Oshkosh of the Menominee Indians. Artifacts and possessions of the late chief, including his hand-painted buffalo robe, are on display.

Washington Island. Off the northern tip of the peninsula lies the country's oldest permanent Icelandic settlement. The Viking Tour Train (a tram, really) stops at Schoolhouse Beach, among other places, on its ninety-minute circuit. Another option: Rent bikes and cycle up to Jackson Harbor and then take a passenger ferry to Rock Island State Park (920–847–2235).

Fishing. Door County offers outstanding perch, walleye, large lake trout, and salmon fishing throughout the year. For a twenty-four-hour fishing report, call the Door County fishing hot line at (920) 743–7046. You can get a list of charter fishing captains from the Chamber of Commerce (920–743–4456).

Boating. For lessons, even landlubbers swear by Sailboats Inc. (800–826–7010). Others worth noting are Bay Breeze Sailing Charters

(920–743–1333) and Classic Yacht Charters (920–743–7200). The Boat House in Ephraim (920–868–3745) rents all kinds of water vehicles.

Golf. There are six courses in the area, including a very good eighteen-hole course in Peninsula State Park; (920) 854–5791. At the southern end of the county, try Cherry Hills, on Highway 42 just north of Sturgeon Bay; (920) 743–3240.

Miniature golf. Pirate's Cove, Highway 42, Sister Bay; (920) 854–4929.

SPECIAL EVENTS

May. Door County Festival of Blossoms, May 1–31. Blossoming orchards and gardens, wild flower hikes, lighthouse walks, and community celebrations. See their Web site at www.doorcountyvacations.com.

May. Maifest. Horsepulling, arts, antiques, 10K run, rides, entertainment. Jacksonport.

June. Old Peninsula Day. Arts, crafts, historic walk, food. Fish Creek.

June. Fyr Bal Festival. Scandinavian festival in Ephraim. Art fair, bonfires on the beach, fish boil.

July. House & Garden Festival. Tour of selected homes throughout the county. Call (920) 743–4456 for tickets.

August. Door County Fair. Exhibits, rides, and games in Sturgeon Bay.

August. Venetian Night Boat Parade and Maritime Festival. Sailboat races, dance, fireworks, food. Sturgeon Bay.

September. Door County Century Weekend. Bike rides of 30, 50, 75, or 100 miles take place throughout the county. Fish boil, entertainment.

OTHER RECOMMENDED RESTAURANTS AND LODGINGS

Baileys Harbor

Florian II, 8048 Highway 57; (920) 839–2361. One of the best-kept secrets in Door County. Lovely waterfront seating. Sophisticated menu (try the sole stuffed with crabmeat and broccoli). Early-bird specials are an especially good buy, with complete dinners available for around $12.

Egg Harbor

Casey's Inn, Highway 42; (920) 868–3038. The atmosphere says "tavern," but the food is much better than that, with upscale entrees such as veal scallopine and veal Oskar. Entrees start at $16.

Village Cafe, Highway 42, (920) 868–3422. A cheery, homey coffee shop known for its great omelets, tasty soups, and excellent burgers. Casual and inexpensive.

Ellison Bay

Griffin Inn, 11976 Mink River Road; (920) 854–4306. Nestled on five acres dotted with sugar maples, this inn typifies the gracious country retreat, from the gazebo on the front lawn to the handmade quilts on the beds. Ten rooms share 2½ baths; the cottages have private baths. Rates: $75 to $95.

Ephraim

Eagle Harbor Inn & Cottages, 9914 Water Street; (800) 324–5427. This white-clapboard inn, lovingly furnished with antiques, is that rare inn that welcomes kids. (You can tell by the swing sets.) Nine guest rooms with private baths, twelve cabins. Full breakfast included. Rates range from $75 to $175 for a cottage; $109 to $129 for a double.

French Country Inn, 3052 Spruce Lane; (920) 854–4001. Lace curtains, period furniture, and lazy ceiling fans can be found at this European-style bed and breakfast. Each of the seven rooms has a pleasant view of the gardens. Take breakfast either in front of the fireplace or on the porch. Rates: $75 to $100.

Fish Creek

Black Locust, 4020 Highway 42 (entrance to Peninsula State Park). The combination of limited hours (dinner only), intimate dining room (fifteen tables), and a talented chef (Christopher Kuhnz) has made this a hot ticket for those with big bankrolls. Specialties: grilled rack of lamb, breast of duck. Desserts: roasted plum in a brioche pastry with chocolate center. Service is very leisurely, so don't choose this for a pretheater dinner. Open daily May through October; weekends only starting November 1, but call first; (920) 868–2999. Expensive.

Thorp House & Inn, 4135 Bluff Road; (920) 868–2444. The word on this meticulously restored country Victorian is getting around. Four guest rooms and six cottages, along with some wonderful common areas, such as a parlor with a stone fireplace and a front porch with a view of the bay. Breakfast includes homemade scones. Not recommended for children. Rates: $90 to $150 per room or two-bedroom cottage. During winter, open on weekends only.

Whistling Swan, 4192 Main Street; (920) 868–3442. The atmosphere is one of spaciousness and luxury (fresh flowers, gleaming wood floors, baby grand piano). Seven decorated rooms and suites, all with private baths. Even if you're not a guest here, you'll want to stop at the Whistling Swan Shoppe, which carries top-of-the-line linens, Crabtree & Evelyn bath products, and other amenities. Rates: $109 to $159 per night.

White Gull Inn, 4225 Main Street; (920) 868–3517. Step into the White Gull and you might as well be stepping back into the nineteenth century. Note the wood-burning fireplace, the period wallpapers, fabrics, and furniture. No wonder it's a fixture on many "best" lists. Rates: $75–$125; cottage (sleeps up to 8) $140–$240.

Jacksonport

Square Rigger Galley, 6332 Highway 57; (920) 823–2408. A fish boil for people who want less of a tour-bus experience and more of an intimate one. Fish are caught that morning by members of this old fishing family. What else sets them apart? Hors d'oeuvres, homemade rye bread, fresh cole slaw, corn on the cob and—here's the best part—complimentary second helpings. Walk on the beach and work up an appetite before dinner. Moderate.

Sister Bay

Sister Bay Bowl, 504 Bay Shore Drive; (920) 854–2841. It doesn't look like much, but it's known for its succulent prime rib. If you arrive on Friday night, you'll see the crowds queuing up for the fish fry. Wind up the evening by bowling a game or two. Open daily year-round, but check for hours in the winter. Moderate.

Sturgeon Bay

Cherry Hills Resort & Golf Course, 5905 Dunn (off Highway 42); (800) 545–2307. A favorite with year-round residents, who love everything from the big picture windows overlooking the ninth green to the creative cuisine. Chef Susan Guthrie (formerly of Chicago's Ritz-Carlton) showcases fish (pecan-crusted trout, grilled salmon). Fine non-seafood options include the herb-covered prime rib. Outstanding Sunday brunch. Open daily seasonally. Call for off-season hours. Moderate.

Dal Santo's, 341 North Third Avenue, Sturgeon Bay; (920) 743–1945. Wonderful pastas and salads. Wash it down with beers that are brewed on the premises at the Cherryland Brewery, which occupies the same building. This microbrewery has gained national attention ever since winning top honors in the Great American Beer Festival in 1991 and 1992. Where else are you going to get to try cherry beer? Guided tours through the brewery are offered daily, 10:00 A.M.–5:00 P.M., and end in the hospitality room—with samples, of course.

The Inn at Cedar Crossing, 336 Louisiana Street; (920) 743–4200 (restaurant, 920–743–4249). Tucked into Sturgeon Bay's historic downtown, this is country Victorian living at its most gracious. The lobby, with its pressed-tin ceiling and crackling fire in the fireplace, instantly welcomes you. Nine rooms are tastefully appointed, and some have double whirlpools. Breakfast features scrumptious frittatas, from-scratch muffins, fresh fruit, granola, and coffee. Rates: $90 to $150 per night.

The Scofield House, 908 Michigan Street; (888) 463–0204. Magnificent Queen Anne–style home filled with antiques, stained glass, and an abundance of Victoriana. Four rooms have oversized whirlpool tubs. For true decadence reserve the 800-square-foot "Room at the Top," with five skylights, double whirlpool, fireplace, and wet bar. Enjoy breakfast on the gazebo. Rates: $93 to $196. Bill and Fran Cecil, owners of The Scofield House, also own a five-acre estate in Baileys Harbor, which includes an 1860 log home on Lake Michigan that has been transformed with Victorian elegance and contemporary amenities.

White Lace Inn, 16 North Fifth Avenue; (920) 743–1105. This fifteen-room Victorian is undeniably romantic and is always mentioned on "ten best inns" lists. It's actually three historic houses connected by a red-brick path that winds through lovely grounds. Breakfast (included) is homemade baked goods, along with Scandinavian fruit soup. Rates range from $98 to $198 per night.

FOR MORE INFORMATION

Door County Chamber of Commerce, Box 406, Sturgeon, WI 54235; (920) 743–4456 or (800) 52–RELAX; www.doorcountyvacations.com.

INDIANA
ESCAPES

Michigan City

DOIN' DUNES COUNTRY

1 NIGHT

Antiques • Shopping • Fishing • Boating • U-pick produce
Golf • Hiking • Cross-country skiing

As you travel through northwest Indiana, it's hard to believe that beyond the grime of the steel mills lies as unspoiled and untamed a landscape as you'll find anywhere in the Midwest. The Indiana Dunes National Lakeshore, which covers 13,000 acres on the southern shore of Lake Michigan, is one of the region's jewels. Carl Sandburg wrote, "The dunes are to the Midwest what the Grand Canyon is to Arizona and Yosemite is to California. They constitute a signature of time and eternity."

The area is easily accessible (not much more than an hour from downtown) and not overly touristed. No two people "do" the Dunes in exactly the same way, so personal discoveries abound for anyone willing to turn off the interstate.

Unlike other weekend trips where everything is usually confined to one quaint little town, this trip can spread over three counties: Lake, Porter, and LaPorte. For this trip we've made Michigan City our base of operations. But you could just as easily opt for Crown Point or Valparaiso (see "There's More"). Also, Michigan City is just a fifteen-minute drive from southwest Michigan, so think nothing of bopping over the border for dinner; the natives certainly don't, especially because the selection is far more extensive.

The first order of business is to zero in on what kind of weekend it's going to be. Hanging out at the beach? Hiking? Outlet shopping? Antiquing? Berry

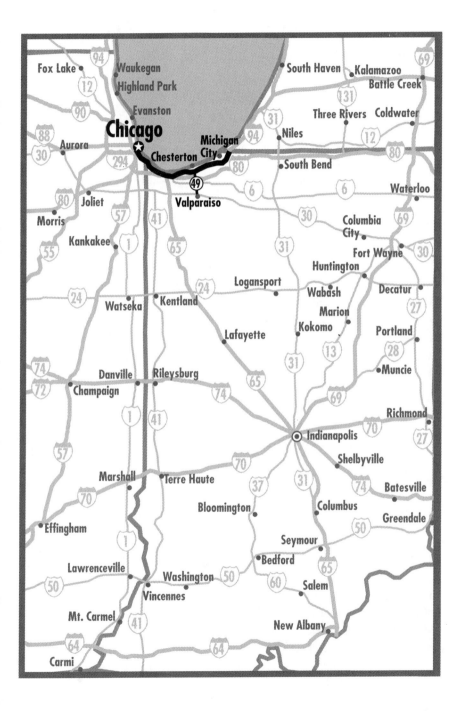

picking? Festival? Once you've determined the focus, the other considerations (lodging, restaurants) will fall into place.

DAY 1

Morning

Hit the road (I–94) early and you should be at your final destination, Michigan City, by afternoon—and that's with a few stops at some of the area's prime antiques malls. One of the advantages of leaving Saturday morning instead of Friday night is that you avoid the horrendous traffic as everyone else heads out of town. If the tie-ups are interminable, get off at I–65 and go north until you hit U.S. Highway 12; then continue traveling east. It's the route people traveled before the days of the superhighways.

Now back to those antiques. Northwest Indiana still has terrific bargains—especially in furniture—because it doesn't get the huge influx of tourists of other areas, such as Galena and Lake Geneva. Indeed, judging by the number of tour buses from far-flung states, northwest Indiana's reputation as a mother lode of antiques is better known outside the Midwest. There are more than 300 antiques dealers in Michigan City and LaPorte alone.

Turn off I–94 to 49 North, exit at Highway 20 East. Go 5 miles and follow the signs to **The Schoolhouse Shops** (278 East 1500 N, 1 block north of Highway 20). There you'll find a setting—a late-nineteenth-century schoolhouse—that is as pleasant as the wares. At **Panozzo's Pantry,** load up on gourmet foods (from pasta sauces to tapenades), while **Glad Rags** offers fabulous contemporary women's clothing and **The Schoolhouse Shops & Antiques** is a treasure trove of furniture, glassware, silver, and art.

If The Schoolhouse has just whetted your appetite for collectibles, return to 49 South and make the 5-mile hop to downtown Chesterton, where you can hit another half dozen or so places, all truly first-rate, all within an easy walk of one another. Here's just a sampling: **Antiques 101** (101 Broadway) and **Antiques 102** (402 Broadway) for Victorian furniture; **Russ & Barb** (302 Lincoln) for glassware; and **Yesterday's Treasures** (700 Broadway), an antiques mall with 130 dealers for just about anything.

One other unusual stop is the **Yellow Brick Road Gift Shop and Museum** (109 East 950 N; 219–926–7048; open Monday through Saturday, 10:00 A.M.–5:00 P.M.). Every September, Chesterton plays host to the Wizard of Oz Festival, which attracts fans of the 1939 film from all over the country. Events include Oz trivia contests and personal appearances by the movie's surviving Munchkins. But even if you're not visiting at festival time, you can still follow the Yellow Brick Road to the museum, which features lots of fascinating memorabilia. Free.

LUNCH: Lucrezia's, 428 South Calumet (219–926–LUCY). You've no doubt worked up quiet an appetite. Lucky that you're right near one of the region's best trattorias. Don't let the modest storefront fool you; fine cooking is the byword here. Recommended: pan-fried polenta, grilled eggplant (for starters). The penne porcini has a rabid following, as do the veal dishes. Great fruit tarts. The only downside: The noise level can be annyoing. If weather permits, opt for outside dining. Moderate.

Afternoon

Get back to I–94 and travel the short distance to Michigan City, largest city in Northern Indiana Harbor Country, which encompasses Michigan City, LaPorte, and surrounding communities in the county.

Make this your designated shopping day and forge ahead to **Prime Outlets at Michigan City,** 601 Wabash Street; (219) 879–6506. With 120 factory outlet stores featuring brand names such as Ralph Lauren, Burberry, Dansk, Eddie Bauer, Anne Klein, Crate & Barrel, DKNY, and J. Crew, this is a shopper's paradise.

Let's face it: Most visitors see little else beyond the outlet mall and the beach. If you want to do some sightseeing, however, head over to the **Barker Mansion and Civic Center,** 631 Washington Street; (219) 873–1520. This opulent thirty-eight-room Victorian estate was home to millionaire industrialist John Barker. You'll admire the rare woods, sleek marble, and lush gardens any time of the year, but at Christmas the home is decorated and especially worth your time. Guided tours during the summer: Monday through Friday at 10:00 A.M., 11:30 A.M., and 1:00 P.M.; Saturday and Sunday at noon and 2:00 P.M. Check hours during the off-season. Admission is $2.00.

If you get hungry, the food service here offers a few options. The **5th Street Deli,** near the Barker Mansion and Civic Center, is a casual eatery with excellent sandwiches, such as "The Three Stooges" and the "Sophia Loren"(431 Washington Street; 219–872–5204). **Klucker's Eatery** (231 West

The Indiana Dunes National Lakeshore boasts one of the best beaches in the Midwest.

Seventh Street; 219–872–8685) and **Lakeshore Coffee** (444 Wabash Street; 219–874–7006, a traditional coffeehouse with poetry readings and such) offer excellent light lunch options.

DINNER: Basil's, 521 Franklin Square; (219) 872–4500. A beautiful bistro with terrific crab cakes, paella, and manicotti. First-rate desserts, especially the crème caramel. Well-priced wine list. Try to get a table by the fireplace. Moderate to expensive.

After dinner check out **Main Street Theatre,** 807 Franklin Street. It has a new home with expanded seating. For a schedule, call the box office at (219) 874–4269.

LODGING: Creekwood Inn, County Road 600 W and Highways 35/20, Michigan City; (219) 872–8357. (Take exit 40B from I–94; then take the first street on the left; then turn left to the inn.) The Creekwood has a casual but elegant atmosphere. The thirty-three-acre wooded setting, complete with a meandering creek (hence the name), can be enjoyed from the inn's patio or screened porch. Classical music adds to the feeling of tranquillity. All rooms have their own baths. Rates range from $120 to $150 (which includes continental breakfast for two).

DAY 2

Morning

BREAKFAST: A continental breakfast of delicious muffins and other baked goods is included in the cost of the room at the Creekwood Inn. A full breakfast is available for an extra charge.

Before heading to the dunes, pick up lunch from the **5th Street Deli.** Or if you're farther south, near Merrillville, **Cafe Venezia** (405 West 81st Avenue) is the region's most authentic Italian grocery (see "Other Recommended Restaurants and Lodgings").

By the way, when people say they're going to the dunes, you have to determine if it's the National Lakeshore or Dunes State Park that they're talking about.

What's the difference? **Dunes State Park** is in Chesterton and is a part of the larger Indiana Dunes National Lakeshore. It's tamer than the National Lakeshore but still lovely, offering a fine swimming beach, cross-country skiing and hiking trails, picnic area, and camping. Of the ten marked trails winding through Indiana Dunes State Park, the longest and most interesting are trails 9 and 10. Call (219) 926–1390 for information or to check water conditions.

Afternoon

LUNCH: Open your picnic basket, enjoy the beautiful surroundings, and maybe even let the waves lull you into an afternoon snooze.

The **Indiana Dunes National Lakeshore** is about a half hour closer to Chicago. (Take I–65 to U.S. Highway 20; west on Highway 20 to Lake Street and go north.) It is larger than the state park and offers nature study, bike/horseback riding trails, one of the best beaches in the Midwest, ranger-led hikes, and picnic areas. (The visitors center is a good place to get oriented.)

Maybe you'd like to try to climb 135-foot-tall **Mount Baldy,** near Michigan City, off of Highway 12, which offers a fine view of Chicago's skyline. The entrance is about 2 miles west of downtown Michigan City on U.S. 12. Farther west, you can visit the **Bailly Homestead,** a Victorian farmhouse, and **Chellberg Farm,** a working nineteenth-century farm. There are horses, goats, and chickens to entertain the little ones. Both are part of the National

Lakeshore park and the site of the popular Maple Sugar Time program each March, when you can tap for syrup. Hours vary with the season. A $3.00 fee per car is charged.

A word of caution: The walk from the parking lot to the beach can be quite a trek, so if you have young children, you may want to bring a stroller. So you don't have to travel home in wet swimsuits, change in the bathhouse. To check on special programs or water conditions, call (219) 926–7561.

DINNER: If you're staying around Michigan City, then make a dinner reservation at **The Ferns at Creekwood Inn** (800–400–1981). Reservations required. In keeping with fine dining tradition, Chef-propietor Cheryl Flynn rolls out a menu of creative flavors, global wines, and pleasant service. Friday and Saturday 6:00–9:00 P.M.

If you are heading back to Chicago, try the **Miller Bakery Cafe,** 555 South Lake Street, Gary; (219) 938–2229 (about a block north of U.S. Highway 12, just over the railroad tracks). This intimate restaurant, with exposed brick and well-chosen antiques, is as good as anything on Chicago's Near North Side at one-third the price. Specialties include fabulous soups (don't miss the Mediterranean tomato), seafood (crab cakes and salmon ravioli), and a decadent flourless chocolate torte. Open Tuesday through Saturday. Prices start at $10 per entree for lunch, $13 for dinner. While you don't need to dress up, you'd feel uncomfortable if you stopped here in beachwear. Not recommended for young children. Reservations essential on weekend nights.

Take I–94 west back to Chicago.

THERE'S MORE

Antiques. If you're into antiques, this is a bonanza. LaPorte County has some two dozen shops within a twenty-minute drive. A few standouts: Coachman Antique Mall (500 Lincolnway; 219–326–5933) is one of the largest in the region, with more than ninety dealers. The largest is The Antique Market (219–879–4084), I–94 and U.S. 421 in Michigan City, which has more than 100 dealers and meeting room space in Preservation Hall. Country Roads (4122 West Small Road; 219–362–5308) has great hickory furniture. Stocking Bale (227 West Seventh Street; 219–873–9270) is a restored Victorian that houses several antiques stores.

In Valparaiso, you'll want to stop at the Valparaiso Antique Mall, 212 East Lincoln Way; (219) 465–1869. Not as large as The Antique Market, but it's still easy to spend a few hours here. About thirty dealers sell an eclectic mix, from late-nineteenth-century furniture to 1950s advertising memorabilia.

Art. The Art Barn, 695 North 400 E, Valparaiso; (219) 462–9009. The gallery exhibits the work of local and national artists. Also known for its Saturday morning children's art class.

The John G. Blank Center for the Arts (312 East Eighth Street, Michigan City; 219–874–4900) is home to the first-ever "Frank Lloyd Wright and Colleagues: Indiana Works" exhibit, showcasing the famous architect's home in Indiana.

Hesston Steam Museum, County Road 1000 N, Hesston; (219) 872–7405. It's small, but younger kids enjoy this unusual outdoor museum with one of the most varied collections of operating steam equipment in the United States. A highlight is a steam engine ride through the surrounding forest, which goes nicely with the fresh-pressed apple cider sold on the premises. Open Memorial Day through the last Sunday in October.

Lake County Courthouse, Courthouse Square, Crown Point. John Dillinger escaped from here. Rudolph Valentino was married here, as was Ronald Reagan (the first time). Today this 1879 courthouse is home to about a dozen shops.

Gambling. If you like to gamble, then you'll love Northwest Indiana, where Las Vegas floats on the shores of Lake Michigan. There are four lakefront casinos: *Harrah's East Chicago Casino* in East Chicago (800–746–9262), *Majestic Star* in Gary (888–2B–LUCKY), *Empress* in Hammond (888–4EMPRESS), and *Blue Chip* in Michigan City (888–879–7711).

Kingsbury Fish and Wildlife Area, 5344 South Hupp Road, LaPorte; (219) 393–3612. This 6,000-acre hunting and fishing preserve offers nature trails, target shooting, bird-watching, and very good mushroom hunting.

Washington Park and Zoo, Michigan City lakefront; (219) 873–1510. One of Indiana's oldest zoos. Small (260 animals), but just the right size for the young set. A tower offers a good view of the Chicago skyline. The zoo is open March through December, but hours vary.

Golf. Northwest Indiana has some excellent courses. In fact, many Chicagoans, finding long lines at their home courses, drive here for tee-off time. With some thirty courses in the area, check with the tourism offices listed in "For More Information."

Horseback riding. Red Arrow Stables, 3848 Academy Road, Michigan City; (219) 872–2114. Horse Country of Galena, 525 East 850 North, LaPorte; (219) 778–4625.

Sailing. Michigan City Sailboat Charters, near the Franklin Street Bridge; (219) 879–7608.

U-pick orchards. LaPorte County alone is home to about twenty-four orchards and berry farms. Crops include blueberries, strawberries, apples, cherries, and peaches. For current harvest information, call (219) 872–5055 or (800) 634–2650. Elsewhere in the region, spots include Anderson's Orchard and Winery in Valparaiso (430 East U.S. Highway 6; 219–464–4936), Garwood Orchards in LaPorte (5911 West County Road 50; 219–362–4385), Andershock's in Chesterton (921 East U.S. Highway 20; 219–926–3141), and Johnson's in Hobart (8960 East Ridge; 219–962–1169).

Christmas tree farms. Cut down your own tree at one of eight farms in the area. Call the Porter County, Lake County, or LaPorte County Tourism Bureaus for details.

SPECIAL EVENTS

July. Porter County Fair. Carnival, entertainment, agriculture. Porter County Fairgrounds, Valparaiso.

August. Chesterton Art Fair. The same artists you'll find at the Gold Coast or Old Town Art Fair without the crowds. Chesterton; (219) 926–4711.

August. Lake County Fair. Arts, crafts, carnival midway, horse show, entertainment. Lake County Fairgrounds, Crown Point.

August. Augustfest. National music acts, ethnic food, rides. Wolfe Lake Park, Hammond.

September. Michigan City holds the first and largest Oktoberfest celebration in the region on Labor Day weekend at the Lake Michigan waterfront in Washington Park. Rides, food, arts and crafts booths. (219) 874–8927.

September. Valparaiso Popcorn Festival. The home of Orville Redenbacher goes all out with entertainments, food, and arts and crafts.

September. Wizard of Oz Festival. Tribute to the MGM classic. Parade, food, contests. Chesterton.

OTHER RECOMMENDED RESTAURANTS AND LODGINGS

Chesterton

Gray Goose Inn, 350 Indian Boundary Road; (219) 926–5781. One of the area's premier B&Bs. Three suites and five doubles (some with fireplace and Jacuzzi) on one hundred wooded acres. Just 2½ miles to Lake Michigan and the dunes. Rates: $80 to $115.

Indian Oak Resort and Spa, 558 Indian Boundary Road; (219) 926–2200. Indoor pool, private balcony. All spa services (facials, massages, etc.) are extra. Many persons report that the service is first-rate. Rates: $100–$125 (generally, rooms on lake side are more expensive than wood side).

Hammond

Phil Smidt and Son, 1205 North Calumet; (219) 659–0025. The epitome of the Calumet Region restaurant. Generations have been making a special trip for the golden, butter-drenched perch and the frogs' legs. If you're hungry, it's well worth the few extra bucks for the all-you-can-eat option.

Merrillville

Cafe Venezia, 405 West 81st Avenue (Ross Plaza); (219) 736–2203. Don't be scared off by the suburban strip mall. This is probably the only spot in the entire region where you can get serious Italian cuisine. Pastas are exceptional, as are the Italian pastries. At the adjacent grocery store, you can pick up the great beginnings (meats, cheeses, breads) of a picnic. Also, given its proximity to the Star Plaza, it's worth remembering when you want to bring a snack back to your room.

Star Plaza Theatre and Resort, I–65 at U.S. Highway 30; (219) 769–6311. A little bit of Vegas comes to the Midwest. A good choice if you're looking for a resort experience. Two pools, whirlpool, and children's indoor playground, but you're better off dining elsewhere. The theater attracts big-name entertainment and frequently offers great room deals when you buy show tickets. Call for a schedule.

Michigan City

Connie's, 1407 Franklin Street; (219) 871–0601. Join Connie and Mr. Connie for casual family breakfasts and lunches, 9:00 A.M.–2:30 P.M.; Sunday brunch, 10:30 A.M.–2:30 P.M. Features homemade soups, breads, and desserts. Credit cards not accepted.

Michigan City Holiday Inn, 5820 South Franklin Street; (219) 879–0311. Best choice if you want to stay near Prime Outlets, but want a hotel with the amenities of pool and sauna. Rates: $89–$169.

Swingbelly's, 104 South Lake Avenue; (219) 874–5718. Burgers, sandwiches, salads. A good stop when you're at the beach. Inexpensive.

Pump's on 12, 3085 West Dunes Highway (Route 12); (219) 874–6201. The hands-down place to go for good pizza. Inexpensive.

Porter

Spring House Inn, 303 North Mineral Springs Road; (219) 929–4600 or (800) 366–4661. About five minutes from the Indiana Dunes National Lakeshore; you'll find this a perfect spot for a relaxing stay. Fifty guest rooms. Indoor pool, whirlpool. Rates: $84 to $97 (includes continental breakfast).

Santiago's, 124 Lincoln; (219) 926–6518. The locals rave about the Mexican food, such as the tampaquina, a seared skirt steak done with cheese enchiladas. Insider's tip: Santiago's sells Valpo Velvet ice cream bars—like Dove Bars, only better. Moderate.

Wagner's Ribs, 361 Wagner Road; (219) 926–7614. As the name suggests, big, meaty, juicy slabs for he-man appetites. Moderate.

Valparaiso

Billy Jack's, 2904 Calumet; (219) 477–3797. Innovative Southwestern cuisine, such as medallions of pork with corn salsa. The house cranberry dressing is yummy. Moderate.

Clayton's, 66 West Lincolnway; (219) 531–0612. A real find where sophisticated cuisine is hard to come by. Recommended: sea scallops, veal dishes. Moderate to expensive.

Coffee & Tea Market, 157 West Lincolnway; (219) 462–7265. Good vegetarian soups, breads and cheeses, and coffee. Casual and inexpensive.

Restaurant Don Quijote, 119 East Lincolnway; (219) 462–7976. The tapas are excellent, as is the paella—or anything with seafood, for that matter. Moderate.

Solé Cafe and Wine Bar, 3300 North Calumet; (219) 462–0992. Trendy pasta dishes and nouvelle cuisine. Moderate to expensive.

Strongbow Inn, 2405 U.S. Highway 30 East; (219) 462–3311. People come here from all over to get turkey with all the trimmings (stuffing, sweet potatoes, cranberries). Family owned since 1940, it's perfect for when you crave a traditional Thanksgiving dinner, even if it's in July. Moderate.

FOR MORE INFORMATION

Lake County Tourism Bureau, 5800 Broadway, Suite S, Merrillville, IN 46410; (219) 980–1617.

LaPorte County Convention and Visitors Bureau, 1503 South Meer Road, Michigan City, IN 46360; (219) 872–5055 or (800) 634–2650. The twenty-four-hour Visitor Information Phoneline is (219) 872–0031.

Porter County Tourism Bureau, 800 Indian Boundary Road, Chesterton, IN 46304; (800) 283–8687; www.duneland.com.

South Bend

HOME OF THE FIGHTING IRISH

2 NIGHTS

Football • Cycling • Golf • Sightseeing
Antiques/flea markets • Amish village

How you feel about South Bend has a lot to do with how you feel about the University of Notre Dame. If you rank it right up there with God and country, it's like heaven on earth. If you couldn't care less about the Fighting Irish, it's just another notch on the Midwest's Rust Belt.

Each fall thousands of visitors from all over the country converge on South Bend to view the perennial gridiron powerhouse. The usual routine for Chicagoans is to make the 90-mile trip for the game and return home the same day. Even people who positively bleed blue and gold will tell you that once you get off campus, the list of diversions in the area is a short one.

But if you add side trips to Amish Acres in Nappanee, there are more than enough activities to make for a fulfilling weekend. If you're more interested in farm life than field goals, you can reverse the emphasis and make the Amish country your base of operations.

A precaution: Don't think you can make a spur-of-the-moment decision to stay over in South Bend after the game. (Hotels are full any weekend the Irish are at home.) If you're not visiting on a Saturday, consider adding "Amish Country" (Indiana Escape Three) to your itinerary. But never on Sunday—the area virtually closes down.

DAY 1

Evening

Make the drive to South Bend on I–80/90 on a Friday evening, so you can be well rested for Saturday's activities and you won't have the pressure of arriving in time for kick-off.

DINNER: One advantage to arriving the night before is that reservations at the **Carriage House,** 24460 Adams Road, which many people consider to be South Bend's finest restaurant, are easier to get on a Friday. The cuisine—from appetizer (crab strudel topped with caviar) to entree (roast duck adorned with cranberries) to dessert (puff pastry with chocolate mousse)—is as serious as you'll find anywhere in the area. Entrees fall in the $18 to $40 range, with a wine list that goes from nominal to stratospheric. Reservations a must. Call (219) 272–9220.

LODGING: South Bend Marriott, 123 North Saint Joseph Street. The accommodations in South Bend are surprisingly limited, considering that it's home to a world-class university. The South Bend Marriott, a five-minute drive from the university, is generally regarded as the best place to stay and was completely renovated in 1993. The reasonable price ($119 per night, which includes a $15 breakfast credit, or $109 per night with no breakfast credit), central location, and indoor pool/Jacuzzi are appealing features. Call (219) 234–2000.

DAY 2

Morning

BREAKFAST: Start your day at **Bibler's Original Pancake House,** 1430 North Ironwood, which is near the stadium and similar to locations in Chicago. The apple pancake is just as decadent, the orange juice is just as fresh, and the coffee is just as piping hot as it is back home. And the lines are shorter—providing you beat the pregame crowd on Saturday and after-church crowd on Sunday. Call (219) 232–3220.

Afternoon

After the game, let everyone make a beeline to the parking lot. Then you can explore the 1,250-acre campus without the crowds. Two popular sights are

particularly conducive to peace and quiet: the **Grotto of Our Lady of Lourdes** (which is a replica of the one in the French Pyrenees) and the **Basilica of the Sacred Heart,** which reopened in 1990 after an extensive renovation. The basilica boasts one of the finest collections of nineteenth-century French stained glass windows.

From the church proceed to the **Snite Museum of Art,** which owns more than 17,000 works, from early African art to twentieth-century. Open Tuesday through Saturday, 10:00 A.M.–4:00 P.M.; Sunday 1:00–4:00 P.M. Free. If you're interested in a student-conducted tour of the campus, call (219) 631–7367.

Or, if your pigskin passion has not yet been satisfied, tour South Bend's new pride and joy, the **College Football Hall of Fame,** at 111 South St. Joseph Street (219–235–7582; 800–444–FAME). The $14 million facility is touted as one of the premier sports shrines, on the order of Cooperstown. Every day will have the feel of a Saturday afternoon in October, right down to the ambient sounds of a roaring stadium. Once seated in the theater, you'll be enveloped by surround-sound projection that takes you into a huddle—for the strategy and the emotion—as two teams slug it out.

The next section of the hall is Training Camp, which consists of the training room (with scorecards to measure your progress), practice field (try hitting the tackling dummy), and strategy clinic. Finally, the Locker Room, designed to replicate locker rooms from the 1890s to the present. (How far are the designers willing to go for authenticity?) Located across from the Century Center.

If the weather is balmy, take advantage of South Bend's excellent county parks. **Potowatomi Zoo,** the oldest in Indiana (500 South Greenlawn Avenue, ¼ mile south of Jefferson Avenue), houses some 400 mammals, reptiles, and fish; (219) 235–9800.

DINNER: About this time, you'll be searching for a good place to eat. If you're still dressed for a football game, then head to **Bruno's,** 2610 Prairie Avenue, which serves up a great thin-crust pizza. Also, if you must choose between a kiss and the garlic bread, opt for the latter. There will be other kisses, but fabulous garlic bread is much less certain. Call (219) 288–3320. Inexpensive.

If you have something more upscale in mind, try the **Beiger Mansion Inn Restaurant** (see "Other Recommended Restaurants and Lodgings").

After dinner, you can find a number of college bars. For a nightcap, check out **Club LaSalle** (115 West Colfax Avenue; 219–288–1155), which has a staggering number of ice cream drinks and coffees (our favorite: cappuccino

Notre Dame's Sacred Heart Church

spiked with Frangelico, topped with grated chocolate). More serious drinkers, take note: Bourbon is the house spirit, with more than twenty brands found on the back bar. The international wine list has earned raves from *The Wine Spectator.*

For live blues and jazz, **Madison Oyster Bar,** 402 East Madison Street, is the only place to go. Call (219) 288–3776. The livelier members in your party may try to talk you into some line dancing at the **Heartland–Chicago Steakhouse** (222 North Michigan Street, 219–234–5200). Go for it.

LODGING: South Bend Marriott.

DAY 3

Morning

BREAKFAST: Bibler's Original Pancake House.

Make sure your route home takes you south on Highway 19 to U.S. Highway 6, so you can stop at **Amish Acres** in Nappanee, an eighty-acre preserved and restored Amish farm. It is open to the public from May until the end of December. This is not the sort of place that would work as a lone destination, but it is just fine as a detour.

If you ignore the frankly commercial qualities and instead regard it as an opportunity to stock up on jams, jellies, sausages, and other foodstuffs, you won't be disappointed. A buggy ride through picturesque woods isn't a bad way to spend a crisp autumn afternoon, either.

The pricing structure is a bit confusing. Depending on what options you want, the tab can range from about $20 for the "total experience" (forty-five-minute house and farm tour, twenty-minute documentary, buggy ride, and dinner) to free if all you do is hit the shops.

LUNCH: Stay at Amish Acres to enjoy the Thresher's Dinner, which is served family style and includes your choice of two entrees per table (turkey, ham, chicken, or roast beef) along with numerous country side dishes, such as mashed potatoes and sage dressing. Dessert consists of authentic shoofly pie, fruit pies, and vanilla date pudding. At $12.95 per adult ($5.00 for kids), this is the best bargain Amish Acres has to offer. Dinner is served Monday through Saturday, 11:00 A.M.–7:00 P.M.; Sunday 11:00 A.M.–6:00 P.M. Call (219) 773–4188.

Return home via I–94.

THERE'S MORE

Northern Indiana Center for History, 808 West Washington Street, South Bend; (219) 235–9664. Really three museums in one: Copshalom, a thirty-eight-room turn-of-the-century mansion, with original furnishings (knowledgeable guides lead hour-long tours); the Center for History, interactive exhibition galleries; and the Worker's Home Museum, a restored two-story cottage celebrating the Polish immigrants who came to the St. Joseph River Valley in the 1930s. Family packages available. Call for admission fees.

East Race Waterway. Located in the heart of downtown South Bend, the East Race Waterway is the first artificial whitewater course in North America and one of only six in the world. It hosts a number of spectator events (such as Olympic regional trials) but is also ideal for recreational sports, including paddling, rafting, and innertubing. Open June through August; fees vary. Call (219) 235–9401.

Studebaker National Museum, 525 South Main Street. A loving tribute to the now-defunct car. Brothers Clem and Henry turned out their first buggy here in 1852 and kept the company going until the last Avanti rolled off the line in 1964. (Perhaps the car's fate was sealed when Mr. Ed was chosen as its spokesman?) The museum's collection includes some seventy-five vehicles, including the carriages of four U.S. presidents. Admission: adults, $5.00; seniors and students over 12, $4.00; children under 12, $2.50. Call (219) 235–9108.

Shipshewana Flea Market, Shipshewana; (219) 768–4129. One of the most famous flea markets in the Midwest, with some 150 vendors. Unfortunately, only open Tuesdays and Wednesdays, May through October. On Wednesdays, everything that isn't sold goes up for auction, which is when you can really find some great furniture buys. (For more details, see Indiana Escape Three.)

Baseball. Catch a minor league game at Stanley Coveleski Baseball Stadium, 501 West South Street, home of the South Bend Silver Hawks, an Arizona Diamondbacks farm team. April through August. (219) 235–9988.

Potato Creek State Park, 7 miles south on U.S. Highway 31; (219) 656–8186. Bike rentals and paved paths. Cross-country skiing rentals; well-groomed trails.

Notre Dame Golf Course, on campus, is open to the public. Phone (219) 631–6425.

SPECIAL EVENTS

June–August. Firefly Festival. St. Patrick's Park, off U.S. Highway 31, just north of South Bend. All summer, outdoor entertainment that ranges from Shakespeare to the Platters.

June. Ethnic Festival. Food, art, crafts. Downtown South Bend.

OTHER RECOMMENDED RESTAURANTS AND LODGINGS

South Bend

Beiger Mansion Inn, 317 Lincolnway East; (219) 256–0365 or (800) 437–0131. Listed on the National Historic Register. Eight rooms offer equal parts romance and nostalgia. All have private baths. Rates: $75 to $195 (master suite, which includes breakfast and champagne).

The B&B is also open to the public for lunch (Tuesday through Friday) and dinner (Thursday, Friday, and Saturday only). Lunch offers endlessly creative sandwiches and salads, accompanied by fresh-baked bread or muffins ($5.00 to $10.00). Dinner is equally artful, with lamb chops marinated in rosemary and garlic as the house specialty, but seafood is also well represented ($15 to $20).

East Bank Emporium, 121 South Niles; (219) 234–9000. The draw here is steaks and seafood, with some attention paid to accompaniments such as homemade salad dressings. Moderate.

Hacienda, 5880 Grape Road; (219) 277–1318. Very good margaritas, salsa, and burritos. There's another location in Scottsdale Mall, on the outskirts of town, but this location has the better atmosphere. Inexpensive.

Jamison Inn, 1404 Ivy Road; (219) 277–9682. Forty-nine rooms, twenty-four of which are suites. Victorian style. Complimentary full buffet breakfast. Rates range from $75 to $110 per night.

Club LaSalle, 115 West Colfax Avenue; (219) 288–1155. A popular nightspot, it also will appeal to the savvy diner. Chef Sean Garrett pays homage to the Midwest with dishes such as roasted sweet corn chowder and veal T-bone. Try the wood oven-roasted pizza for starters. Classic cocktails, premium cigars, and live music. Moderate to expensive.

Queen Anne Inn, 420 West Washington; (219) 234–5959. Five rooms, some with fireplaces, all with private baths. Victorian style. Full breakfast included with cost of room. Rates range from $70 to $109.

Tippecanoe Place, 620 West Washington Street; (219) 234–9077. South Bend's best-known restaurant and the original home of Clement Studebaker. With its forty rooms and twenty fireplaces, the decor dazzles. Stick to Midwestern basics (such as prime rib at an incredible $14.95) and you'll get your money's worth.

INDIANA

FOR MORE INFORMATION

South Bend–Mishawaka Area Convention and Visitors Bureau, 401 East Colfax, Suite 310, South Bend, IN 46617; (219) 234–0051 or (800) 828–7881.

INDIANA

Elkhart and Crystal Valley

A WEEKEND IN AMISH COUNTRY

2 NIGHTS

*Crafts • Quilts • Golf • Sightseeing • Amish village
Antiques/flea markets*

Many overworked urbanites pay thousands of dollars to go to faraway retreats in search of solitude, when all they have to do is turn off the interstate and explore Indiana's Amish country. There you can enjoy a slow-paced weekend amid beautiful, rolling countryside.

The Crystal Valley area is home to about 20,000 Amish and Mennonites. Today their life-style remains virtually the same as it was a century ago. They still drive horse-drawn buggies (something to keep in mind as you approach a hill), milk their cows by hand, and shun adornment. But the simple life here is more than just a hiatus from traffic jams. It's an attitude that permeates the entire community. You can feel it from tours that include stops at "real" people's homes to accommodations that treat guests like family.

If, however, your time is short and you just want to get an overview of the area, take the Heritage Trail Audio-Cassette Driving Tour, a 100-mile loop that begins and ends at the Elkhart County Visitors Center (219 Caravan Drive). It takes about a full day of travel to do the trail—and that's without stopping at all the sites along the way. The tape is available for a $10 refundable deposit. Visitors center hours: weekdays, 8:00 A.M. to 5:00 P.M.; weekends, 9:00 A.M. to 4:00 P.M. Call (219) 262–8161.

If you want an even more condensed experience, it can be had at Amish Acres in Nappanee, located in the southwest corner of Elkhart County (see Indiana Escape Two).

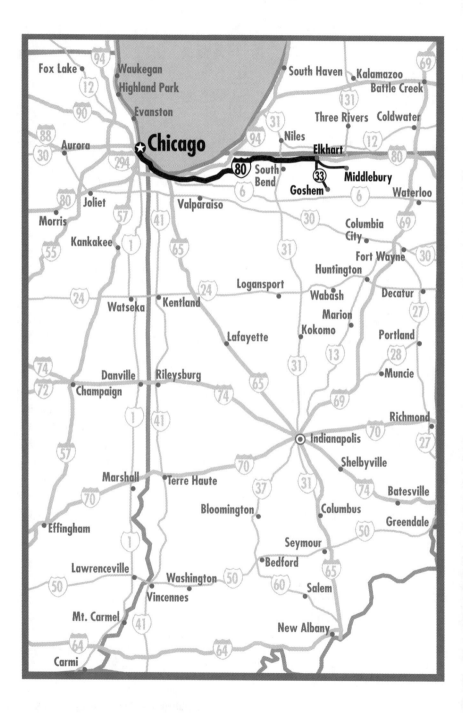

A few caveats: This getaway to Indiana's Amish country is one that you may want to schedule in the middle of the week. That is the only way to see the famous Shipshewana Flea Market and Auction, which operates only on Tuesday and Wednesday, and the county virtually closes down on Sunday. Also, while you'll find people to be hospitable, they ask that visitors respect their beliefs by not taking their photographs.

DAY 1

Morning

Take I–80/90 east to exit 92 into Elkhart, a prosperous city that makes more than half of the nation's band instruments and almost as many mobile homes and pharmaceuticals.

There are several exceptionally good small museums here. The **Ruthmere Museum** (9302 East Beardsley Avenue; 219–264–0330) is another reason for planning a midweek excursion. This lovely Beaux Arts mansion belonged to Albert Beardsley, one of the founders of Miles Laboratories. Built in 1908, the house combines old money with modern conveniences. Furnishings include china and Tiffany lamps from Presidents Hayes, Jackson, and Harding. Don't miss the classic cars in the garage. The museum is open Tuesday through Saturday (guided tours only at 10:00 A.M., 1:00, 2:00, and 3:00 P.M.). Admission: adults, $6.00; seniors, $5.00; children 5–12, $3.00.

LUNCH: The **Exchange Bakery,** 109 West Lexington; (219) 293–5175. Quality soups, salads, and other goodies (like spinach en croute) make this a delightful stop. Inexpensive to moderate.

Afternoon

If you're a rail fan, you'll want to include the **National New York Central Railroad Museum** (721 South Main Street; 219–294–3001) on your itinerary. You'll see the ongoing restoration of locomotives and railcars and a display that details the story of "Curly Top," a young Elkhart girl who achieved fame in the 1930s by waving to the passing Twentieth Century Limited every day. Celebrities on board responded by throwing autographed menus to her as the train rumbled by. The museum, which opened in 1989, is open from 10:00 A.M. to 2:00 P.M., Tuesday through Friday; 10:00 A.M. to 4:00 P.M., Saturday, and noon to 4:00 P.M., Sunday. Admission is $2.00 for adults, $1.00 for seniors, students, and children 6–12 years old.

The **Midwest Museum of American Art** (429 South Main Street; 219–293–6660) is also worth a stop. Located in a renovated bank building downtown, the museum gives you a good overview of American art styles (Norman Rockwell rates his own gallery). Allow an hour to tour. Admission is $3.00 for adults, $2.00 for seniors, $1.00 for students. Open Tuesday through Friday 11:00 A.M. to 5:00 P.M., Saturday and Sunday until 4:00 P.M.

Travel about 15 miles east of Elkhart on U.S. Highway 20, right into Middlebury, in the heart of what is called the Crystal Valley, home to about 20,000 Amish and Mennonites.

DINNER AND LODGING: Checkerberry Inn, 62644 County Road 37, Goshen; (219) 642–4445. This is another spot that makes it onto everybody's "best" lists for its exceptional facilities and European approach, from the food (duck breast in orange port wine sauce and frozen chocolate Kahlua mousse) to the Swiss-milled soap in the bath. You'll find a curious marriage of decor here: Amish hats hang on the walls above the sleek, contemporary beds. Some rooms have whirlpools and fireplaces. The inn sits on one-hundred wooded acres. Four-course dinners are in the $25 to $35 range. Room rates range from $130 for a double to $350 for a two-bedroom suite. To reach Goshen, take Highway 13 south from Middlebury to Highway 4 west. For a more scenic route, take County Road 22 from Middlebury.

DAY 2

Morning

BREAKFAST: Checkerberry Inn. Continental breakfast of muffins, fruits, juices, and coffee is included in the cost of the room.

After breakfast, head to the **Menno-Hof Visitors Center** to get oriented. The center, which resembles a farmhouse and barn, explains the history of the Plain People. You can even experience a model dungeon, where early converts were punished for their beliefs, or a tornado room (the floor actually moves), which illuminates disaster-relief efforts. It's right across from the Shipshewana Flea Market on Highway 5. Call (219) 768–4117.

The **Shipshewana Flea Market and Auction** is held every Tuesday and Wednesday from May through October. It is one of the largest flea markets in the country, with more than 1,000 vendors.

Visitors who arrive by 8:00 A.M. on Wednesdays also can bid for great finds at an indoor antiques auction, where up to twelve auctioneers work simultaneously. While the flea market certainly can boast size and scope, many people grumble that the merchandise has slipped in recent years and there are more manufacturer's closeouts (such as cookware and tube socks) than antiques. They skip the flea market altogether and stick to the auction. If you're looking for quality, also add **Rebecca Haarer Arts & Antiques** (165 Morton Street; 219–768–4787) to your list. Open 9:30 A.M. to 5:00 P.M. Monday through Saturday. Closed on Sunday.

Across from the flea market, in the Shipshewana Center, you'll find some local fixtures, including Yoder's Department Store, Yoder's Hardware, and Yoder's Supermarket.

LUNCH: Buggy Wheel Restaurant. Morton Street; (219) 768–4444. Pass the platters of fried chicken, please. This is just plain good cooking, served by young Mennonite women. But you may want to skip that second helping of mashed potatoes to leave room for a slice of pie (there are more than twenty varieties to choose from) or fresh-baked cinnamon rolls. Make your lunch reservation early in the morning to guarantee you'll get in. But even if the lines are long, the **Bread Box Bake Shop** right next door means you can buy a bag of goodies to munch on while you wait.

Afternoon

Veterans of the flea market/auction generally consider it a full day's attraction. (Many recommend if you really want to see the Amish and Mennonite way of life, you scrupulously avoid flea market days, when a steady stream of traffic all but overwhelms the horse-drawn buggies.)

Still, the same things that primarily draw people to the flea market and auction—good food, antiques, and fine furniture—are available at any time in Amish country. The **Old Bag Factory** in Goshen, 1100 Chicago Avenue, a renovated warehouse, is home to numerous arts-and-crafts shops. Standouts include **Quilt Designs,** where custom quilts are made (219–534–5111), and **Swartzendrubber,** a fine woodshop and showroom where you can watch craftsworkers ply their trade (219–534–2502).

In Shipshewana there are two complexes worth noting. The **Crafter's Marketplace,** 210 North Van Buren Street, houses almost a dozen shops. The **Craft Barn Furniture Shop** (219–768–4725) is known for its oak furniture, which you can watch take shape in the woodshop. Open 9:00 A.M.–6:00 P.M. Monday through Saturday.

The unhurried pace of Amish country is an antidote to urban stress.

The **Davis Mercantile,** at the corner of Harrison and Main Streets, is named after the founder of Shipshewana. The two-story building is joined to the Old Davis Hotel, for decades the center of commerce for the community. Of the fifteen shops, arts-and-crafts lovers should hit the **Craft Patch** (219–768–7012) and **A Touch of Country** (219–768–7222).

Not all purchases have to be family heirlooms in the making. At **Yoder's Popcorn Shoppe,** on County Road 200S, just 4 miles south of Shipshewana, you can choose from many varieties of popcorn. The shop's kernels are shipped all over the country—including Soldier Field and Comiskey Park; (800) 537–1194. Open 9:00 A.M.–5:00 P.M. Monday through Friday and 9:00 A.M.–4:00 P.M. on Saturday. Closed Sunday.

DINNER: Patchwork Quilt Country Inn, 11748 County Road 2, Middle-bury; (219) 825–2417. The inn, which is actually a century-old farmhouse, is known for its award-winning buttermilk pecan chicken. It's also worth remembering for lodging (four-poster beds). The lobby is comfortably furnished, with a huge fireplace as its centerpiece. Rates: $70 to $85 (shared bath); suites, $85 to $110.

LODGING: Checkerberry Inn.

DAY 3

Morning

BREAKFAST: Checkerberry Inn. Homemade breads, fresh fruit, and juices are at the heart of Checkerberry's good country breakfasts.

After breakfast take one of the "back roads tours," which depart from the Patchwork Quilt Inn. The four-hour tours are structured according to your interests. For instance, the gourmet tour includes heartland foods, farm markets, and a bakery, while the arts-and-crafts tour includes quilt, crafts, and woodworking shops. Many of the families you'll visit will be friends and neighbors of the tour guide, adding a warmth that you don't get at many tourist attractions.

LUNCH: When in Rome . . . and when people are in Amish Country, they eat hearty, hefty fare. **Das Dutchman Essenhaus** (literally "eating house") is a popular, albeit touristy, choice. Meals include roast beef or ham *and* fried chicken, dressing, and mashed potatoes with gravy. All is served family-style. Amish baking skills really shine, with a pie menu that goes from apple to shoofly; 240 U.S. Highway 20, Middlebury (219–825–9471). There are a number of stores (bakery, craft, country, clothing) in the Essenhaus complex. It's a fun finale before heading back to the city. It also is a popular inn (see "Other Recommended Restaurants and Lodgings").

THERE'S MORE

Bonneyville Mill Park, Bristol. Visit the oldest continually operating gristmill in Indiana. Built in 1832, the mill still grinds corn, wheat, and rye (flour is for sale). Milling takes place hourly between 10:00 A.M. and 5:00 P.M., May through October; (219) 534–3541. On the Little Elkhart River, 2½ miles east on Highway 120, then ½ mile south on Highway 131.

Ideal Beach Family Water Park, Elkhart. Water activities. 56-foot corkscrew slide, beach, playground, miniature golf. Open daily, 10:00 A.M.–7:00 P.M., Memorial Day through Labor Day; (219) 262–1769.

Roller skating. Eby's Pines, Bristol.

Bristol Opera House. Elkhart Civic Theatre performs year-round. Call for schedule; (219) 848–4116.

SPECIAL EVENTS

March. Maple Syrup Festival. Wakarusa. The ultimate pancake breakfast.

June. Elkhart Jazz Festival. A major regional showcase for the best jazz in six places. Downtown Elkhart.

July. Elkhart County Fair. One of the largest county fairs in the country. Music, carnival, livestock, harness racing, food. Elkhart County Fairgrounds, Goshen.

August. Amish Acres Arts & Crafts Festival. Artists, entertainment, farmer's market, and buggy rides. Nappanee.

September. Michiana Mennonite Relief Sale. Hundreds of quilts go on sale. Crafts, homemade foods, and furniture are also part of this lively event at the 4-H Fairgrounds in Goshen.

November. Crystal Valley Country Christmas. Country crafts, merchant open houses. A weekend showcase of Amish culture that takes place in Bristol, Middlebury, and Shipshewana.

OTHER RECOMMENDED RESTAURANTS AND LODGINGS

Goshen

Olympia Candy Kitchen, 136 North Main Street; (219) 533–5040. An old-fashioned (circa 1912) candy shop, with a lunch counter that serves sandwiches.

South Side Soda Shop, 1122 South Main Street; (219) 534–3790. Noted for its award-winning chili, but the ice cream sodas shouldn't be overlooked, either (try the Green River). The jukebox and the peanut machine add to the fun.

Middlebury

Essenhaus Country Inn, 240 U.S. Highway 20; (219) 825–9447. About thirty rooms, including five suites (some with whirlpools). Lots of lovely touches, such as luxurious towels and soaps. Most of the bleached-pine furniture is made by local craftworkers. Rates: $89–$145.

Harley's Soda Shop and Antiques, 422 South Main; (219) 825–2565. Maker of Vic's ice cream, a local favorite for decades. Also, some fine vintage wicker and maple pieces. Stop for a soda, come home with an armoire.

FOR MORE INFORMATION

Elkhart County Convention and Visitors Bureau, 219 Caravan, Elkhart, IN 46514; (219) 262–8161 or (800) 262–8161.

Crystal Valley Tourist Association, P.O. Box 55, Middlebury, IN 46540.

Indianapolis

A CITY FOR ALL SEASONS

2 NIGHTS

Museums • Sightseeing • Speedway • Theater • Ballet
Amateur and professional sports

Indianapolis may sound like an odd destination for a weekend escape. Why head for an urban landscape when you already live in one? Because Indianapolis offers a lot of the perks of city life with none of the hassles. In about three hours you can put yourself squarely in a place that offers an incredible amount of variety at a very affordable price—and you'll never have to search for a parking place.

The latest addition to the city is the NCAA's Hall of Champions, located in White River State Park, which opened in March 2000. This interactive, multimedia museum celebrates intercollegiate athletics and the spirit of competition. More than seventy cities campaigned for the facility, but the NCAA chose Indianapolis because of the city's love of sports, both amateur and professional.

Elsewhere you'll see the civic pride Hoosiers take in preserving their old landmarks. One of the most eye-catching is the 284-foot-tall Indiana State Soldiers and Sailors Monument, which was built in 1902 but updated into a lovely downtown plaza. Its lower level recently became home to the Colonel Eli Lilly Civil War Museum, highlighting the Hoosier war experience. In the summer it is the perfect place for a carriage ride, picnic, and people watching. In the winter the monument is draped in thousands of tiny lights, while carolers and brass ensembles usher in the holiday season.

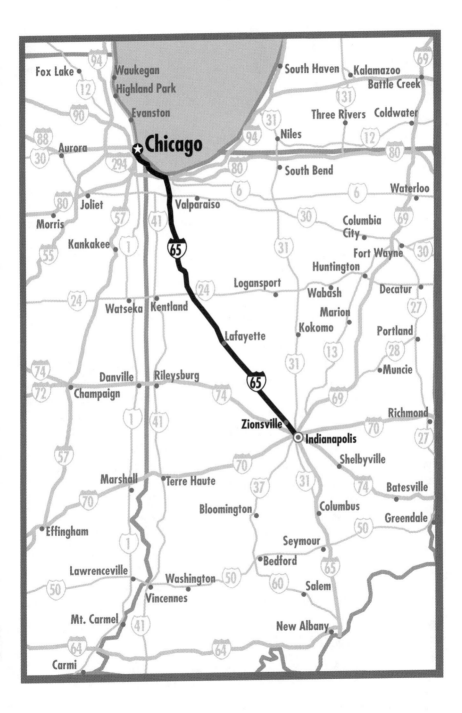

What else is new in Indianapolis? Since 1996 there's been a dining renaissance, as well. More than a dozen new restaurants have opened downtown, giving the city a far more cosmopolitan air. The selection runs the gamut from Planet Hollywood (across from Circle Centre) to the Mikado Japanese Restaurant and Sushi bar. (See "Other Recommended Restaurants and Lodgings" for some of the best.)

In addition, there's a lot more new just in the last year, including the new Conseco Field House, which opened for the Indiana Pacers' 1999 season, and White River Gardens, a $13.5 million conservatory and garden at the Indianapolis Zoo, which opened in June 1999.

Also note that the towns of Noblesville (home of Conner Prairie; see Indiana Escape Six) and Zionsville are worthy detours, which can be scheduled en route to Indianapolis or on the way home (or hit one each way). If logistics make that impossible, they are both close enough to Indianapolis to qualify as day trips.

DAY 1

Take I–94 to I–65 to Indianapolis.

Head right over to the number-one attraction: the **Children's Museum,** 3000 North Meridian Street, which consistently ranks among the top museums in the country. The largest children's museum in the world, these five floors of magic are alone worth the trip—even if you don't have kids. Once you've bartered for goods in a 1700s French fur-trading post or sat behind the wheel of a race car or gone spelunking in a limestone cave, it's doubtful you'll have time to see much of anything else. But try not to leave without checking out the model train and antique doll collections—both claim to be the largest in the country.

The hand-carved carousel, which dates back to the 1900s, is well worth the extra 50 cents. The museum also has a terrific playscape gallery for preschoolers.

Science Works is a $2.5 million gallery, in which kids can climb a 22-foot limestone rock wall, dig for fossils, or move bricks and fossils around a construction site using a pedal-operated dump truck and other equipment.

LUNCH: The restaurant at the museum, **Reflections,** is surprisingly good. Even eating is seen as an opportunity to learn, as kids watch the bakers at work.

Insider's tip: The scope here is really closer to a Museum of Science and Industry, so some extra planning is necessary. Schedule in mini-breaks, so everyone's circuits don't get overloaded. On weekends arrive when the museum opens, otherwise the lines at the most popular exhibits are interminable. If you need a well-timed bribe, the gift shop has nifty toys (educational, of course) that you'll find nowhere else. Open Tuesday through Sunday, 10:00 A.M.–5:00 P.M. Open every day from March 6 to Labor Day. Admission: adults, $8.00; children, $3.50; under 2, free. Call (800) 208–KIDS.

If your idea of a hands-on activity is whipping out your credit card, then head over to **Circle Centre Mall,** 49 West Maryland Street. The mall, anchored by Nordstrom and Parisian stores, includes dozens of specialty shops, restaurants, and a multi-screen cinema.

DINNER: The **Restaurant at the Canterbury,** 123 South Illinois Street; (317) 634–3000. Although the food at this sophisticated spot is pricey by Hoosier standards, it is reasonable for Chicagoans who have become accustomed to $20 entrees. Signature dishes are Dover sole, rack of lamb, lobster, and veal Tivoli, as well as dessert soufflés. Try the freshly baked croissants and buttery Danish pastries for breakfast. It's also open for afternoon tea. Open daily. Moderate to expensive.

LODGING: The **Canterbury Hotel,** 123 South Illinois Street; (317) 634–3000. This hotel has ninety-nine individually decorated rooms with Chippendale reproductions, four-poster beds, and marble baths. Most charming is the parlor, which has a carved wooden fireplace and a bookcase with the works of Shakespeare, Dickens, and Kipling. The Canterbury hits just the right balance between British sophistication and down-home Hoosier hospitality. Rates range from $150 to $500 per night.

DAY 2

Morning

BREAKFAST: Breakfast at the Canterbury. Try the freshly baked croissants and pastries.

On today's agenda is the **Indianapolis Museum of Art,** 1200 West 38th Street. This is really four different art pavilions in one. The Mary Fendrich Hulman Pavilion houses the Eiteljorg Collection of African Art. The Clowes Pavilion features medieval and Renaissance art. The Krannert features eighteenth-

and twentieth-century European and American paintings. And the fourth pavilion, the Lilly, boasts extensive decorative arts shown in period settings.

Consider the 152 acres of lush grounds and botanical gardens as a bonus. Admission is free. A fee is charged for special exhibits, however, and a donation is requested at the Lilly Pavilion. Call (317) 923–1331. Open Tuesday through Saturday, 10:00 A.M.–5:00 P.M.; Thursday, 10:00 A.M.–8:30 P.M.; Sunday, noon–5:00 P.M.

LUNCH: The **Garden on the Green,** located on the museum grounds, is a perfect spot for sandwiches, soups, and salads. Brunch is also served on Sundays, but reservations are required. Call (317) 926–2628.

Afternoon

After lunch, head back toward downtown, for a tour of the **James Whitcomb Riley Home,** 528 Lockerbie Street. Built in 1872 and located in the 6-block historic Lockerbie Square neighborhood (just north of New York Street), this house is generally regarded as one of the best Victorian preservations in the country. The Hoosier poet's pen remains on his desk and his hat on the bed, as if he were due back any minute. Open Tuesday through Saturday, 10:00 A.M.–3:30 P.M.; Sunday, noon–3:00 P.M. Closed holidays. Admission: adults, $3.00; seniors $2.00; children under 17, 50 cents; children under 7, free. Call (317) 631–5885.

If you are a fan of old homes, then make it a point to take in the **President Benjamin Harrison Home,** 1230 North Delaware Street (north of I–65); (317) 631–1898. The residence of the twenty-third president has been lovingly restored, right down to much of the original furniture. Also worth noting is the collection of gowns belonging to Mrs. Harrison and her daughter. Open Monday through Saturday, 10:00 A.M.–3:30 P.M.; Sunday, noon–3:30 P.M. Closed most holidays. Admission: adults, $5.00; seniors, $4.00; children, $1.00.

If history doesn't stand a chance against shopping, then head back to Circle Centre, which attracted 12 million visitors in its first year. Or take in a larger-than-life movie at the IMAX 3-D theater, located in Indiana's only urban state park, **White River.**

Itinerary note: If you are leaving for Conner Prairie or Zionsville tomorrow, you may want to fit in the two following suggestions today. If not, save them for your third day.

If Indianapolis means a checkered flag to you, then no visit here would be complete without a stop at what many consider a shrine: the **Indianapolis Motor Speedway,** 4790 West 16th Street, just west of downtown, home to the Indianapolis 500, the Brickyard 400, and the Forumula One U.S. Grand Prix. You can get a driver's-eye view of the track by taking a bus tour around the 2½-mile oval. Adjacent to the track, the **Hall of Fame Museum** displays all kinds of cars (racing, antique, and classic) and enough motor memorabilia to last a lifetime. Open daily, 9:00 A.M.–5:00 P.M. Closed Christmas. Admission: $2.00 (bus ride is an additional $3.00 adults. $1.00 children). Call (317) 484–6747.

If you think cars are merely a way to get from Point A to Point B, however, consider taking in the **Indianapolis Zoo,** 1200 West Washington Street; it's large enough to be stimulating but not so large that it's intimidating. The sixty-four-acre "cageless" facility includes the state's largest aquarium, an enclosed dolphin and whale pavilion, and animals in their natural habitats. There's also a critter "encounter" area where kids can have a hands-on experience with their furry friends. Open daily, 9:00 A.M.–6:00 P.M., June 1 through Labor Day; 9:00 A.M.–4:00 P.M. the rest of the year. Admission: adults, $9.00; children 3 to 12, $5.50; parking, $2.00. Call (317) 630–2030.

DINNER: Stay close to the hotel and dine at **St. Elmo's Steak House,** 127 South Illinois Street; (317) 635–0636. This quintessential steakhouse has been a local tradition since 1902. Sprawling twenty-ounce sirloins plus thick double filet mignons are the big draws, but the juicy veal chop shouldn't be ignored, either. Dinner only. Expensive.

There are a number of options for after-dinner activities. The easiest is a stroll along the White River Canal Walk. Or rent a "pedalboat" ($12 per hour; 317–632–1824) and work off dinner. Theater and concert lovers can feast in Indianapolis—and at bargain prices, as well. If music is your passion, you should know that Indianapolis has a first-rate symphony that plays in the **Hilbert Circle Theater,** 45 Monument Circle. Not only is this venue considered acoustically superb, but an average seat will set you back only about $20. The season runs from October to May, with the annual Yuletide concert drawing an audience from all over the state. Call (317) 639–4300.

First stop for theater fans should be the **Indiana Repertory Theater,** 140 West Washington Street, the state's only full-season resident theater. The six-play season goes from October to May. Call (317) 636–2669.

The **Indianapolis Opera** is highly regarded, mounting four operas a year at **Clowes Hall** on the campus of Butler University, 4600 Sunset Avenue. For ticket information, call (317) 283–9696.

Even dance—hard to come by in all but the largest cities—is well represented with **Ballet Internationale–Indianapolis.** The company stages several major ballets each year, also at Butler, which is recognized as one of the premier ballet schools in the country. The Ballet Internationale spends about half of its August-through-April season on national tour, so the best way to keep on top of the schedule is to call the box office at (317) 637–8979.

LODGING: Canterbury Hotel.

DAY 3

Morning

Get an early start for **Conner Prairie** in Fishers. Take I–465 north to exit 35, then go 6 miles north. You feel as if you stepped into a time machine and set the dial for 1836 as you enter this living-history museum. Like Greenfield Village in Detroit (see Michigan Escape Five), the meticulous attention to detail is what makes this one of the state's best attractions.

The other on-the-road option is **Zionsville,** which is really a northern suburb of Indianapolis (take I–65 north to the Zionsville exit). There is no shortage of fun shops along the brick-paved streets of the 125-year-old Victorian business district. Though only 6 blocks, you'll find the ambience (window boxes overflowing with flowers, candlelit windows) most pleasant. You can pick up a shopping and dining guide at the Chamber of Commerce, 135 South Elm Street; (317) 873–3836.

Adventurous palate alert: The heart of downtown Zionsville may seem like an unlikely place for an exotic restaurant, but there is one there called **Adam's Rib and Seafood House,** at 40 South Main Street. The menu includes delicacies such as black bear, alligator, lion, and antelope. Of course, tamer selections are available (prime rib, barbecued ribs, fresh fish), and all are expertly prepared. Moderate to expensive. Open Tuesday through Saturday, 11:30 A.M. to 2:00 P.M. for lunch and 5:00 to 10:00 P.M. for dinner. Call (317) 873–3301.

THERE'S MORE

Eiteljorg Museum of American Indians and Western Art, 500 West Washington Street at the entrance to White River State Park; (317)

Capitol Commons epitomizes spruced-up and blooming downtown Indianapolis.

636–9378. Home to one of the nation's finest collections of American Western and Native American art and artifacts. If your time is limited, peruse the paintings from the Southwest, particularly the work by the Taos, New Mexico, artists. The museum hosts an annual chili cookoff and an Indian Market. Open Monday through Saturday, 10:00 A.M.–5:00 P.M.; Sunday, noon–5:00 P.M. Admission: adults, $5.00; children, $2.00 (under 4, free); seniors, $4.00. Closed Monday, except during summer months.

Madame Walker Urban Life Center, 617 Indiana Avenue; (317) 236–2099. Named after the country's first black woman millionaire, this fabulous 1927 art deco building was originally used as a stage for vaudeville, but fell into disrepair after World War II. In 1988 it received a $3.2 million face-lift and now serves as an arts and cultural center for the African-American community, as well as home to the popular weekly "Jazz on the Avenue" concerts.

Professional and semipro sports. Indianapolis offers sports fans a lot to choose from. The Indiana Pacers tip off at the new Conseco Field House and the Indianapolis Colts kick off at the RCA Dome (100 South Capitol Avenue), but the number for tickets is the same (317–239–5151). And just

because there is no major league club here, that doesn't mean baseball fans are shut out. The Indianapolis Indians, the Triple A affiliate of the Cincinnati Reds, play at Victory Field, a 15,500-seat open-air downtown ballpark, which opened in 1996. Designed by the same firm responsible for the Baltimore Orioles' park at Camden Yards, the $18 million field has both traditional features, such as real grass, and modern amenities, such as a picnic area. Call (317) 269–3545.

geokids. Since most visitors coming from the Chicago area don't come through the airport, make a special stop at Indianapolis International to check out this interactive exhibit. geokids painlessly teaches youngsters about geography, the environment, and weather as they roam over a huge floor map, "hike" the Appalachian Trail, or use computers to check climatic conditions all over the world. It's open around the clock.

Broad Ripple neighborhood. About twenty minutes north of downtown, this charming community features a concentration of eclectic boutiques, galleries, sidewalk cafes, ethnic restaurants, and antiques shops, many housed in renovated clapboard homes. Ask your hotel for directions.

SPECIAL EVENTS

Memorial Day. Indianapolis 500. The granddaddy of all auto races. Make sure you get your tickets well in advance. If you can't get tickets to the world's second-largest sporting event, the first day of qualifications is considered to be the next best thing.

June. Midsummer Fest. Entertainment and dozens of food booths from local restaurants.

July. Indiana Black Expo's Summer Celebration. Showcases the achievements of African-Americans in culture, art, history, and business. The three-day event at the Indiana Convention Center is the largest event of its kind in the United States.

August. Indiana State Fair. Carnival fun, horse shows, entertainment. State fairgrounds.

August. NASCAR Brickyard 400. In addition to the 500-mile race on the Sunday before Memorial Day, there is now a second major auto racing event held annually at the Speedway. The first Brickyard 400 was held in August 1994.

September. Penrod Arts Fair. A giant celebration, featuring music, dance, opera, and theater, plus hundreds of artisans' booths and food stalls, all sprawling across the lush grounds of the Indianapolis Museum of Art.

September. Formula One U.S. Grand Prix. The third motor sports event at the Indianapolis Motor Speedway. The premier road-racing series in the world.

OTHER RECOMMENDED RESTAURANTS AND LODGINGS

Indianapolis

Bazbeaux Pizza, 334 Massachusetts Avenue; (317) 636–7662. Keep this in mind when you're downtown. Bazbeaux uses homemade sauces and offers a staggering selection of fifty-two toppings—enough flair to impress even the most chauvinistic Chicagoans.

Bertolini's Italian Trattoria, City Centre Mall; (317) 638–1800. Wood-fired pizzas, pastas, and other Italian specialties. A good place for a casual lunch or dinner. Moderate.

Chanteclair, in the Holiday Inn–Airport, 2501 South High School Road; (317) 243–1040. Another special-occasion place, with the accent on French cooking. The strolling violinist sets the stage for romance. Expensive.

Courtyard at the Capitol, 320 Senate Avenue; (317) 684–7733. New in 1997; quality lodging at an affordable price. Rates: $90 to $160.

Crowne Plaza Indianapolis at Union Station (123 West Louisiana Street; 317–631–2221) provides the opportunity to stay in one of twenty-six authentic Pullman sleeper cars that have been transformed into period hotel rooms. The rooms are meticulously appointed and probably would be quite pleasing if you were traveling by rail. But it may be hard to accept a narrow, claustrophobic room when you know more spacious accommodations exist just across the hall in conventional hotel rooms—and for about $20 less per night. The inconveniences (for example, only one person can watch TV at a time) likely will outweigh the comforts for all but the most passionate railroad buffs. There are also an indoor pool and whirlpool. Rates range from $91 to $195 per night.

Hubbard & Cravens Coffee Co., corner of Georgia and Illinois Streets; (317) 383–9705. Wonderful coffees and desserts (attention carrot-cake lovers) in comfy art deco surroundings. Inexpensive.

Hyatt Regency–Indianapolis, 1 South Capitol Avenue; (317) 632–1234. One of the largest hotels in Indianapolis. Health club; luxury level available. Concierge on duty. Rates: $155 to $200 per night.

Mikado Japanese Restaurant and Sushi Bar, 148 South Illinois Street; (317) 972–4180. Authentic Japanese food in a serene atmosphere. Excellent sushi. Patrons can expect to find seasonal changes to the menu, the artwork, and even the china. Moderate to expensive.

Omni Severin, 40 West Jackson Street; (317) 634–6664. A first-rate hotel in a great location. Also has a charming cafe, called 40 West, which is perfect for people-watching. Rates: $140–$190 per night.

Palomino's, 49 West Maryland; (317) 974–0400. Euro-bistro cuisine, lots of vegetarian options, and innovative soups, pastas, and salads. Moderate to expensive.

Radisson Hotel City Center, Ohio and Meridian Streets; (317) 635–2000. Deluxe accommodations just 1 block north of Monument Circle. Rates: $119 to $135 per night.

Renee's, 839 East Westfield Boulevard; (317) 255–0863. Lovely dining in the Broad Ripple neighborhood. Recommendations include chicken Dijonnais and beef Burgundy; don't miss the chocolate mousse. Good, affordable wine list. Open for lunch and dinner. Moderate.

Residence Inn Downtown by the Canal, 350 West New York Street; (317) 822–0840. Opened in late 1997, this suite hotel is well located and a good choice for families. Rates: $100–$225.

Ruth's Chris Steakhouse, Circle Center Mall; (317) 663–1313. The classic steakhouse, which started in New York and now has opened across the country. There is another location in nearby Carmel, Indiana. Expensive.

Shapiro's, 808 South Meridian; (317) 631–4041. An authentic delicatessen that has been in the family for four generations, where you can find such ethnic specialties as juicy brisket, cabbage borscht, and cheesecake. Also good for breakfast. Inexpensive to moderate.

Westin Indianapolis, 50 South Capitol Avenue; (317) 262–8100. Everything you would want from a full-service, large (572 units) hotel. Heated indoor pool, whirlpool, health club privileges. Adjacent to the RCA Dome and Convention Center. Luxury level available, which includes a continental breakfast. Rates: $100 to $175 per night.

FOR MORE INFORMATION

Indianapolis Convention and Visitors Association, 1 RCA Dome, Suite 100, Indianapolis, IN 46225; (317) 323–4639 or (800) 323–INDY; www.indy. org.

Brown County

AUTUMN ADVENTURE

2 NIGHTS

Fall foliage • Hiking • Antiques shops • Shopping • Galleries
Fishing • Horseback riding

Autumn is to Brown County what skiing is to Aspen and the Derby is to Kentucky. The blazing of the colors in these richly forested foothills of the Cumberlands has become such a big event that it is not uncommon to find October weekends booked more than a year in advance.

While the drive to south-central Indiana is on the long side (a little more than four hours from the Loop) and there undoubtedly are closer locales for viewing fall foliage, Brown County has enough other selling points to make it worth the trek.

For starters, it has enjoyed a reputation as a crafts mecca ever since it became a retreat for impressionist painters in the early 1900s. That same reputation endures today, and it is one the natives take very seriously. When you consider that Nashville has a population of only 800—but more than 300 shops—you can see that art is Nashville's meal ticket.

The following itinerary confines shopping to just one day. If you really are an addict, however, rest assured that you can spend your entire weekend in downtown Nashville and not do it all. Also, be forewarned that if you visit during a peak autumn weekend, you will probably encounter a preponderance of tour groups. If you're looking for Walden Pond, head to the state park.

Any visit to Brown County may easily be combined with the two counties that border it on both sides. To the east is Bartholomew County, home of Columbus, Indiana, one of the showplaces of American architecture (see Indi-

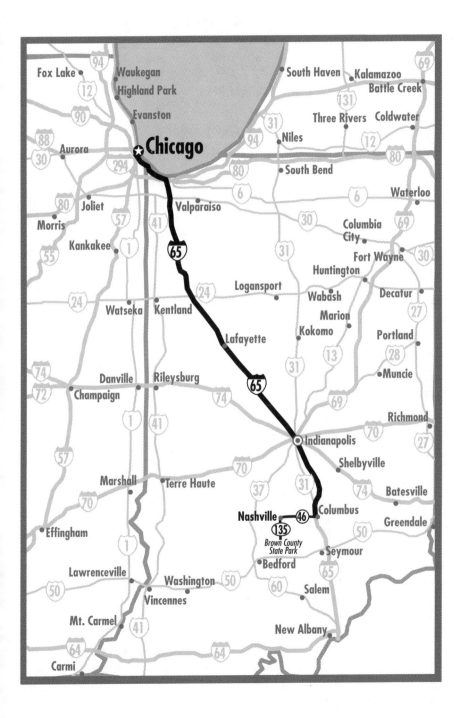

ana Escape Six). To the west is Monroe County, anchored by Lake Monroe (the state's largest lake) and Indiana University in Bloomington. You'll find several good ethnic restaurants in Bloomington, antiques malls, and an opera house that rates rave reviews from *The New Yorker*. All are worthy of a side trip or just a stop as you're coming or going.

DAY 1

Morning

About the quickest way to get to Indianapolis is to take I–94 to I–65 south. Then take Highway 46 west right into **Nashville.** It is most efficient to get an early start and stop along the way for breakfast in Lafayette, Indiana, which has a number of chain restaurants not far off the interstate.

The sheer volume of boutiques, antiques shops, and galleries in Nashville can overwhelm even the most hard-core shopper. Get oriented at the **Brown County Convention and Visitors Bureau,** on the corner of Main Street and Van Buren. If you haven't picked up a free copy of the *Brown County Almanack* at your hotel, get it here. It will be an invaluable source, particularly if you're searching for something specific, such as cornshuck wreaths or stained glass.

LUNCH: Gather up all your brochures, so you can read them over lunch at the **Hob Nob,** right across the street from the visitors bureau. Don't confuse this one-of-a-kind eatery with the chain restaurants of the same name in Chicago's suburbs. This former apothecary shop is loaded with charm, from the wooden booths to the soda fountain. Lighter fare includes quiche and homemade soups and sandwiches, so you can leave room for the wickedly good sodas and sundaes. Call (812) 988–4114. Open 8:00 A.M.–9:00 P.M.

Afternoon

Right above the Hob Nob is the **Brown County Craft Gallery,** a cooperative that showcases crafts made exclusively by local artists. If your time is limited and your concern is design integrity rather than just picking up a few knickknacks, the gallery's knowledgeable staff will help you plan the rest of your artistic itinerary.

If you do start here, then continue traveling north on Van Buren. There are about two dozen shops, which cover the craft spectrum from Shaker to Southwest. Taking even the smallest detour off the main drag can yield some delights, such as handcrafted dulcimers at **Mountain Made Music** on West Main Street.

Going south on Van Buren, there are several clusters of shops (Calvin Place, Artists Colony) that are just made for exploring. Once again, get off the beaten track. If you go west on Franklin, you'll hit **Reflections,** a historic building that features ten rooms filled with prints, floral designs, and accessories. Right across the street is **Honeysuckle Place,** where you can check out Ditte Val-bourg's lovely tapestries. Continue south a block and you'll come upon **The Courtyard** and the **Barnyard Shops.**

DINNER: Brown County Inn, Highways 46 and 135. This family restaurant is a convenient spot to end your shopping spree, since it is located at the end of Van Buren Street. The inn features fried chicken, prime rib, and fried cat-fish; moderate prices (most entrees fall in the $12 to $18 range); and plentiful portions (soup and salad bar are included). The hash browns and the fruit cob-blers are standouts.

From June through July the Brown County Inn holds a backyard barbecue every Saturday from 4:00 to 7:00 P.M. The buffet, which includes everything right down to the watermelon, is about $13.95 for adults ($6.50 for kids). With a playground nearby, Mom and Dad can linger over coffee and still keep an eye on the little ones. Call (812) 988–2291.

LODGING: Brown County Inn, Highways 46 and 135; (812) 988–2291 or (800) 772–5249. The most popular choice for families, the Brown County Inn offers many of the activities and amenities (cable TV, indoor pool, tennis) that younger travelers want. Ongoing renovations are updating the facility, which has one hundred rooms and is the largest in the area. Rates: $109–$139 per night.

DAY 2

Morning

BREAKFAST: A full and fortifying breakfast at **The Seasons Lodge** (Highway 46; 812–988–2284). The specialty of the house is hot fried biscuits and apple butter. Try to get a seat near the window, where the bluffs provide the best floor show in town.

Presuming you've gotten all the shopping out of your system, make this your outdoorsy day. City dwellers will find everything from hayrides to hik-ing readily available at **Brown County State Park,** the largest in Indiana. It's located on Highway 46, 16 miles west of I-65. You can easily spend a day amid the lush 16,000 acres, including Weed Patch Hill, one of the state's highest elevations. There's also fishing, swimming (Olympic-size outdoor pool), a nature center that provides hands-on experiences and programs on wildlife, and eight well-marked trails where you may catch a glimpse of white-tailed deer. The 2-mile trek starts at the lodge and includes the North Lookout Tower; this is a good route for the average hiker. More advanced hikers may prefer the more rugged terrain that loops around the Ogle Hollow Nature Preserve. Be sure to pick up a trail map at the lodge.

LUNCH: Abe Martin Lodge, Brown County State Park. Built in 1932 of hand-hewn native stone and oak, the dining room offers soups, salads, and sandwiches at very affordable prices. Call (812) 988–7316. Lunch is served from 11:30 A.M. to 2:00 P.M., dinner from 5:00 to 8:00 P.M.

Afternoon

Outside Nashville, visit the **home and studio of T. C. Steele,** considered one of Indiana's most esteemed artists, about 2 miles south of Belmont, off Highway 46. Steele's home and studio, all set amid 200-plus acres of beautiful gardens, can be toured. Open Tuesday through Saturday, 9:00 A.M.–5:00 P.M.; Sunday, 1:00–5:00 P.M. Free. Call (812) 988–2785.

If you're not planning a trip back to central Indiana soon, save the afternoon—or the whole second day—for a visit to Columbus. The architectural tour, which leaves by minibus from the Columbus Visitors Center at Fifth and Franklin Streets, is conducted by knowledgeable guides. Or if you prefer, pick up a map and wander at your own pace (see Indiana Escape Six).

DINNER: Story Inn, Highway 135; (812) 988–2273. The best place to satisfy the sophisticated palate, this turn-of-the-century general store has carved out a reputation throughout the entire Midwest. Menus change monthly and the kitchen does it all, from fettuccine to rack of lamb; specialty of the house: Poulet Printemps (chicken breast breaded in crushed pecans and sautéed in a rhubarb wine sauce). Service would be called leisurely by some, slow by others. Open year-round except Mondays. Reservations are a must for dinner; walk-ins accepted for breakfast and lunch. Moderate to expensive. It is also considered a first-rate place to stay (see "Other Recommended Restaurants and Lodgings").

The emphasis on the visual arts has spilled over to the performing arts, which means that there are more entertainment options than you usually find in a town this size.

The **Brown County Playhouse,** operated by the theater department of Indiana University, has been going strong, from June through October, for thirty years. The repertoire is bound to have something by Neil Simon, and at about $14.00 a ticket ($7.00 for children), it represents one of the area's best buys. Call (812) 988–2123.

If your tastes run more toward country than cabaret, check out the **Little Nashville Opry,** located off Highway 46, which attracts big names at small-town prices. Saturday nights from May through November. Call (812) 988–2235.

LODGING: Brown County Inn.

THERE'S MORE

Tours. If you're staying at one of the big hotels (Brown County Inn, Seasons Lodge), you can take a tram, called the Nashville Express, to Richard's Ice Cream, right in the center of town. The tram makes a 2-mile loop and runs from May through October, 10:00 A.M.–5:00 P.M. Tours by carriage are also available.

Antiques. While Brown County itself is one big antiques fair, there are some malls devoted exclusively to antiques. One of the largest is Alberts' Mall, with fourteen rooms of antiques from 1800 through 1920. It's located 1 mile from Nashville on Highway 46W; (812) 988–2397. Others include Brown County Antique Mall I (located downtown) and II (3 miles east of town). If that's not enough, there are more antiques malls in nearby Columbus, Morgantown, and Bloomington.

Golf. Salt Creek, an eighteen-hole course, is located adjacent to Brown County State Park, north entrance on Highway 46, just 2 miles east of Nashville; call (812) 988–7888.

Duffers should also know that down the road in Columbus is Otter Creek Golf Course, which has been consistently ranked as one of the top twenty-five public courses in the country by *Golf Digest* magazine. 11522 East 50 North; call (812) 579–5227.

Fishing. Ogle Lake provides mostly bass and bluegill. State license is required; one can be obtained at the Brown County State Park office.

Horseback riding. Schooner Valley Stables, Inc. Moonlight and overnight riding can also be arranged. Call (812) 988–2859.

Skiing. Ski World. Seven slopes, a bunny slope for beginners, chairlifts, rope tows, lodge, and dining facilities. Open mid-December to early March, weather permitting. In the summer, go-carts and a water slide are the off-season options. Call (812) 988–6638.

SPECIAL EVENTS

April. Spring Blossom Festival. Arts, crafts, food, entertainment.

June. Log Cabin Tour. Tour a half dozen of the area's log cabins.

November and December. Christmas in Brown County. Special open houses at all shops and galleries.

OTHER RECOMMENDED RESTAURANTS AND LODGINGS

Three of Brown County's best-known restaurants—The Ordinary, The Nashville House, and The Seasons—are all under the same ownership. If you're looking for cuisine that's more sophisticated, seek out the bed and breakfasts mentioned here and in Columbus (Indiana Escape Six).

Nashville

Abe Martin Lodge, located in Brown County State Park; (812) 988–7316. Like most state park inns, prices are moderate (rates start at $80).

The Allison House Inn, 90 South Jefferson Street; (812) 988–0814. A restored Victorian home, located within walking distance from downtown. Five bedrooms, all with private baths. Breakfast included (the caramel nut rolls are especially tasty). Rate: $95 per night, two-night minimum.

The Daily Grind, in Calvin Place, near Van Buren and Franklin; (812) 988–4808. The best cup of coffee in town, regardless of which of the twenty varieties you choose. This place feels like the coffeehouses of the sixties right down to the live folk and bluegrass music, which are featured on the weekends.

Hotel Nashville, Highway 135 and Mound Street; (812) 988–0740. In the heart of downtown. Year-round pool, sauna, and spa. Suites available. Rates: $119 to $169 per night.

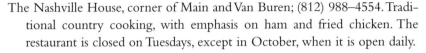
The Nashville House, corner of Main and Van Buren; (812) 988–4554. Traditional country cooking, with emphasis on ham and fried chicken. The restaurant is closed on Tuesdays, except in October, when it is open daily.

The Ordinary, on Van Buren a block north of Franklin; (812) 988–6166. A good lunch stop. The tenderloin sandwiches and chicken salad are local favorites. Note that the restaurant is closed on Mondays, except in October, when it is open daily.

Seasons Lodge and Conference Center, Highway 46, ¼ mile east of State Road; (812) 988–2284. With eighty rooms, this lodge offers extras such as a pool and gameroom, and some of the rooms have fireplaces. Known for its rustic surroundings. Rates: $89 to $119 per night.

Story Inn, Highway 135 South; (812) 988–2273. Located on the edge of Brown County State Park, the Story Inn is best known for its restaurant. Built in 1850 as a general store, accommodations include four suites, three double rooms, and six cottages. (No children under 12 are allowed in the Main House.) Breakfast (try the banana pancakes) is included. Rates: $87–$140 per night.

FOR MORE INFORMATION

Brown County Convention and Visitors Bureau, corner of Main and Van Buren Streets, P.O. Box 840, Nashville, IN 47448; (800) 753–3255 or (812) 988–7303.

INDIANA

Columbus

SHOWPLACE OF AMERICAN ARCHITECTURE

2 NIGHTS

Architecture • Antiques • Sightseeing • Hiking
Fishing • Historic village

Columbus is the one town that can lay claim to that overworked adjective *unique*. When the American Institute of Architects recently asked its members to rate U.S. cities based on design quality, Columbus ranked sixth nationwide. Not bad for a town of 35,000 people in central Indiana.

How did Columbus become "the Athens of the prairie," snaring such famous architects as Harry Weese, I. M. Pei, and Cesar Pelli? The answer goes back to Joseph Irwin Miller, chair of Cummins Engine Company, one of the town's biggest employers. Miller commissioned Eliel Saarinen, the well-known architect, to design the First Christian Church. In 1942 the striking brick-and-limestone structure tower was completed, and the town's reputation was born.

Twelve years later Miller again sought out a Saarinen. This time it was Eliel's son, Eero, who was Miller's classmate at Yale, and the project was the Irwin Union Bank. Miller was so delighted with the glassy, lushly landscaped structure that he set up a foundation to attract top-notch talent to Columbus. Today more than fifty buildings are a testimony to his vision.

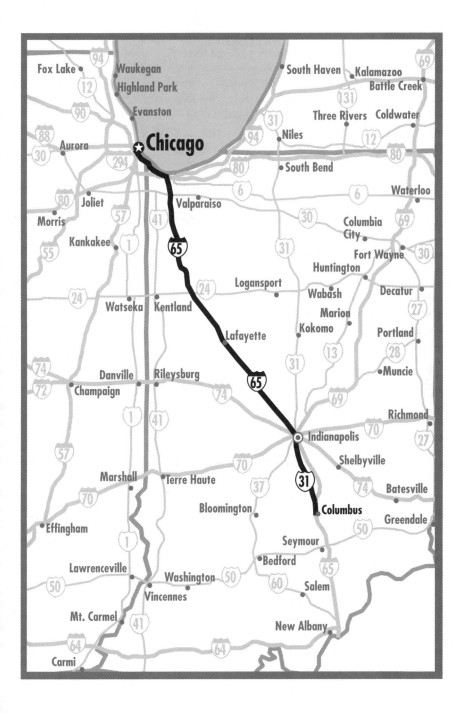

INDIANA

DAY 1

Morning

Take I–94 east to I–65 south. Then get on Highway 46 and head east into Columbus, 45 miles south of Indianapolis. The traveling time—four hours—is almost identical to that of Nashville (Indiana Escape Five). In fact, many people tack on an extra day and combine the two.

Since most visitors are too tired to "do" the architecture tour the day of arrival, you may find it more efficient to plan a side trip for the first day and save the Columbus sightseeing for the second day.

A stop at **Conner Prairie,** a living-history museum in Noblesville—about 10 miles north of Indianapolis—fills the bill quite nicely. Turn off I–65 at Lebanon and take Highway 32 about 20 miles east to 13400 Allisonville Road, Noblesville.

LUNCH: Start your visit at the museum center, where you'll find **Governor Noble's Eating Place,** which offers traditional cooking. There's a bakery adjacent to the restaurant, if you want to pick up a bag of goodies to nosh on during the afternoon.

Afternoon

After lunch you can peruse the galleries and gift shop at the museum center before touring the historic buildings. Here, first-generation Indiana settlers come to life in the schoolhouse, blacksmith shops, and gardens. Costumed guides and lots of hands-on activities make this more a personal encounter than a history lesson.

Conner Prairie also holds many special events, from weddings to performances by the Indianapolis Symphony Orchestra. The **Candlelight Christmas Tours,** held at 5:30 P.M. during most of December, are especially popular. Call (317) 776–6000 for a schedule. Admission: Adults $9.75; kids 5–12, $5.75; seniors $8.75.

For an entirely different kind of experience, you can hit **Prime Outlets** at Edinburgh on I–65 (take exit 76B), about a half hour north of Columbus. Compared with similar outlet malls in Wisconsin at Michigan City and Kenosha, the prices here are noticeably cheaper, probably because the clientele comes primarily from Louisville and Indianapolis instead of Chicago.

Get back on I–65 to Columbus.

The Irwin Union Bank and Trust, a landmark on the Columbus architectural tour.

DINNER: Tired from all that shopping? Go casual for dinner. The **Columbus Bar,** known locally as "the C.B.," fits the bill. Its pork tenderloin sandwiches and onion rings get rave reviews; 322 Fourth Street (812–376–7046).

LODGING: Columbus Inn, 445 Fifth Street; (812) 378–4289. This is one of the most acclaimed B&Bs in the country and the only one to have been awarded four diamonds by the AAA. In keeping with the town's architectural theme, the Columbus Inn is, appropriately enough, the old city hall, but you'd never guess. The guest rooms are spacious and scrupulously clean, decorated in reproduction American Empire. All rooms (five suites, twenty doubles, nine singles) have private baths. Afternoon tea will give you a wonderful feeling of welcome. Unlike many other elegant inns, the Columbus welcomes children, and even babysitting can be arranged with the front desk. Rates run from $96 to $210 per night (buffet breakfast included).

DAY 2

Morning

BREAKFAST: Breakfast buffet at the Columbus Inn includes everything from juices to scrambled eggs to pastries and bread pudding.

Begin your architectural tour at the **Columbus Visitors Center,** located in a nineteenth-century home at 506 Fifth Street (812–378–2622 or 800–468–6564). Here you can pick up maps for self-guided tours. For a more formal orientation, take the two-hour guided bus tour, which leaves from the visitors center daily during the summer. Departures Monday through Friday, 10:00 A.M.; Saturday, 10:00 A.M., 2:00 P.M.; Sunday, 11:00 P.M. (Sunday, March through November). Arrive a little before departure time to catch the video. (Check for tour hours during the off-season). Admission: adults, $9.50 ($8.50 for AAA members); children 6–12, $3.50; children under 6, free. There is a one-hour tour option.

Thirty-five of the area's guidebook buildings are in Columbus; fifteen others are within a 12-mile radius of the city limits. According to the late *Chicago Tribune* architecture critic Paul Gapp, "Structures range from the brilliant to the commonplace and . . . at least a couple are absolute bombs." In addition to the Irwin Union Bank, Gapp cited the following buildings as especially noteworthy:

The **First Christian Church,** designed by Eliel Saarinen and where the whole effort began, is on the corner of Fifth and Lafayette. (You won't have any trouble finding it; the 166-foot-tall chimes tower can be seen for miles around.) Across the street is the **Cleo Rogers Memorial Library,** designed by I.M. Pei. On the same block is **Lincoln Elementary School,** by Gunnar Birkerts. Said Gapp of the school: "It completes the ensemble of structures with satisfying harmony. Nowhere else in Columbus, perhaps, do buildings visually interact so well."

Rounding out the list is the **North Christian Church,** a few miles away at 850 Tipton Lane. It is Eero Saarinen's last work before his death and arguably Columbus' most famous building. Chicagoans should note that while most of the architects are represented by one or two designs, Chicago architect Harry Weese is credited with ten of the 102 buildings and sculptures listed in the guidebook.

If you skip the outlying buildings, the driving time takes between two and four hours, depending on how long you linger at each stop.

If you'd rather sit back and leave the driving to someone else, however, try the bus tour. Reservations may be made in advance of the tour, which leaves from the visitors center daily from March through November (no Sunday tours December through February). Arrangements can be made at the visitors center.

When you return you may also want to spend some additional time at the visitors center, which also sells interesting architectural gifts and Columbus merchandise.

LUNCH: A Columbus tradition, **Zaharako's Confectionery** has been located at the same address (329 Washington Street) since 1900. This amazing ice cream parlor features a Mexican onyx soda fountain (courtesy of the St. Louis World Exposition in 1905), Tiffany lamps, a working pipe organ, sandwiches (limited to the grilled cheese–sloppy joe variety), and luscious fountain creations. Call (812) 379–9329.

Afternoon

Across the street from Zaharako's is the **Commons,** designed by Cesar Pelli. This mall includes the usual stores, as well as an indoor playground that will be tough to tear the kids away from. The other big draw is the 30-foot-tall, seven-ton kinetic sculpture by Jean Tinguely. Appropriately called "Chaos," the sculpture has a strangely hypnotic effect.

Stop in **kidscommons,** the children's museum (812–378–3046). Before leaving the mall, reserve some time for the **Indianapolis Museum of Art/Columbus Gallery** on the second floor. After almost two decades at the visitors center, the gallery moved into its state-of-the-art space. You're always assured of seeing several good exhibits.

For recreation, go west on Fifth Street to **Mill Race Park.** In 1992, the city gave itself this $8 million gift to mark the 500th anniversary of Christopher Columbus' voyage. The lovely green, located by going west on Fifth Street, has something for everyone—paddleboats, playground, bike trails, and an amphitheater, where concerts and movies are a summer fixture.

DINNER: Peter's Bay, right in the Commons (812–372–2270). Opened at the end of 1990 by Marty Dittman, who was raised on a fishing boat. Fish is flown in daily from his family's boat near Boston. Moderate to expensive.

LODGING: The Columbus Inn.

DAY 3

Morning

BREAKFAST: The Columbus Inn.

Make this your outdoorsy day. While architecture may take center stage in Columbus, the recreational opportunities represent one of the Midwest's best-kept secrets.

Depending on the season, the 16,000 acres at **Brown County State Park** offer hiking, boating, swimming, horse trails (see Indiana Escape Five). And if you're a serious angler, **Lake Monroe,** Indiana's largest body of water, is such a mother lode for bass and bluegill that it was listed as one of the top twenty-five locations for a fishing vacation in the angler's guidebook *Fishing Hotspots*.

Boaters should note that the lake has two different characters, divided by Highway 446. Head to the western side—a.k.a. "the fast side"—for boating and waterskiing. The east side is more tranquil, with boat speed limits held to a minimum. **Lake Lemon,** which borders Brown and Monroe counties, is smaller than Lake Monroe, but it has the same splendid scenery and facilities. For information, contact the visitors center at (800) 678–9828.

LUNCH: Many of the area restaurants will pack you a picnic lunch, perfect for enjoying the area's beautiful vistas.

Afternoon

Wend your way home via I–65. If you haven't browsed Nashville's 250 galleries and shops, this is the time to break out those credit cards—depending on your budget, patience, or feet (or all of the above).

THERE'S MORE

Bicycling. There are plenty of places to pedal in both Brown and Monroe counties, but if you're into cycling in a big way, Bloomington should be on your itinerary. *Bicycle* magazine ranked it the seventh-best city in the United States. The "Little 500" (remember the film *Breaking Away?*), held every April, and the "Hilly Hundred" are two of the premier events on the cyclist's calendar. Bartholomew County also holds "Hope Ride" every September to benefit a local food bank.

Camping. Fourteen public and private campgrounds are available throughout the Lake Monroe area. For information contact the Convention and
Visitors Bureau, 441 Gourley Pike, Bloomington (812–334–8900). (See
also Brown County State Park, Indiana Escape Five.)

Otter Creek Golf Course, the only Robert Trent Jones–designed course in
the state, has been ranked as one of the top twenty-five courses in the
country by *Golf Digest*. An additional nine-hole course designed by Jones'
son Reece, opened in the spring of 1995. For information call (812)
579–5227.

Fishing. There are a number of charter services that will take you out on Lake
Monroe.

SPECIAL EVENTS

May. Historic Homes Tour. Families living in historically significant homes
open their doors to the public. Sponsored by Bartholomew County Historical Society and held every other year (in the even-numbered years).
Call (812) 372–3541.

June. Popfest. The Indianapolis Symphony Orchestra and the Columbus, Indiana, Philharmonic play in the public library plaza. Attracts up to 10,000
visitors.

October. Ethnic Expo. On the second weekend of October, a three-day festival of food, cultural exhibits, and entertainment, plus a kite-flying contest, all of which celebrate the city's cultural diversity.

Thanksgiving through early January. Festival of Lights. Public displays
transform Columbus into a winter wonderland.

OTHER RECOMMENDED RESTAURANTS AND LODGINGS

Columbus

Holiday Inn Conference Center, 2480 Jonathon Moore Pike; (812) 372–1541.
Indoor pool, sauna, exercise equipment. Rates: $90 to $125.

Ramada Inn Plaza Hotel, 2485 Jonathon Moore Pike; (812) 376–3051. Pool,
free continental breakfast, tennis. Rates: $75 to $100, some suites also
available.

FOR MORE INFORMATION

Columbus Visitors Center, 506 Fifth Street, Columbus, IN 47201; (812) 378–2622 or (800) 468–6564; www.columbus.in.us.

MICHIGAN
ESCAPES

Southwest Michigan

HARBOR COUNTRY

2 NIGHTS

*Antiques • Bicycling • Sailing • Orchards • Hang gliding
Swimming • Winery tours • Hiking • Camping*

Harbor Country—the chamber of commerce moniker—extends from the Indiana border on the south through New Buffalo, Union Pier, Lakeside, and Bridgman. It has been a vacation haven for Chicagoans for more than a century, but it was only during the 1980s that the area got a giant dose of glamour, thanks to an influx of celebrities such as movie critic Roger Ebert and novelist Andrew Greeley.

Today pricey condos line the largest full-service marina on Lake Michigan, and there are long lines at restaurants on the weekends. Even so, Harbor Country is blessed with sand, surf, and breathtaking sunsets. Everything moves just a little bit more slowly (except your watch; don't forget that Michigan is an hour ahead of Chicago). In every other way, however, the state line is virtually meaningless. It's just as easy to dine in Michigan City, Indiana, as it is in Michigan, so check out the offerings there (Indiana Escape One) as well.

One lodging note: For a popular resort area, Harbor Country is almost completely free of large hotels, which also adds to its charm. But if you're traveling with kids, you may need the amenities that a national chain has to offer.

MICHIGAN

DAY 1

Evening

You'll want to make the quick trip right from work, taking I–94 to the Union Pier exit.

DINNER: Miller's Country House, 16409 Red Arrow Highway, 3 miles north of New Buffalo; (616) 469–5950. A fixture of the Harbor Country dining scene, Miller's is the place to go for charbroiled specialties. The steaks are the calling card, but the chef turns out a mean grilled salmon. The grill room is more clubby and casual, with a menu to match. Not open Tuesday. Moderate to expensive.

After dinner, head over to **Oinks,** 227 West Buffalo; (616) 469–3535. Forget nightlife. This is the place to see and be seen in the evening, and with fifty-five flavors of ice cream, it's no wonder that this is one of the first stops on any weekend itinerary. Don't be intimidated by the long lines; they move quickly. Around back is a new addition, Oink's Chocolate Pig, which sells every candy imaginable, from Pez to truffles. Hours: noon–11 P.M., Monday through Thursday; noon–11:30 P.M., Friday; 11:30 A.M.–11:30 P.M., Saturday; 11:30 A.M.–11:00 P.M., Sunday.

LODGING: Opened in 1997 the **Harbor Grand,** 111 West Water Street (616–469–7700), is the first luxury hotel built between Chicago and South Haven since the 1920s. With a nod to the prairie style of Frank Lloyd Wright, the fifty-seven rooms are nicely appointed, especially if you get a fireplace and a harbor view. The location—on the water, but in the heart of New Buffalo's shopping district—is a dream. The price includes a full breakfast buffet and an indoor pool that can save a rainy weekend. Rates: $135 to $225.

DAY 2

Morning

BREAKFAST: Harbor Grand.

Once you park your car, you can forget about it. Every conceivable creature comfort in New Buffalo is within walking distance. Set up camp on the beach, go shopping, grab some lunch, covet the yachts. You can even get a massage (**Harbor Country Day Spa,** 11 Mechanic Street; 616–469–7761), then walk a couple of blocks back to your beach towel for a midday snooze.

LUNCH: Brewster's, 11 West Merchant Street, just off Whittaker; (616) 469–3005. The food is very good—pastas, wood-fired pizza, and a few salads—and it is designed for the adult palate. The penne with pesto, sun-dried tomatoes, and pine nuts is first-rate, as is the gnocchi. Skip the odd herb pan bread in favor of more conventional Italian bread.

The other choice, if you don't want to stray too far from the beach, is **Nancy's** (142 North Whittaker; 616–469–4240). Good shakes, too.

Afternoon

The afternoon is prime time for browsing. If you are up for a short ride, you can hit some of the boutiques and galleries, clustered along Red Arrow Highway.

Lakeside Gallery, 15486 Red Arrow Highway, is the best known. This is a serious gallery that attracts serious artists (you'll frequently see announcements in the *Chicago Tribune's* Friday calendar). There's also a rustic hotel (translation: no phones, TVs, or air-conditioning). It originally was set up to house visiting artists but now takes people who haven't even held a paintbrush since kindergarten. Call (616) 469–3022.

Equally well known in the collectibles department is **Rabbit Run Antiques,** 15460 Red Arrow Highway, which has a terrific selection of English and Irish pine furniture. There are also quilts, rugs, and country folk arts.

Other worthwhile destinations: **Royal Veil Antiques** for fine collectibles and **Filoni Vestimenti,** which sells fashionable clothing and accessories. Both are at 15300 Red Arrow Highway. Serious gardeners should head to **Riviera Gardens,** 16024 Red Arrow Highway, where you'll also find handcrafted birdhouses, terra-cotta pots, and earthenware. Other wonderful pieces for home and garden can be found at **Lovell & Whyte,** 14950 Lakeside Road; (616) 469–5900.

If you're sticking around the waterfront in New Buffalo, it's easy to get in your shopping quota. The main drag, Whittaker, is lined with chic shops, such as **Trillium, Whittaker House,** and the **Silver Crane Gallery,** which has the best selection of silver this side of Santa Fe. As for home accessories, there's tons of cool stuff at **The Climbing Monkey.** Gourmet shoppers should check out the **Shops at Michigan Thyme** (gourmet vinegars, olive oils, pates, etc.).

Be forewarned: While this may look like Mayberry, the prices are closer to Manhattan, so bring plenty of plastic. The only real bargains are the decadent potato salad and a to-die-for bread pudding at **Naturally New Orleans,** a

Untamed beaches at Warren Dunes attract sunseekers and hang gliders alike.

take-out shop, which opened in 1997. Definitely a welcome addition to Whittaker Street.

DINNER: Jenny's, 15460 Red Arrow Highway, Lakeside; (616) 469–6545. Widely regarded as the best in the area, and with good reason. With a modernized bar and lounge (the ceiling and beams are replete with stencils based on local Native American designs), the setting enhances the innovative cuisine. Thai sea bass, and grilled steak with mounds of fried shoestring potatoes are hugely popular. Grand finale: perfect profiteroles. Saturday night reservations are tough during the summer season.

LODGING: Harbor Grand.

DAY 3

Morning

BREAKFAST: People travel a long distance to reach the **Blue Plate Cafe,** 15288 Red Arrow Highway, and Linda Beck's smoked turkey breast hash, frittatas, freshly baked goodies, and juice bar. If you can't make it for breakfast,

lunch offers a fine selection of homemade soups and sandwiches. (Dinner is a very family-friendly noodle bar, available Fridays only, from Memorial Day to Labor Day.)

Head away from the coast by traveling east on Highway 12. About 7 miles away is Three Oaks, where you'll find the **Three Oaks Bicycle Museum and Information Center** right downtown at 110 Elm Street (616–756–3361). Not only does this quirky museum include all kinds of relics and memorabilia, but it also offers very reasonable rates ($12 per day) for its well-maintained bikes. It also has toddler seats, helmets, and any other accessories you might need. In addition, you can get a map of bike routes in the area; it is designed for people who are just weekend riders as well as serious cyclists.

In fact, Three Oaks tourism is almost entirely built on the humble bike—especially during the third week of September, when some 7,000 cyclists flock to town for the **Apple Cider Century,** a 100-mile bicycle tour through the colorful back roads of Berrien County.

Also on Elm Street (which intersects with U.S. Highway 12), you'll find the only meat market that qualifies as a tourist attraction. **Drier's Meat Market** (14 Elm Street; 616–756–3101) sells hot dogs, sausages, and cheeses amid antiques, art, and homespun philosophy. Load up for the way home.

Froehlich's, 26 North Elm Street (616–756–6002), is just down the street and is a great place to pick up some terrific sandwiches (try the tuna), brownies, or any other noshes. Just behind the restaurant there's a picnic table in a lovely shaded park.

Or, if you're eager to explore more of the region, go back to U.S. Highway 12 to Bridgman. Go north to Lake Street (which becomes Shawnee Road), and then go east and follow the signs to **Tabor Hill Winery and Vineyard.**

LUNCH: At Tabor Hill, you can either picnic on the grounds or eat at the restaurant, which has creative fare such as chicken breast breaded in crushed pecans as well as simple grilled foods, including soft-shell crab. Prices range from $9.00 to $16.00.

Afternoon

After lunch you'll be ready to join the tour of the winery. Tabor Hill began when two Chicago salesmen brought a selection of hybrid grapevines back from France in the late sixties. They chose Southwest Michigan because they

thought the gentle breezes off the lake would closely duplicate the conditions of the French provinces. Their hunch was right. The transplanted vines grew into a successful venture that produces about 40,000 gallons a year, making it the second-busiest winery in the state, behind St. Julian in Paw Paw (which also operates a tasting center in Union Pier).

The half-hour tour begins where workers bottle the wine and then heads out into the vineyard. Next is a descent into the wine cellar for a look at the hand-carved oak casks (which depict scenes from Tabor Hill's history). The tour winds up in everyone's favorite place—the tasting room—for samples of some whites, reds, and blends.

The winery is open daily June through mid-September; otherwise weekends only. Call (616) 422–1161.

If you have time on your way home, even a brief stop is worthwhile at **Fernwood,** a nature facility and botanical garden (13988 Range Line Road, between Berrien Springs and Buchanan). This little six-acre gem includes a lilac garden, a boxwood garden, a perennial garden, a fern trail, and a rock garden. The new visitors center has a sunny plant room, a gift shop, and a tearoom. Call (616) 683–8653.

THERE'S MORE

Cook's Energy Information Center, Red Arrow Highway, 3 miles north of New Buffalo; (616) 465–6101. Worth remembering on a rainy day, the Cook Nuclear Plant is one of the largest in the country. The center features three video presentations, including a robot-led trip through time. Open daily during the season; check off-season.

Lemon Creek Fruit Farms, Vineyards, and Winery, 533 Lemon Creek, east of Baroda. (From I–94, take the Bridgman exit.) What used to be strictly a produce operation has been turning out credible medium-priced wines since the early 1980s. Lemon Creek supplies Tabor Hill, St. Julian, and other local wineries with grapes, as well. Much less showmanship than other winery tours, which some folks will find appealing. It's a seasonal operation, so check for hours by calling (616) 471–1321.

Michiana Antiques Mall, 2423 South 11th Street, Niles; (616) 684–7001. Some of the first-rate antiques stores have been mentioned, but the Michiana Antiques Mall is worth remembering for its one hundred dealers and one-stop shopping.

Berrien Springs Courthouse, on U.S. Highway 31 (Cass) at Union Street, 3 blocks north of downtown Berrien Springs. The 1839 Greek Revival courthouse is the oldest county government building in Michigan. It holds a worthy collection of artifacts, from Native American to Civil War memorabilia to information on how the area became a mecca for Seventh-Day Adventists. The complex includes a sheriff's office and a log home. Admission is free. Call (616) 471–1202.

Tree-Mendus Fruit, East Eureka Road, 5 miles northeast of Berrien Springs. In a land of orchards and produce markets, this is the granddaddy of them all. You can have a delightful one-hour orchard tour, watch an apple cider press in action, or do nothing more taxing than buy jams and jellies. There are also 560 acres of U-pick orchards, a nature park with hiking trails and swings for the kids, and even a chapel in the woods in case you feel like getting married. Call (616) 782–7101.

Warren Dunes State Park (12032 Red Arrow Highway; 616–426–4013), Michigan's busiest state park. Each year thousands of visitors enjoy the more than 2 miles of beach, with dunes so high that the area has become a hotbed of hang gliding. The gentle breezes that blow off the lake combined with the soft "landing pad" below attract dozens of colorful gliders, especially in the fall and spring.

If you want to stay closer to downtown New Buffalo, the city beach, at the foot of Whittaker Street, is just fine, especially for people- and boat-watching.

SPECIAL EVENTS

June. Three Oaks Flag Day. Billed as the largest Flag Day celebration in the country. Includes an old-fashioned tent circus. Downtown Three Oaks.

July. International Cherry Pit-Spitting Contest. Doesn't the name tell you everything you want to know? Tree-Mendus Fruit Orchards, Eau Claire.

August. Ship and Shore Festival. Entertainment, food, art. Downtown New Buffalo.

December. Harbor Country Christmas Walk. Parade of homes throughout the area.

OTHER RECOMMENDED RESTAURANTS AND LODGINGS

Bridgman

Hyerdall's, 9673 Red Arrow Highway; (616) 465–5546. A very popular restaurant that turns out basic American fare, such as meat loaf or chicken with mashed potatoes and gravy, polished off with apple pie. The bread basket—abundant with rolls and muffins—could qualify as a meal in itself. Inexpensive.

Grand Beach

Tall Oaks Inn, 19400 Ravine Drive; (616) 469–0097. Spacious rooms, most with private baths; may include Jacuzzis for two, fireplaces, and decks. Full breakfast included. Lounge on the private beach or explore nearby trails on bikes or cross-country skis, both available to guests. Rates: $120 to $190.

Lakeside

The Pebble House, 15093 Lake Shore Road; (616) 469–1416. This seven-room inn is known for its pared-down Arts & Crafts style. In fact, special weekends that celebrate this early twentieth-century design movement are held here. The beach is across the street. Full breakfast buffet includes meats and cheeses. Rates: room, $110–$160 per night; cottage, $250.

New Buffalo

Casey's, 136 North Whittaker Street; (616) 469–5800. Worth remembering for drinks and appetizers (particularly the chicken wings) because it has one of the loveliest outdoor patios, tucked away behind the restaurant and a world away from street noise.

Comfort Inn, exit 1 at I–94; (616) 469–4440. This is a spot to remember if you're traveling with kids, since many B&Bs are for adults only. Even though Comfort Inn has a reputation as a national chain, this property is more upscale and even offers king-size suites that include in-room Jacuzzis, refrigerators, and wet bars. Pool/sundeck. Continental breakfast included. Rates: $89 to $179.

Dakota's, 203 West Buffalo; (616) 469–4001. Fine American regional cuisine in a casual atmosphere. Known for its pastas, fresh seafood, and wood-fired grilled meats. Moderate.

Redamak's, 616 East Buffalo; (616) 469–4522. Redamak's and New Buffalo are synonymous. Anyone who has waited in the long lines here knows that this hamburger haven needs little introduction. The burgers are delicious, the fries are crispy, and it's all a terrific buy, especially if you're there during the week when "the workingman's special" kicks in (burger and fries for around $3.50). Stick to the basics and you won't be disappointed. In balmy weather, try for a table on the patio.

Skip's Other Place, Red Arrow Highway between New Buffalo and Union Pier; (616) 469–3330. Skip's is a longtime establishment with a loyal clientele. The place to go for prime rib. Moderate.

Sawyer

Horsefeather's, Red Arrow Highway at Three Oaks Road; (616) 426–3237. Word spread quickly about this casual spot, which opened in 1996. Fresh seafood (jambalaya and crab cakes), pastas, and salads (try the roasted garlic dressing). The garlic mashed potatoes and yams with the restaurant's own maple butter are other top picks. During the season, breakfast is also served daily here. Moderate.

Union Pier

The Inn at Union Pier, 9708 Berrien Street (just off Lakeshore Drive); (616) 469–4700. Ranks with Pine Garth as one of the area's best-known inns; it is located just 200 steps from the beach. Swedish ceramic fireplaces (called "kakelugn") grace the five second-floor rooms of the main house and the six rooms in the pier house, which makes this an especially worthy destination in fall and winter. Enjoy a hearty homemade breakfast in the morning, Michigan wines and popcorn in the evening. Rates: $135–$205 per night (less midweek).

Pine Garth Inn, 15790 Lakeshore Road, Union Pier; (616) 469–1642. (Take Red Arrow Highway south.) All rooms but one have a captivating view of the lake. Each room is individually decorated, so even repeat visits have a different feel. Several rooms on the main floor have lookout decks, just made for stargazing. Or browse the shelves in the library and pick out an old movie, which you can take up to your room and pop into the VCR (hidden in the armoire). Rates range from $125 to $170 per night for rooms and $200 to $240 for cottages (children permitted in cottages only).

Red Arrow Roadhouse, 15710 Red Arrow Highway; (616) 469–3939. Fresh fish, pastas, and salads. A good medium-price selection.

FOR MORE INFORMATION

Harbor Country Chamber of Commerce, 3 West Buffalo, New Buffalo, MI 49117; (616) 469–5409.

Southwest Michigan Tourism Council, 2300 Pipestone Road, Benton Harbor, MI 49022; (616) 925–6301; www.swmichigan.org.

South Haven

FROM BIKES TO BLUEBERRIES

3 NIGHTS

Antiques • Biking • Fishing • Watersports • Museums

As recently as a decade ago, the only thing South Haven had to offer was nostalgia. From the 1920s until the late 1960s, South Haven was a popular vacation spot. But a variety of factors conspired to turn South Haven into a ghost town. Young baby boomers didn't want to go where their parents went—and they certainly didn't want to go where the activities centered around eating, card playing, and seeing third-rate comedians. They wanted tennis courts, golf courses, and aerobics classes. With the advent of cheap airfares, they could have any of these—and at prices that weren't much different from a South Haven weekend. When those stinky little fish called alewives washed up on Lake Michigan's shores during the 1970s, the beaches were off-limits and so was South Haven. Hotels were boarded up, and lawns became choked with weeds.

Fast-forward to the 1990s. The time crunch put South Haven back into the tourism business. The same baby boomers are bringing their own children to its pristine beaches, casual ambience, and easy commute (about two hours from the Loop).

The South Haven of the 1990s is different because most hotels and resorts have been replaced by condominiums (watch the Sunday paper for rental information). The list of good accommodations is short, but if you're shut out, check out the larger neighboring communities of Saugatuck and Holland.

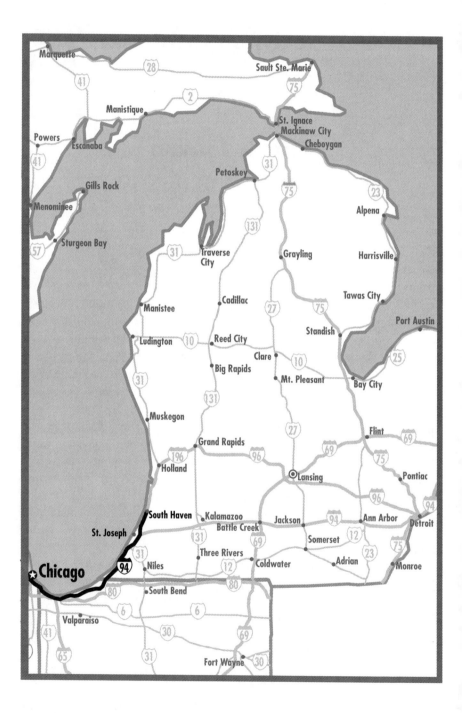

DAY 1

Morning

Head east on I–94 to St. Joseph. Founded as a shipping port in the 1830s, St. Joe (as nearly everyone calls it) has a genteel air. The downtown with its early twentieth-century architecture features landmarks such as the People's State Bank and the once-grand Whitcomb Hotel (now a retirement home). True history buffs will want to pick up a visitor's guide and follow the entire walking tour.

If you want something a little more hands-on, try the **Curious Kids Museum,** 415 Lake Boulevard (between Broad and Elm Streets); (616) 983–CKID. While it doesn't have the five floors of spectacle you'll find at the Children's Museum in Indianapolis, there is plenty here to warrant a stop, especially if your kids like—and you can stand—messy (bubbles and face painting) and noisy (musical instruments) activities. The gift shop is a nifty opportunity to pick up some educational toys. Open Monday through Saturday, 10:00 A.M.–5:00 P.M.; Sunday, noon–5:00 P.M. Admission: adults, $3.50; children, $2.50 (under 1, free).

Or try the new **Color Me Yours** studio, 202 Center Street. Do-it-yourself pottery. You paint it, they fire it. Therapeutic and a rainy-day lifesaver.

LUNCH: Two possibilities. **Hollywood Hi's,** 214 State Street; (616) 983–3607. About 3 blocks from the Curious Kids Museum is a local version of Planet Hollywood. Movie memorabilia from Sylvester Stallone and Kevin Costner, among others, and good fajitas and grazing food (onion rings, chicken fingers), to boot.

Stroll through **Lake Bluff Park** for a splendid view of Lake Michigan as well as a crash course in the city's past. The park is dotted with monuments, including a bronze firefighter carrying a child, which commemorates twelve city firefighters who perished in an opera house fire at the turn of the century.

Afternoon

Just a few blocks away, at 707 Lake Boulevard, is the **Krasl Art Center.** The Krasl is another well-run, accessible museum. The exhibits are constantly changing, from fine arts to folk arts. The **Holly Market,** the center's Christmas crafts fair, attracts a huge following. Free. Call for a schedule: (616) 983–0271. Open Monday through Thursday and Saturday, 10:00 A.M.–4:00 P.M.; Friday, 10:00 A.M.–4:00 P.M.; Sunday, 1:00–4:00 P.M.

Get back on I–94 west to exit 34, where you pick up I–196, and follow that right into South Haven (exit 20).

DINNER: Sea Wolf, Blue Star Highway, 3 miles north of downtown South Haven. Considered one of the best restaurants in southwest Michigan. Choose from whitefish prepared five different ways. Blueberry pie and other desserts provide a taste of the region's produce, as does this famous Suzie Salad with blueberries, raspberries, and apples. Complete dinners include matzo ball soup, reflecting the restaurant's earlier lineage as the well-known Weinstein's Resort. Prices start at about $13. Open for dinner, but it also turns out a stellar Sunday brunch. May through Labor Day. Call (616) 637–2007.

LODGING: Yelton Manor Bed and Breakfast, 140 North Shore Drive; (616) 637–5220. This lovely Victorian inn has a great location (right across from the beach), as well as charming rooms (some with Jacuzzis, fireplaces, and balconies) and gracious hospitality. A full breakfast and hors d'oeuvres are included with the cost of a room. If you stay in midsummer, you'll be greeted by 110 rose bushes; between Thanksgiving and mid-January, you'll find a Christmas tree in every room. Rated by Amoco as one of the top twelve B&Bs in the country. Rates range from $125 to $220 per night.

DAY 2

Morning

BREAKFAST: Yelton Manor Bed and Breakfast. A multicourse affair, from fresh fruit to eggs and American fries to warm-from-the-oven coffee cake. If you're not a guest, try **Pigozzi's** (see page 245).

People come to South Haven for relaxation. At **North Beach,** 5 miles of sand and gentle waves (Lake Michigan averages five degrees warmer on the Michigan side than on the Illinois side) make it easy to mellow out. Type-A personalities, however, can always get into a lively game of volleyball or participate in a variety of watersports. **Outdoor Sports** (114 Dyckman Avenue; 616–637–5555), just a few blocks from the beach, rents sailboards and bikes and has certified instructors in kayaking.

Afternoon

Lake Michigan Maritime Museum, right next door to Captain Lou's, provides a good overview of the link between shipping and the Great Lakes. Boats

South Haven's marina and beaches make it a baby-boomer favorite.

are displayed outside as well. Admission: $2.50; children 5–12, $1.50. Call for hours: (616) 637–8078.

Adjacent to the museum is **Old Harbor Village,** a retail complex that is part of the South Haven renaissance. While the shopping is long on tacky T-shirts, the ambience will make you feel as if you're really on vacation.

From Old Harbor Village, you're just a few blocks from Phoenix, the main drag. There's a sprinkling of interesting antiques and gift shops, most notably the **Arkins Book Store** (where you can find lots of books about the shore), **The Painted Turtle** (cool cards and papers), and the **Blueberry Store,** which sells everything from soup to soap in South Haven's favorite flavor and scent.

Decadent Dogs is full of unique yuppie paraphernalia for dogs. Remember Rover with a South Haven souvenir. This place has every conceivable toy, as well as a deli case stocked with healthy doggy delights. The **Kerry Mark Salon and Day Spa** is a pampering place for facials, massages, wraps, and other stuff for body and soul. Before leaving Phoenix Street stop in at Ode to Joy for pottery and one-of-a-kind picture frames.

DINNER: While you're here, you might as well put your name on the list at **Clementine's Saloon** (500 Phoenix; 616–637–4755). Tourists and natives

alike are drawn to the moderate prices and large portions, so count on long lines between Memorial Day and Labor Day. During the summer the grilled chicken salad is a good bet, but when the mercury drops, go for the home-made soups. Specialty of the house is the golden onion rings, which are served on a wooden peg and are stacked vertically.

After dinner walk across the street and browse through the artsy paper goods and clothing at **Renaissance** (507 Phoenix; 616–637–7033). Right above Renaissance is **Mersonis,** a local gallery with well-edited, well-priced home accessories. Or rediscover the charm of going to a small-town movie theater (as opposed to the concrete bunker at the mall). **The Michigan** shows first-run movies, and you'll pay a few bucks less and get real butter on your popcorn, to boot. Prices are two for one on Mondays; bring your own bag on Tuesdays and the popcorn is free.

After the movies, end up the evening with an ice cream cone. You have a couple of options. **Sherman's Dairy Bar** (on the corner of Phoenix and I–196; 616–637–8251) is the place for a late-night run (open until 11:00 P.M. daily during the summer). But if you don't want to drive (the store is next to the actual dairy on the outskirts of town), satisfy your sweet tooth at **Macdonald's,** the drugstore on Phoenix, which has an old-fashioned soda fountain.

But if an ice cream drink is more what you had in mind, then board the *Idler,* an 1897 riverboat docked at Old Harbor Village (616–637–8435). Built by a wealthy merchant as a pleasure craft, it hasn't changed its function a bit almost a century later. A hipper choice: **Captain Lou's** (just over the Dyck-man drawbridge.) By day this is just a place to grab a soft drink and watch the bridge go up. But by night, it transforms into a Key West–inspired dance club, so grab a rum runner and boogie under the stars.

LODGING: Yelton Manor.

DAY 3

Morning

BREAKFAST: Yelton Manor. If you tried the egg casserole yesterday, go for the stuffed French toast today.

Pick up a picnic lunch at **The Depot** (616) 637–8319; it shares the same building with Outpost Sports) and hit the **Kal-Haven Trail,** which many people consider to be one of the best bike paths in western Michigan. The former Penn Central Railroad bed offers 34 miles of smooth, level riding, making it accessible to even young cyclists. In addition, the landscape boasts many changes and is spectacular for viewing fall foliage. The trail passes by the small towns of Lacota, Grand Junction, Bloomingdale, Gobles, Kendall, and Alamo before ending in Kalamazoo. It's also a favorite of hikers and snowmobilers. Be forewarned: If you decide to ride to Kalamazoo, there's little in the way of accommodations beyond the **Kal-Haven Bed and Breakfast** in Gobles (23491 Paulson Road; 616–628–4932).

The start of the trail is at Wells Street, ½ mile from Blue Star Highway. Trail fee: $2.00 per person per day; $5.00 per family. For an illustrated map, call (616) 637–2788.

Afternoon

If you've totally exhausted yourself, head back to the beach. If not, muster up the energy to visit the **Bangor Antique Mall,** 215 West Monroe (616–427–8557).

DINNER: New this year is the **Inn at HawksHead,** 6959 105th Avenue; (616) 639–2146. This 1928 English Tudor mansion overlooks a championship eighteen-hole golf course. Townies recommend the lobster bisque or lamb chops with mashed sweet potatoes sumptuous enough to eat as dessert. Moderate to expensive.

Walk off dinner on South Haven's **South Pier,** which is now adorned with twinkling lights. It's a romantic stroll down to the lighthouse at the end of the pier, but do pay attention to the weather. The waves have been known to sweep visitors off the pier.

Still have that spring in your step? Check out **Tello's,** 1701 North Shore Drive, about a mile down from Yelton Manor on North Shore Drive, for late-night dancing. Reports are coming back that the Italian food here is first-rate.

LODGING: Yelton Manor.

DAY 4

Morning

BREAKFAST: You can't leave South Haven without having breakfast at **Pigozzi's North Beach Inn** (51 North Shore Drive; 616–637–6738). The pancakes and waffles are bursting with blueberries, and motherly waitresses make sure your coffee cup is never empty. The lines here can be long, but they move quickly. This Victorian home is also a B&B. People have been known to check in here strictly to ensure that they get a terrific breakfast. (The dinners are pretty spectacular, too.)

Head to **Anchor Antiques,** 517 Phoenix (616–637–1500), which offers very good prices and high-quality merchandise.

If that breakfast whetted your appetite for blueberries, you're in luck. The last stop before you go home is **DeGrandchamps Blueberry Plantation,** 3 miles south of South Haven on Blue Star Highway (616–637–3915). Picking your own isn't much cheaper than buying produce, but it's a lot more fun. With one hundred acres, DeGrandchamps is the largest in the region. You can also watch the processing and packing operations.

THERE'S MORE

Arcade/amusements. Fideland Fun Park, (3 miles east of South Haven). Go-carts, batting cage, driving range, miniature golf. Call (616) 637–3123.

Golf. South Haven Golf Club (616–637–3896), on Blue Star Highway, just north of South Haven. (See also Inn at HawksHead.)

Fishing. Captain Nichols, primarily perch. Can arrange any type of charter. Call (616) 637–2507.

Racing. Ginger Man Raceway, 5 miles out of town on Phoenix. A 2-mile, eleven-turn motor sports complex with Porsche, Mercedes, and Rolls Royce show that attracts a crowd. April through October.

Van Buren State Park, Blue Star Highway, 3 miles south of South Haven. Camping, hiking.

SPECIAL EVENTS

June. Harborfest. Dragonboat races, "Blues on the Black River," crafts fair, family entertainment. Riverfront Park, South Haven.

August. Blueberry Festival. Crafts, entertainment, and a blueberry-pie-eating contest. Downtown South Haven.

September. All Crafts Fair. 250 local crafts booths. Stanley Johnston Park.

OTHER RECOMMENDED RESTAURANTS AND LODGINGS

South Haven

A Country Place, North Shore Drive, about 1 mile from downtown; (616) 637–5523. A very sweet place, just as the name implies. "Innkeepers are so delightful that they actually make the weekend," said one visitor. Full breakfasts (such as Southwest egg casserole and heavenly cinnamon rolls) are served on the deck in summer and by the fireplace in winter. Breakfast, in fact, is such a big deal here that a card file is kept on hand, just to make sure guests don't get the same entree twice. About 1 block from the beach. Rates: $70 to $105 per night.

Golden Brown Bakery, 421 Phoenix; (616) 637–3418. Right downtown; a good place to pick up rolls and juice for a breakfast outing. English muffin bread makes for great beginnings.

Hello Dolly's, 524 Phoenix; (616) 637–6742. This little diner, which opened in 1997, features terrifically big burgers and sliders, ultrathick malts, and a faithful-to-the '50s ambience replete with vinyl booths and a jukebox.

The Inn at HawksHead, 6959 105th Avenue; (616) 639–2146. Nine rooms, all with English decor, some with fireplaces and kitchenettes. Good for golfers and corporate outings. Rates: $80 to $130 per night.

Old Harbor Inn, 515 Williams; (616) 637–8480. Located at the drawbridge, this is a good selection for those who want more hotel and less inn. None of the thirty-seven rooms has the same decor as any other room. Most rooms have balconies that overlook the river. Some have Jacuzzis and fireplaces. Peak season rates range from $98 to $190 per night.

FOR MORE INFORMATION

South Haven/Van Buren County Lakeshore Convention and Visitors Bureau, 415 Phoenix Street, South Haven, MI 49090; (616) 637–5252; www.southhaven.org.

Southwest Michigan Tourism Council, 2300 Pipestone, Benton Harbor, MI 49022; (616) 925–6301.

Saugatuck

THE ARTISTS' COLONY

2 NIGHTS

Ferry rides • Galleries • Boating • Shopping
Fishing • Golf

Saugatuck's name has been linked with painters and sculptors since 1910, when the Art Institute of Chicago opened an artists' camp there. Creative types were drawn by the same balmy breezes, untamed marshes, and slightly bohemian atmosphere that attract tourists today.

To truly savor the area's unspoiled beauty, consider off-season. As in Lake Geneva and Door County, the crowds can make you think you never left the city. Off-season does not mean dead of winter, however. Mid-September can be early enough. One word of caution: Saugatuck can be a very tough place in which to find lodging, so book reservations well in advance. Also, more accommodations are available in Holland, just fifteen minutes away. Because there is so much to do in both towns, they are listed here as separate destinations, but you can easily combine the two for one terrific weekend.

DAY 1

Morning

Take I–94 east to I–196 north into Saugatuck. (If the trip is leisurely and you'd like to make some stops along the way, see Indiana Escape One and Michigan Escapes One and Two.)

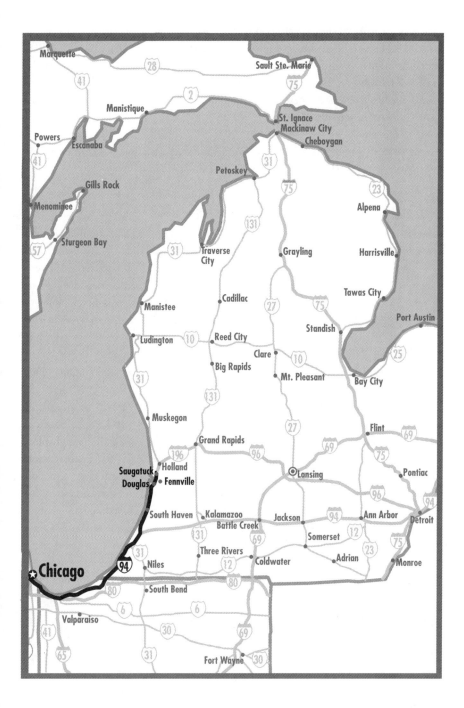

LUNCH: Stop for lunch at the **Loaf & Mug**, 236 Culver Street. Walk right through the dining room to the backyard terrace, where the umbrella tables and wrought-iron furniture are the perfect complement to the fresh salads, just-baked muffins, and tall, cool glasses of lemonade and iced tea. The house specialty is a hollowed-out round loaf that serves as a "bowl" for the soup du jour (which is actually closer to stew du jour). Casual and inexpensive. Call (616) 857–2974.

If your day is too busy for a sit-down lunch, grab a packed brown bag at Gourmet Garden, 322 Culver Street; (616) 857–4885.

Afternoon

Because Saugatuck has some fifty shops, your eyes can easily glaze over. A better strategy is to divide your shopping over two days.

The main street is Butler, where virtually every craft is represented. There are also numerous antiques shops. Don't expect to find any real bargains because of the large Chicago clientele, but the looking is great fun.

An especially interesting spot is the **Old Post Office Shop** (238 Butler Street), a fantastic stationery store, which carries everything from beautiful gift wraps to hand-illustrated Florentine paper.

Also stop in at **Saugatuck Drug**, 201 Butler Street (616–857–2300). This is really a department store masquerading as a drugstore. It has everything from beach towels to video rentals—even an old-fashioned ice cream fountain and a video arcade, tucked in the back. If it's a rainy day and you have kids, this is your best bet.

Other standouts include **Goods Goods Gallery** (106 Mason Street; 616–857–1557), which stays true to its motto, "art for creative living." This colorful gallery is enough to inspire anyone to remodel a room or two.

Cain Gallery (322 Butler Street; 616–857–4353) is another spot to find wonderful jewelry as well as sculpture and art glass. This is the summer home of a gallery of the same name in Oak Park (at 111 North Marion), and items are always being shuttled between the two—good to remember if you see something you love on vacation and want to kick yourself later for not buying it.

DINNER: Chequers, 220 Culver Street, is a comfortable English-style pub with a convivial atmosphere. Fish and chips, shepherd's pie, and mixed grill are hearty and fairly inexpensive. An ample selection of beers and ales. Come early, or be prepared to wait. Call (616) 857–1868.

Food ok - london Broil - nice atmosphere.

Savvy tourists gather on **Oval Beach** (one of the prettiest beaches in the Midwest) at dusk to see the sun put on its splendid show as it disappears into Lake Michigan. Of course, you don't have to be sedentary. Climb all 282 steps up to **Mount Baldhead,** a 250-foot dune near Oval Beach, for a cardiovascular workout, to say nothing of a great vantage point.

LODGING: The accommodations in Saugatuck vary from the most elegant inns to no-frills motels. Here are two options: one for a romantic weekend, the other for a family outing.

The **Wickwood Inn,** 510 Butler Street, offers terrific creature comforts and a location to match (on the edge of the business district, but one sand dune away from the beach). Country-English furniture will make you feel as if you're in the Cotswolds, not southwestern Michigan. While many resort hostelries operate in a halfhearted manner during the winter months, the Wickwood turns Christmas into a two-month-long affair. From mid-November until mid-January, there's a tree in every bedroom. But don't count on waking up in one of the four-poster canopy beds on Christmas Day. It's closed. Rates range from $150 to $195. Call (616) 857–1097.

When the kids are in tow, consider the **Beachway** (106 Perryman; 616–857–3331), which is the closest resort to the public beach. The casual, friendly atmosphere is very suitable for families. While the decor is more bargain basement than Laura Ashley, the rooms have the comfortable feel of your own summer rental. Inflatable toys and air mattresses float in the pool—thus saving the expense when you discover that you've left yours at home. Rates range from $85 to $175 (suites).

DAY 2

Morning

BREAKFAST: Continental breakfast at the Wickwood. Or start the day at **Ida Red's** (631 Water Street; 616–857–5803), considered the best breakfast in town. You can smell the bacon sizzling two blocks away. (Hours are cut back after October, so call first.) Inexpensive.

Check out **Saugatuck Dunes State Park,** located 3½ miles north of Saugatuck. Its remote location makes it one of the best-kept secrets in western Michigan, and it's especially tranquil in the morning. The 1,100 acres include more than 2 miles of Lake Michigan beach and 14 miles of hiking trails, where you can find wonderful dunetop views of the lake. It's an outstanding place for a picnic lunch, which a number of Saugatuck restaurants can arrange.

Afternoon

This would be an opportune time to take a ride aboard that nostalgic Michigan tradition, **Saugatuck Dune Rides.** The sixteen-seat, open-air vehicle is more scenic than scary, although you still don't want to let go of the grip bar. Find it ½ mile west of I–196; (616) 857–2253. Adults, $10.00; children 10 and under, $6.50.

After the half-hour ride, head into Douglas, just a few miles from Saugatuck. Douglas does not have the business district of its more famous neighbor, but it does have the **SS *Keewatin*** ship museum. The 336-foot vessel is permanently moored here and is a fine example of a luxury passenger boat from back in the days when steamships regularly crossed Lake Michigan. The Edwardian dining room and ornate mahogany make you yearn for a more elegant era. Tours: 10:30 A.M.–4:30 P.M. daily. Open Memorial Day through Labor Day. Admission: adults, $4.50; kids under 12, $2.00. Call (616) 857–2107.

While you're longing for the open seas, head back to Saugatuck for a ninety-minute cruise on the *Star of Saugatuck.* The eighty-two-passenger stern-wheeler travels down the Kalamazoo River to Lake Michigan as the captain furnishes fact and folklore. In July and August, weather permitting, cruises depart every two hours, Monday through Saturday, from 10:00 A.M. until 5:00 P.M., with a sunset sojourn pushing off at 7:30 P.M. On Sundays, the first cruise sails at 1:00 P.M. The schedule is more abbreviated in May, June, September, and October. The pier is at 716 Water Street; call (616) 857–4261. Rates are $9.00 for adults, $5.00 for children 2–12.

DINNER: Clearbrook Golf Course, 6494 Clearbrook Drive, just a few minutes from the center of town. Many residents consider this Saugatuck's best restaurant. Specialties include rack of lamb, beef tenderloin, and fresh walleye. Insider's tip: Tuck this place away for lunch, too; you can enjoy grilled food on the patio, which overlooks the first tee. Reservations recommended. Call (616) 857–2000. Moderate to expensive.

Unlike many resort towns that roll up the sidewalks at dusk, Saugatuck has a bustling nightlife. **Coral Gables,** 220 Water Street, boasts four bars and is a late-night magnet. The **Crow Bar** gets a younger (and louder) crowd, while the **Rathskeller** gets the over-30 set.

If the bar scene isn't for you, peruse the marquee at the **Red Barn Playhouse** (3657 63rd Street), where you can see surprisingly polished musicals, despite the fact that stagehands hand out lemonade at intermission. Season is from Memorial Day through October. Call for schedule: (616) 857–7707.

DAY 3

Morning

BREAKFAST: Continental breakfast at Wickwood Inn. Or check out **Pumpernickels,** 202 Butler Street (just 2 blocks from the Wickwood Inn). This family-oriented, no-smoking restaurant is known for its giant cinnamon rolls. Drive up and grab a few to go or sit down for a continental breakfast.

After breakfast, stop at any of the Saugatuck boutiques you couldn't fit in the first day before heading out of town.

Travel south on I–196 and take Highway 89 east to Fennville, about 6 miles southeast of Saugatuck. A stop in Fennville—either coming or going—is a must. To be in the vicinity and not stop at **Crane's Orchards and Pie Pantry Restaurant,** 6054 124th Avenue, would be to miss out on one of the best orchards in Michigan. Call (616) 561–2297.

It is well worth your time, whether you're there to cool off with an apple cider popsicle on a July afternoon, to take the bite off an October morning with a cup of hot cider (watch it being pressed), or to pick a bushel of apples to bring home (usually late September to mid-October). Try to arrange your departure so you're here for lunch. The food is basic good cooking—homemade soups, chili, and roast beef and turkey sandwiches on freshly baked bread, all washed down with Crane's trademark cider, which arrives in a pitcher. Save room for apple, red raspberry, and cherry crisps and pies, but if you can't loosen your belt another notch, you can always buy one to take home.

THERE'S MORE

Ballooning. One of the fastest-growing sports in western Michigan, balloon rides can be arranged by the hour or the day. For rates and information call (616) 335–3363.

Boating. Tower Marine (616–857–2151), Sergeant Marine (616–857–2873), and West Shore Marine (616–857–2181) all have boats to rent. Call them for specific information.

A chain ferry brings visitors across the Saugatuck River.

Fishing. Sportfishing (chinook and coho salmon; lake, brook, and steelhead trout) is very big in these parts. The season starts in early April and winds up around November 20. A number of charters provide everything you need, right down to the box lunch. (They'll even clean and package your catch.) "Best Chance" Charters (616–857–4762) or CoHooker (616–335–2076).

Golf. West Shore Golf Club, Douglas. The second–oldest golf course (1917) in the state of Michigan. Call (616) 857–2500. Or try Clearbrook and Ravines (616–857–2000).

Hunting. Allegan State Game Area, 4590 118th Avenue. About 45,000 acres of marshes and fields between Fennville and Allegan. Canada geese migrate here each fall, making it one of Michigan's largest and most popular hunting areas. In addition to waterfowl, hunters recommend it for deer, turkey, and small game. For information, call (616) 673–2430.

Skiing. The tourism folks are doing their best to market the area as more than just a summer resort town. Saugatuck State Park has well-groomed, marked trails, as does Allegan State Game Area.

SPECIAL EVENTS

July. Harbor Days/Venetian Night. Decorated boats, entertainment. Saugatuck.

October. Gallery Stroll Weekend. Galleries and craft shows host special exhibits, complete with hors d'oeuvres and wine. Saugatuck.

October. Halloween Harvest. Craft bazaar, pie eating, country music, and Saturday-night parade. Fennville.

Mid-October. Fennville Goose Festival. A celebration of the goose migration at Allegan State Game Area. Arts and crafts, Dixieland band, goose-calling contest, cook-your-goose cooking demonstration.

OTHER RECOMMENDED RESTAURANTS AND LODGINGS

Douglas

Everyday People Cafe, 11 Center Street; (616) 857–4240. Great breakfasts, truly worth a detour. Daily vegetarian specials, too. The entire restaurant is nonsmoking. *Casey's Cosey said lunch was wonderful.*

M&Ms, 141 Blue Star Highway; (616) 857–1030. Take-out Macedonian food in an old Tastee-Freez? Believe it. Tasty, fresh, and heaven for vegetarians.

Kirby House, 294 Center Street; (616) 857–2904. Oak woodwork, four fireplaces, antiques with 1990s conveniences (hot tubs). About a twenty-minute walk from downtown Saugatuck. Rates include a full buffet breakfast (quiche, meats, cheeses, cereal, fruit). Rates: $90 to $135, some private baths.

Sherwood Forest, 938 Center Street; (616) 857–1246 or (800) 838–1246. The giant mural in one of the five guest rooms is like being in a treeloft, surrounded by woods. Each room has a bath; swimming pool. Expanded continental breakfast. Rates: $90 to $140.

Fennville

Kingsley House, 626 West Main Street; (616) 561–6425. Guest rooms are named after varieties of apples. During the winter you can cross-country ski in the orchards behind the house. A winding oak staircase leads to five rooms decorated with Victorian antiques. Family-style breakfast. Rates: $80 to $165.

Saugatuck

Bayside, 618 Water Street; (800) 548–0077. If it's not a vacation without a view of the water, this converted boathouse is for you. Rates: $95–$235 (suites).

Billie's Boathouse, 449 Water Street; (616) 857–1188. Nothing fancy, but it does have better-than-average seafood. Great location. Moderate.

Restaurant Tollhouse, 248 Culver Street; (616) 857–1561. An elegant French find. The menu has original creations like duck breast in a sweet confit. Who could resist a chocolate voodoo dessert? Moderate to expensive.

Kemah Inn, 633 Pleasant Street; (616) 857–2919. The Kemah is known for its lovely interiors, including stained glass windows. Lots of details—newspaper in the morning, mints at night, and thick, thirsty towels—make this an especially nice choice. Breakfast is on the simple side (fruit, baked goods, coffee), but it tastes especially good when sitting on white wicker on the sunporch. Walking distance from downtown shops. Rates: $95–$175.

Marro's, 147 Water Street; (616) 857–4248. A haven for boaters. Great pizza and lasagna. Inexpensive to moderate. *Everyone said food very good.*

Monroe's, 320 Culver Street; (616) 857–1242. A 1950s diner atmosphere, the winners here are the barbecued ribs and chicken. Open May to late October. Inexpensive.

Twin Oaks, 227 Griffith Street; (616) 857–1600. Every room has large private bath, TV, and VCR (there's a large film library). Outdoor hot tub. Full breakfast on weekends ("Everyone takes home the French toast recipe"); expanded continental breakfast on weekdays. Rates: $85–$115.

Wally's, 156 Hoffman Street; (616) 857–5641. A genuine (not yuppified) bar that is loved by the locals. Fantastic perch and burgers; equally good music. Open for lunch and dinner.

Willa, the Innkeeper was a great cook. Off main drag, only 7 rooms, nicely decorated and baths were large. French toast & blueberry coffee cake.

FOR MORE INFORMATION

Fennville Area Chamber of Commerce, P.O. Box 84, Fennville, MI 49408; (616) 561–2036.

Saugatuck/Douglas Convention and Visitors Bureau, P.O. Box 28, Saugatuck, MI 49453; (616) 857–5801.

Mermaid's - casual - food good, noisy

twinoaks @ sirus.com

Holland and Grand Haven

A TOUCH OF DUTCH

2 NIGHTS

Boating • Shopping • Fishing • Museums • Galleries
Wooden-shoe factory

It's time to hit the road and head to Holland, a mere fifteen-minute drive from Saugatuck. Nestled in tulip country, the village is replete with Dutch nostalgia, including wooden-shoe dancers and flower pastures dotted with old windmills spinning in the breeze. The countryside is particularly spectacular in May, when acres of tulips proudly display their magnificent charm.

The townsfolk are still of Dutch ancestry—all you have to do is open the phone book and see the pages of "vans" and "vons." Indeed, some families have roots in the area that go back to the 1840s, when tens of thousands of Dutch separatists fled the Netherlands for the United States. What many visitors don't realize, however, is that Holland boasts the largest concentration of Hispanics in the state, as well.

Visitors like Holland for its combination of attractions and leisure activities. The pace here progresses at a comfortable speed, slow enough to jump aboard but quick enough to take you to another world.

About 20 miles up the road is Grand Haven, a city that has done an excellent job of coaxing the fun out of its lakefront without killing it with overdevelopment. The focal point is a magnificent new boardwalk that stretches for almost 3 miles. While Grand Haven is the end of this swing around Lake Michigan, it can be the jumping-off point for exploring the northern reaches (Muskegon, Ludington, and beyond) when you have more time.

DAY 1

Morning

Take I–94 to I–196 and into Holland. For stops along the way, see Indiana Escape One and Michigan Escapes One, Two, and Three.

If you visit Holland in May, you'll know you're in the right place by the millions of colorful tulips (and about an equal number of tourists). The whole town rolls out the red carpet, from the street scrubbers to the costumed dancers who clip-clop down those same streets in their wooden shoes. There are flaky pastries and a parade of bands—all the elements for the quintessential ethnic festival.

But Holland is in full flower even after the Tulip Festival is over. There's plenty of Dutch charm to go around all year long—especially at **Dutch Village,** your first stop, which mirrors a Netherlands town from a century ago. But after the 2½-hour ride from Chicago, the first order of business is lunch.

LUNCH: Queen's Inn (U.S. Highway 31 at James Street) claims to be the only restaurant in Holland to serve authentic Dutch fare. Try Pigs in a Blanket, served only at lunch, which comes with pea soup and Dutch apple pie. Prices are about $7.00 for lunch and about $12.00 for dinner. Reservations are recommended for weekend dining. Call (616) 393–0310.

Afternoon

You'll find Dutch Village to be that slightly hokey type of family attraction. A genuine re-creation of an old-fashioned street fair delights folks with a carousel; two enormous, elaborately carved street organs; and an ornate *Zweefmolen* swing. You'll encounter the wooden-shoed "klompen" dancers, whose foot-stomping style is accompanied by the Gouden Engel street organ for four performances daily (11:00 A.M., 1:00, 3:00 and 5:00 P.M.), which may inspire you to buy a pair of hand-carved clogs at one of the gift shops nearby.

There are lots of activities to keep the younger set amused. They can feed live animals in the kid-size barn near an old-fashioned Dutch farmhouse and a pond that bobs with ducks.

From kitsch to class, Holland's gift stores offer a souvenir to suit every taste. The high-end market has everything from carved porcelain figures and costumed dolls to delftware, lead crystal, and Dutch lace. On the lower end, you'll find the usual trinkets and T-shirts. Some of the shops extend their hours from 9:00 A.M. to 7:00 P.M. daily, from May 1 to Labor Day. Hours fall back to 9:00

A.M. to 5:00 P.M. during the rest of the year. Admission is $6.50 for adults and $4.50 for children 3–11. For more information, call (616) 396–1475.

DINNER: Piper's, 2225 Shore Drive; (616) 335–5866. Overlooking the lake, its atmosphere is sophisticated but affordable. Named the best restaurant in Southwest Michigan by *Grand Rapids* magazine. The menu includes sandwiches and wood-fired pizza. Moderate. *We say a very good*

LODGING: The **Old Holland Inn,** 133 West 11th Street; (616) 396–6601. Antiques are displayed throughout the guest rooms and common areas of this nationally registered Victorian home constructed by Dutch wood-carvers at the turn of the century. The inn offers five private rooms, all but one sharing a bath. Rates (including a continental breakfast) range from $70 to $110 per night.

The **Hope Summer Repertory Theater** (DeWitt Cultural Center, 141 East 12th Street) is a delightful way to spend a summer evening. The repertoire ranges from Shakespeare to Simon, and it is extremely popular. If you know that you want to make theater a part of your weekend, be sure to call ahead for tickets (616–395–7890).

DAY 2

Morning

BREAKFAST: The Old Holland Inn. In the summer, guests take a breakfast of fruit, muffins, and breads out on the deck.

You can tiptoe through the **Veldheer Tulip Gardens** (12755 Quincy Street, a couple of miles northeast on U.S. Highway 31), where a glorious spectacle of sights and scents of some one hundred varieties of tulips and other bulbous blossoms are displayed. It's best to come during April and May, for a truly splendid sight. During the off-season, other flowers take over. You can also buy bulbs and flowering plants. Admission, charged only during April and May, $6.00 per person. The gardens open at 8:00 A.M. daily and close around 6:00 P.M. Call (616) 399–1900.

Right next to the tulip gardens is **DeKlomp Wooden Shoe and Delftware Factory,** where you can see the trademark blue-and-white china, as well as wooden shoes, being made.

Windmill Island Municipal Park, just northeast of downtown, provides an even more in-depth experience. It's a unique municipal park that

sits on a thirty-six-acre island. A replica of a Dutch village, the island boasts a working drawbridge and tulip gardens. Its 230-year-old operating windmill, which was shipped here in 1964, is the last windmill the Dutch government allowed to leave the Netherlands. Called DeZwaan, the mill cranks out a fine graham flour, which can be purchased at the park's concession stands.

The post house is a re-creation of a fourteenth-century Netherlands wayside inn, furnished with an interesting collection of Dutch furniture. The half-hour documentary will bore all but the most die-hard nationalists, but the klompen dancing is mildly entertaining. The park, located at Seventh and Lincoln Streets, is open from May to Labor Day, Monday to Saturday, 9:00 A.M.–6:00 P.M.; Sunday, 11:30 A.M.–6:00 P.M. Limited hours from Labor Day to October 31. Tickets are $6.00 for adults, $3.00 for children. Call (616) 355–1030. The **Original Wooden Shoe Factory** at 16th and U.S. Highway 31 is free of charge and open 8:00 A.M.–6:00 P.M. daily.

If you've had enough Dutch culture and want to steep yourself in good old American shopping, swing over to downtown Holland. Its business district boasts a number of upscale retailers. **Sand Castle Toys,** 2 East Eighth Street (616–396–5955), is filled with wonderful diversions—especially useful on rainy weekends. Literary types will love thumbing through the volumes at **Booksellers on Main Street,** 49 East Eighth Street (616–396–0043).

In addition to the small boutiques, outlet fever has swept Holland, too. The **Horizon Outlet Center,** on James Street just east of U.S. Highway 31 (616–396–1808), features fifty factory-direct stores in a re-created old Dutch village.

DINNER: **Til Midnight,** 208 College Avenue. A great choice for either lunch or dinner. Known for its sophisticated pastas. Don't miss the scallop and shrimp linguine with prosciutto, shrimp, sun-dried tomatoes, and a touch of saffron. Sandwiches start at about $7.00; full dinners start at $16.75. Don't miss the Midnight Cake, a rich, dense chocolate confection that is as close to pudding as cake. As the name implies, Til Midnight is also one of the few late-night spots around. Call (616) 392–6883. Moderate to expensive.

Since Grand Haven is just a half hour away, leave after dinner so you can get in a full day of activity. Take U.S. Highway 31 straight north into downtown.

LODGING: **Harbor House Inn,** corner of Harbor and Clinton, Grand Haven; (616) 846–0610 or (800) 841–0610. Sit out and enjoy continental breakfast or just breathe in the evening air from the wraparound porch. Great

A 1780s operating windmill brought to Holland, Michigan, from the Netherlands.

location overlooking the boardwalk and the harbor, but if it's tranquility you're after, you may want to stay a little more off the beaten track. Most rooms are furnished with fireplaces and whirlpools. There's also a separate two-unit cottage, steeped in luxury. Rates range from $125 to $200 per night.

DAY 3

Morning

BREAKFAST: Dockside Gallery, 301 North Harbor Drive; (616) 846–3300. On the boardwalk downtown, has great French toast, omeletes, and other hearty fare. Try the house specialty—the Farmer's Market Omelete.

After breakfast explore the **boardwalk** which extends for 2½ miles from Chinook Pier to the Grand Haven pier. Here you can find an eclectic range of attractions. First, get your bearings by perusing the brass sidewalk map, which highlights the waterways that feed into the Grand River, all fabricated in brass. (In a display of civic pride, employees of the Grand Haven Brass Foundry donated time to the project.)

Of course, if you really want to get oriented, hop the **harbor trolley,** which takes visitors on short guided tours of the area daily from 11:00 A.M. to 10:00 P.M. and is one of the best bargains in town ($2.00 for adults, $1.00 for children). The red trolley leaves every thirty minutes and tours Grand Haven; the blue one leaves every forty minutes and tours nearby Spring Lake and Ferrysburg.

Washington Street, the main boulevard, is lined with chic boutiques, such as **Carriage House Antiques,** 122 Franklin (616–844–0580), specializing in Victorian and country furniture and accessories; **Baas Clothier for Men,** 100 North Third Street (616–842–5110); **The Dockside Shop** in Harborfront Place (616–846–9116), featuring sportswear for men and women; and **Michigan Rag Company,** 121 Washington (616–846–3510), which features unique hand-printed clothing made exclusively in Grand Haven. **Carlyn Gallery** (134 Washington), specializing in Southwest art; and the **Gallery Upstairs,** a cooperative of the area's best artisans, where you'll find reasonable prices, partly because the artists donate one day a month to run the gallery.

Turn into **Harborfront Place,** formerly the Story & Clark Piano Company, which has upscale shops, restaurants, and condominiums.

LUNCH: Pass on the usual food court offerings and try **Morning Star Cafe,** 711 Washington (616–844–1131). It specializes in Southwestern cuisine and has homemade desserts and fresh-brewed specialty coffee. Open for breakfast, too. Moderately priced.

Afternoon

Now, for a little enlightenment. The **Tri-Cities Historical Museum,** 1 North Harbor (616–842–0700), has something for everyone, whether your interests run from railroads (it's housed in an old train depot) to Victoriana. Hours vary, so call for information. Admission is a suggested donation.

There's also some shopping with personality in Nunica, located 4 miles east of Grand Haven. People all over western Michigan make a special trip to **Moser's Dried Flowers,** 14065 Cleveland (616–842–0641), especially during the holiday season. Dutch native Reini Moser decks the halls with boughs of holly, as well as fir, juniper, and cedar. Open January 1 through March, Tuesday through Saturday, 10:00 A.M.–5:00 P.M.; balance of year, seven days a week, 9:00 A.M.–5:00 P.M.

DINNER: Arboreal Inn, 18191 174th Avenue; (616) 842–3800. A classic country inn tucked into a woodland setting. The mushroom bisque is ultra-silky, the seafood is always fresh, and the wine list is exhaustive (with more than 175 varieties to choose from). Recognized as one of the best dining experiences this side of Lake Michigan. Expensive.

The **Musical Fountain,** located on the boardwalk at the foot of Washington, is Grand Haven's pride and joy. While it's hopelessly corny, it seems to be a must for tourists. For about a half hour, computer-generated music is matched with computer-synchronized fountain light. Tuesday nights feature rock music; Sundays feature gospel and hymns accompanied by the rising of a large cross. Suffice it to say that it borders on the campy. Daily performances Memorial Day to Labor Day; weekends only through the rest of September.

Return to Chicago. If your schedule permits, check out the suggestions for the trip back to Chicago in Michigan Escapes One, Two, or Three or Indiana Escape One.

THERE'S MORE

Amusements. Craig's Cruisers, U.S. Highway 31 at Pontaluna Road, Norton Shores; (616) 798–4936. Go-carts, batting cages, gameroom, miniature golf.

Antiques. Tulip City Antique Mall, 3500 U.S. Highway 31, Holland. About 200 dealers with a better-than-average range of collectibles, furniture, books, and jewelry.

Bicycling. In Holland you can enjoy a most picturesque drive on the Park Township bike path, which is parallel with Ottawa Beach Road and Lake Shore Drive. It ends in Grand Haven. For a free map, call Holland CVB at (800) 506–1299.

In Grand Haven a bike is a great way to get around Bicentennial Park. No bike? No problem. Try Rock 'n Road, 300 North Seventh Street; (616) 846–2800.

Farmer's Market in Grand Haven, off Harbor Drive, is a terrific farmer's market. Open Wednesday and Saturday mornings, June to November.

Fishing. Sportfishing (chinook and coho salmon; lake, brook, and steelhead trout) is a major draw in Grand Haven. Head to Chinook Pier, 2 blocks north of Washington on Harbor Drive, and you'll find anything and everything that has to do with fishing, right down to the party snacks. For charters, try Chinook Pier Sport Fishing (616–842–2229) Bolhouse Charter Service (616–361–0704).

Golf. Grand Haven Golf Club, 17000 Lincoln, Grand Haven; (616) 842–4040. Play eighteen holes amid the dunes and the pines. Holland Country Club, 51 Country Club Road, Holland; (616) 392–1844.

Parks. Grand Haven State Park (1 mile west of Grand Haven, off U.S. Highway 31) is one of the largest beaches in southwest Michigan. Another popular beach is P. J. Hoffmaster State Park (10 miles northwest of Grand Haven, off U.S. Highway 31), which houses the Gillette Nature Center and provides hiking, biking, and cross-country skiing trails. Kirk Park (between Lake Michigan and Lakeshore Drive) and Kitchel Dune Reserve in Ferrysburg are frequently mentioned recreational areas. Kitchel's fifty-two acres is the perfect spot for tranquility, but watch out for poison ivy.

Skiing. Mulligan's Hollow Ski Bowl, 519 Washington, Grand Haven, (616) 842–7051. Has six runs; its longest run is 700 feet. A dozen Grand Haven parks have cross-country trails. For conditions, check with the visitors bureau.

Gillette Nature Center, 1 mile west of U.S. Highway 31, in P. J. Hoffmaster State Park; (616) 798–3573. One of the world's largest accumulations of sand dunes. Lots of hands-on exhibits. Nature trails and observation deck. Park entrance fee: $4.00 per car.

Holland Museum, 31 West Tenth Street, Holland; (616) 392–9084. Share local pride in this landmark building, listed on the National Register of Historic Places. On view: delftware, pewter, a hand-carved carousel, dollhouses, and an 11-foot bronze clock. Admission: adults, $4.00; family, $8.00; under 6, free. Monday, Wednesday, Friday, and Saturday, 10:00 A.M.–5:00 P.M.; Thursday, 10:00 A.M.–8:00 P.M.; Sunday, 11:00 A.M.–5:00 P.M. Closed on Tuesday.

SPECIAL EVENTS

January. Polar Ice Cap Golf Tournament. This unique winter tournament is for brave and hardy golf fanatics who want to test their skills on Spring Lake's challenging course.

May. Tulip Festival, three parades, 1,500 klompen dancers, and tens of thousands of blossoms. Make sure you have reservations in advance. Holland.

August. Coast Guard Festival. Boats, entertainment, foods, parade, and fireworks. Grand Haven.

Late November–December. Dutch WinterFest. A three-week holiday festival celebration.

December. Classic Homes Holiday Tour. Grand Haven's Victorian homes dressed in their holiday best. Call (616) 842–0700 for information.

OTHER RECOMMENDED RESTAURANTS AND LODGINGS

Grand Haven

Bil-Mar Inn Supper Club, 1223 Harbor Avenue; (616) 842–5920. Dining on the shore of Lake Michigan. Prime rib and fresh whitefish are specialties of the house. Moderate.

Charlie Marlin's Caribbean Cuisine, 1 Harbor Island Drive; (616) 847–0200. Moderate.

Grand Haven Area Bed & Breakfasts is a consortium of eight B&Bs, assuring a high level of quality: Boyden House Inn (616–840–3538), Lakeshore B&B (616–844–2697), Harbor House Inn (616–846–0610), Royal Pontaluna (616–798–7271), Seascape B&B (616–842–8409), Village Park B&B (616–865–6289), Washington Street Inn (616–842–1075), and Looking Glass Inn (800–951–6427).

Grand Harbor Resort and Yacht Club–Spring Lake, 940 West Savidge Street, Spring Lake (Highway 104 at U.S. Highway 31); (616) 846–1000. Overlooking Grand River. Most rooms with balconies. Two heated pools, sauna, marina. Rates: $70 to $130 per night.

Kirby Grill, Washington at Harbor Drive; (616) 846–3299. Another good pasta place, especially for fettuccine Alfredo.

Rosebud Pizza & Prime Rib, 100 Washington; (616) 846–7788. Moderate.

Holland

Beechwood Inn, 380 Douglas; (616) 396–2355. The place to go for fresh lake perch. Very popular; closed Sunday. Moderate.

The Hatch, 1870 Ottawa Beach Road; (616) 399–9120. Delicious steaks and seafood. Reservations strongly recommended. Moderate.

Pereddie's, 447 Washington Square (between 18th and 19th Streets); (616) 394–3061. Classic old Italian restaurant—casual, chic, and comfortable. A real favorite of the locals. Moderate.

FOR MORE INFORMATION

Holland Convention and Visitors Bureau, 76 East Eighth Street, Holland, MI 49423; (800) 506–1299; www.holland.org.

Grand Haven/Spring Lake Area Visitors Bureau, 1 South Harbor, Grand Haven, MI 49417; (800) 303–4090 or (616) 842–4499; www.grandhavenchamber.org.

Marshall

AN ARCHITECTURAL FANTASY

1 NIGHT

Historic homes • Antique shopping • Museums

Marshall is to historic house lovers what Las Vegas is to gamblers. Located halfway between Chicago and Detroit, this little jewel of a town has been hailed as a textbook example of nineteenth- and early-twentieth-century small-town architecture.

With 867 buildings designated a National Historic Landmark District, many Marshall residents see themselves more as curators than homeowners. True students of design will want to allow themselves two days. To peek at the interiors, however, schedule your visit for the first weekend after Labor Day, when the annual historic house tour takes place.

The tour began in the 1950s when a group of churchwomen opened their kitchens to show off the latest in postwar appliances. The kitchen tour expanded into a house tour, which now attracts some 15,000 visitors and has become so popular that the Marshall Historical Society has taken it under its wing.

It's poetic justice for a town that had always planned for a crowd. In 1847 the citizens of Marshall expected the town to be named the capital of Michigan. Their dreams, however, were dashed by a fickle legislature that gave the nod to Lansing instead. The area of town known as Capitol Hill—particularly the "Governors Mansion" at 612 South Marshall Avenue—is a testimony to what might have been.

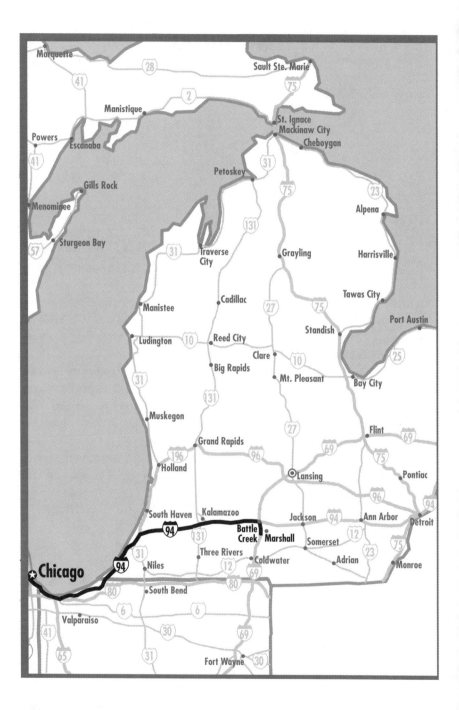

Morning

To get to Marshall take I–94 east to the juncture of I–94 and I–69. The exit for Marshall is just beyond this juncture. The town is about three hours from Chicago.

The main thing to do in Marshall is to walk and gawk. There are guided tours offered here, but there's no reason why a traveler armed with a *Historic Marshall* brochure (available free at the Chamber of Commerce and other spots around town) and a pair of sensible shoes can't do it solo.

The brochure features addresses and details of 103 homes as well as a guide to the town cemetery and historical markers.

The first stop on your list should be the **Honolulu House** at 107 North Kalamazoo Avenue. This tropical confection is painted in ivory, red, and three shades of green (its style is listed in guidebooks as "eclectic"). The house was built in 1860 for Abner Pratt, a former United States consul to the Sandwich (now Hawaiian) Islands. Now a museum, it is also the headquarters of the Marshall Historical Society. Open daily, noon–5:00 P.M., May 1 to September 30. At other times, by appointment.

Adjacent to the Honolulu House is the **Brooks Memorial Fountain,** which anchors Michigan Avenue. Dedicated in 1930 by its mayor and name-sake Harold Brooks, the fountain was badly in need of restoration by 1976. Once again, the then 91-year-old Brooks came through to save what has become the symbol of the community.

LUNCH: Espresso Yourself, 301 East Michigan Avenue; (616) 789–1136. A good time to stop for a light lunch (soups, salads, and sandwiches). Terrific coffee drinks and desserts. If your pace is truly leisurely, board games and newspapers are available to patrons. Inexpensive.

After lunch, either continue on the house tour or shift gears for shopping.

The downtown district is a mecca for antiques lovers, representing one of the strongest concentrations of dealers in the Midwest. There are a dozen shops within a few blocks of Michigan Avenue alone; enough to fill a week-end, much less an afternoon. (Several dealers are closed Sundays or are open by appointment only, so check first.)

I found not only good prices, but a dazzling variety of goods, as well. Since Michigan is the birthplace of the automobile, this is the place for "motorstal-gia"—be it a hood ornament or an ad for the Edsel. With Battle Creek (home of Kellogg) nearby, it also has a wealth of cereal collectibles: boxes, bowls, premiums, you name it.

Space cannot do justice to each dealer's strong suit, but here is just a brief rundown of what the largest shops have to offer: **Smithfield-Banque** (616–781–6969), English furniture; **J.H. Cronin Antique Center** (616–789–0077), signage, World War II memorabilia, slot machines, jukeboxes, and leaded windows; **Heirlooms** (616–781–1234), glassware and china; **J&J Antiques** (616–781–5581), postcards, rare books, primitives, and furniture. Open Friday and Saturday only, 11:00 A.M.–4:00 P.M.

Two smaller museums—both open by appointment only—are also located downtown. The **American Museum of Magic** (107 East Michigan Avenue; 616–781–7674), was founded in 1978. It's the only museum of its kind in the world, filled with three floors of artifacts and props used by the greatest stage magicians of the nineteenth and twentieth centuries. Be forewarned: This is not a place for children, and the owner clearly made us feel unwelcome with a 9-year-old in tow. If you are an adult with a passion for the history of magic, however, this is a worthy destination.

The **Postal Museum** (202 East Michigan Avenue; 616–781–2859) is also for lovers of the arcane. It houses an entire post office, as well as mail memorabilia from the last 150 years.

DINNER: Just a few blocks away from the museums is **Malia,** 130 West Michigan Avenue (616–781–2171), a charming Italian bistro in the heart of the downtown shopping district. Highly recommended: all the pastas, especially the smoked salmon fettucini and the shrimp linguine. An abundant breadbasket, a fresh salad accompanied by a crisp wine, and what else do you need? Maybe dessert? No problem. The tortes in the display case are well worth the calories. Moderate.

LODGING: The **National House Inn,** 102 South Parkview Street. Built in 1835 as a stagecoach stop, the National House is the oldest operating inn in Michigan. This solid Greek Revival building is perfectly situated at the end of Michigan Avenue, Marshall's main street.

There are sixteen rooms with airy 12-foot ceilings. All are tastefully furnished with authentic antiques, in a style consistent with the era. A midafternoon snack of lemon cookies, fresh fruit tart, and iced tea tasted especially fine on a sweltering summer day. Rates range from $66 (shared shower) to $145, and include a full breakfast. Call (616) 781–7374.

DAY 2

BREAKFAST: The **National House Inn** serves an egg strata that is so popular that printed recipe cards are available. Also have some muffins or fresh fruit, then it's time to hit more homes.

Side trips can be made from Marshall to Battle Creek, Kalamazoo, or any of the stops along the way. See Indiana Escape One (Michigan City) and Michigan Escapes One through Four (Harbor Country, South Haven, Saugatuck, or Holland/Grand Haven).

THERE'S MORE

Binder Park Zoo, 7400 Division Drive, Battle Creek; (616) 979–1351. Home to more than 250 animals, all roaming freely in a lush forest setting. Highlights include the Butterfly Zone, where hundreds of beautiful butterflies flit freely through a walk-through habitat.

Cornwell's Turkeyville USA, 18935 Half-Mile Road, Marshall; (800) 228–4315. A place to get homespun entertainment and a delicious home-style turkey dinner. The menu also has such variations as turkey ruben and turkey stir-fry. Theatrical selections run toward musicals and comedy. Dinner/show, $29.95. Show only, $21.00.

Kellogg's Cereal City U.S.A., Battle Creek; (616) 962–6230. $6.50 adults, $5.50 senior citizens, $4.50 children. Open year-round; Tuesday through Friday, 10:00 A.M.–4:00 P.M.; Saturday and Sunday, 10:00 A.M.–5:00 P.M.

OTHER RECOMMENDED RESTAURANTS AND LODGINGS

Rose Hill Inn, 1110 Verona Road; (616) 789–1992. Rates: $99 to $125. Visit the inn on the Web at www.B-B.com/Rosehill.

Schuler's Restaurant and Pub, 115 South Eagle Street; (616) 781–0600. A Michigan historic landmark for dining and tourism. The original, where prime rib reigns supreme and people still fill up on freshly baked breads, including California Sourdough and Farmer's Bavarian. A Southwest Michigan tradition. Moderate to expensive.

FOR MORE INFORMATION

Marshall Area Chamber of Commerce, 424 East Michigan Avenue, Marshall, MI 49068; (616) 781–5163 or (800) 877–5163.

MICHIGAN

Traverse City/Petoskey

THE BEAUTY OF THE OTHER

NORTH SHORE

3 NIGHTS

*Biking • Hiking • Galleries/Shopping • Golf
Fishing • Theaters/Concerts*

In the northwest corner of Michigan's Lower Peninsula lies a large area of astonishing vistas, gorgeous natural wonders, and unparalleled amenities that may not exist anywhere else in the Midwest. Sound like just a bit of an over-statement? Not when you experience the beauty of Lake Michigan's other North Shore—the 100-mile stretch of coastline that extends from Sleeping Bear Dunes National Park north to Petoskey State Park.

Once considered only as a destination for ruggedly hearty outdoorsmen, the area now is home to the stately manors of some members of the Ford and Upjohn families, as well as the contemporary developments and resorts of Harbor Springs, Traverse Bay, and Cheboygan. Two-lane roads wind their way along the Leelanau Peninsula coast through dozens of resort villages—each claiming the best dining and views of Lake Michigan. On the smaller Old Mission Peninsula, the larger port of Traverse City forms the starting point for investigating the cherry orchards, historic lighthouses, and gently rolling farm-lands that line the eastern and western peninsula shores.

From Chicago, it's almost a six-hour drive up to Sleeping Bear Dunes National Lakeshore, but it's well worth the time to experience a destination that will satisfy both the active travelers and the relaxation seekers in the

family. There's too much to do in Northwest Michigan to squeeze it all into a three-day weekend, so save this for when you've banked a little vacation time.

DAY 1

Morning

Start your drive east on I–94 and exit north on I–196, which turns into U.S. Highway 31 past Holland. Stay on I–31 all the way up to Traverse City, about a five-hour drive north of Chicago. Don't hesitate to stop along the way for that familiar Michigan staple, the roadside farmstand—especially when cherries are in season.

Afternoon

LUNCH: One of the most popular spots in downtown Traverse City is **Poppy-cock's,** 128 East Front Street (231–941–7632), a moderately priced cafe serving homemade soups, pastas, and hearty sandwiches. And, of course, cherry pie.

You'll need all the strength and carbo-loading you can muster, for just forty-five minutes west of Traverse City is **Sleeping Bear Dunes National Lakeshore**, a 70,000-acre National Park, featuring more than 35 miles of coastal dunes and two uninhabited islands 5 miles off the coast. The dunes are named after a Chippewa Indian legend that tells of a mother bear and her two cubs that tried to escape a forest fire by swimming across Lake Michigan. The two cubs drowned and later became the outer Manitou Islands. The huge Sleeping Bear Dune became the spot where the mother bear awaited the return of her cubs.

Today, many tourists attempt the dune climb (actually a crawl) up from the lakeshore—an oxygen-depleting journey and definitely not for those fresh out of cardiac rehab. But if you're lucky enough to make it to the top, the views of Lake Michigan and the surrounding Lakeshore Park are well worth the gasping.

There's also the 7.4-mile **Pierce Stocking Scenic Drive** through the park, which affords hikers and bikers many opportunities to explore the dunes and forest along the lakeshore. There's a $7.50 admission fee per car to get into the park; stop by the **National Park Service Visitors Center** for free maps and lots of information. Though open from April to November, call (231) 334–2000 for a list of hours and programs available throughout the summer.

North of the dunes is **Manitou Island Transit** (231–256–9061) in Leland, which offers camping trips to North and South Manitou Islands for those interested in investigating pristine beaches and old shipwreck sites.

DINNER: La Becasse is a gem of a restaurant, offering French country cuisine in the village of Burdickville, west of Traverse City near Glen Lake, off M–675. Call (231) 334–3944 for reservations and directions. The prices are high, but the steak frites and the bouillabaisse are worth it. After a day of negotiating the dunes, you've earned dessert. Try the gateau of the day.

LODGING: The **Bayshore Resort,** 833 East Front Street (800–634–4401), offers spacious rooms in an elegant Victorian setting right on the beach. Located along the lakefront highway in Traverse City. Some of the rooms have fireplaces and spas. There's also a large indoor pool and a fitness area. Rates vary from $120 to $350, depending on the view and the season.

[handwritten note: Dinner: Bowers Harbor Inn - very good, nice service, dress! Expensive $16 ~ 32 entrees. Huge portions!! Behind the inn is the Brewery - casual, less expensive - or food]

DAY 2

Morning

BREAKFAST: If you decide to opt out of the continental at the Bayshore, try **The Omelette Shoppe,** 1209 East Front Street in Traverse City; (231) 946–0590. Need we say more? Generous and varied omelettes, along with strong coffee and other standard breakfast fare. Try the cherry and blueberry pastries. It's a popular and usually busy spot, but the staff is friendly and loves to chat with all the visitors. Moderately priced.

Shopping opportunities abound in Northwest Michigan and run the gamut from rustic antiques to nouveau art. Traverse City in particular has several antiques stores and an eclectic downtown shopping district. The renovated **Traverse City Gas Company Building** at 301 Grand View Parkway, which dates back to 1901, houses several interesting shops, including **The Candle Factory** (231–946–2280) and **Home Elements** (231–946–2850).

Feeling cultural? Traverse City also has three excellent spots for an educational interlude. The **Dennos Museum Center** of Northwestern Michigan University, 1701 East Front Street (231–922–1055), has one of the largest Eskimo art collections in the lower forty-eight states. There's also a children's gallery that could be a lifesaver if you run into a rainy day. Also check out the schedule of concerts and gallery exhibitions at the **Interlochen Center of the Arts** (231–276–7200), about a twenty-minute drive south of Traverse

City. **The Music House,** 7377 Highway 31 (231–938–9300), is an unusual museum of restored and antique musical instruments. There are also nostalgic radio and phonograph galleries. This jewel of a collection is open only during the busy tourist season, so call ahead for hours and admission prices.

Afternoon

LUNCH: If you're ready for lunch, head north on Route 22 to one of the peninsula's more popular tourist destinations, Leland, and one of its most famous restaurants, the **Blue Bird,** 102 River Road; (231) 256–9081. The Great Lakes whitefish is legendary, and see if you can find room for the dune-size cinnamon rolls. Moderate.

There are a couple of shopping spots to investigate. One is the **Fishtown** area, which features little shops in red-shingled shacks along a pier. There are also the Main Street shops, which include **Tampico,** at 112 North Main Street (231–256–7747), featuring an unusual selection of wares from all over South America, and **Becky Thatcher Designs,** 110 North Lake Street (231–256–2229), with a large selection of Native American jewelry.

DINNER: Head south, then east on Route 204 around Leelanau Lake to the town of Sutton's Bay, the largest town on the peninsula's eastern shore. Find your way to **Hattie's,** 111 St. Joseph Street; (231) 271–6222. This is one of the nicer places along the peninsula, and reservations are recommended. The menu is fresh and eclectic (try the scallops), and you won't go wrong with any chocolate dessert. Expensive.

If you're feeling a little lucky tonight, try the **Leelanau Sands Casino,** 2521 North West Bay Shore Drive in Sutton Bay; (888) 951–8946. It features all the standard casino gaming fare, and it's open till 3:00 A.M. nightly. You must be 18 years old to enter.

LODGING: Open Windows B&B in Sutton Bay, at 613 St. Mary's Avenue (231–271–4300), is a charming restored nineteenth-century home near downtown. Rates are $115 to $160 and include a full breakfast.

We recommend, however was sold out.
off main road.

DAY 3

Morning

BREAKFAST: Head about an hour north on Highway 31 to the charming town of Petoskey and get your appetite warmed up for some of the best pancakes in the Midwest at the **Flap Jack Shack,** 314 West Mitchell Street; (231) 347–1260. You want pancakes? They've got pancakes—from blueberry and buckwheat to sourdough and blintzes. Inexpensive.

Petoskey and nearby Harbor Springs have been home to summer vacationers for more than one hundred years. As with many of the resorts of Northwest Michigan, the area's natural, picturesque beauty and pristine lake waters have long attracted many of the well-to-do families of the Midwest—including the Fords and the Wrigleys. As they were a century ago, the beaches continue to be a magnet for hunters of Michigan's unique state rock: Petoskey stone, which is actually shiny-smooth fossilized coral with a noticeable and distinct ring pattern. These stones are thought to be 350 million years old, and the best hunting sites are **Petoskey State Park** (800–543–2937) and **Magnus City Park.**

Today the area is also a haven for cyclists and home to the **Petoskey Waterfront Path.** In the fall, the **Tunnel of Trees Road** overlooking Lake Michigan and off Route 119 is spectacular, a must for novices and seasoned pros. The area is also popular in the winter due to the ski action at nearby **Boyne Mountain** and **Boyne Highlands,** southwest of Petoskey. Follow the signs down Highway 131. Lift tickets are $34 during the week and $40 on the weekend. Open 9:00 A.M.–4:30 P.M. Call (800) 462–6963 for reservations.

If you're still not shopped out, visit Petoskey's **Gas Light District,** which offers distinctive galleries and boutiques among historic turn-of-the-century storefronts. For Ernest Hemingway fans, stop by the **Horton Bay General Store** (231–582–7827), in Boyne City for a large collection of Hemingway memorabilia. Hemingway married his first wife, Hadley Richardson, in nearby Horton Bay, where the author spent many summers of his youth. Call (231) 347–2620 for seasonal updates of ongoing Hemingway tours and activities. (For more Hemingway memorabilia, also check out the Petoskey Historical Society.)

Afternoon

LUNCH: In the midst of the Gas Light District is a spot that specializes in healthy food: the **Roast and Toast,** 309 Lake Street; (231) 347–7767. Featuring homemade soups, original salads, and fresh-baked pastries, this moderately priced gem also boasts its own daily roasted coffee and is a perennial in *Traverse* magazine's top ten reader favorites in Northern Michigan.

On the outskirts of Petoskey lies the small village of **Bay View,** which was founded in 1875 as a summer retreat for members of the Methodist Church and today is notable for its large number of restored Victorian buildings. The community's restoration efforts earned it a designation as a National Historic Landmark, with the most charming structures highlighted on walking and trolley tours. Take your time wandering through this wonderfully restored village, and stop by the town museum (231–348–2599) for more information on the history of Bay View. Or try the **Bay View Association** (231–347–4210) for schedules and ticket prices of concerts, lectures on the entire history of Bay View, and recitals.

DINNER: The region's crowning jewel is hidden away about 15 miles south of Charlevoix down U.S. Highway 31 and off State Highway C–48 in the tiny town of Ellsworth. **Tapawingo,** 9502 Lake Street (231–588–7971), is rated by *Gourmet* magazine readers as one of the country's top country dining experiences. The restaurant offers nouvelle American fare, featuring Lake Michigan fish sautéed with local fresh vegetables and fruit. Expensive.

LODGING: The **Weathervane Terrace Inn** on Pine River Lane in Charlevoix (231–547–9955) sits on a bluff overlooking Lake Michigan. The inn is evocative of a small medieval castle, and the views of the lake and the surrounding vistas are breathtaking. Room prices vary depending on the season but range on the high side. Call for exact rates.

THERE'S MORE

Ballooning. Here's an opportunity to get a once-in-a-lifetime view of the Old Mission Peninsula. Grand Traverse Balloons, 225 Cross Country Trail in Traverse City (231–947–7433), offers one-hour sunrise and sunset flights, along with subsequent champagne celebrations and photos. Prices vary depending on the time and day of the week.

Canoes. Bear River Canoe, 2517 McDougall Road in Petoskey (231–347–9038), and Crystal River Canoe, 6052 West Harbor Road in Glen Arbor (231–334–3090), both offer trips and pointers for excursions on local lakes and rivers. It's for adults and children, and they provide the life vests.

Ferries and tours. Bay Water Ferry and Tours, in Petoskey and Bay Harbor (231–347–5550), offers ferry service on Little Traverse Bay. Tours are also available from May until mid-October.

Fish hatchery. Oden State Fish Hatchery, on U.S. Highway 31 North near Oden (231–347–4689), is free and offers self-guided tours through outdoor pond areas for rainbow and brown trout. The kids in the family can feed the fish for 10 cents. That's right, *cents.*

Golf. Northern Michigan has quickly built a reputation for top-class golf, replete with challenging courses designed by famous golf architects. Three area courses—Boyne Highlands Heather (near Harbor Springs), a Robert Trent Jones, Sr., course; High Pointe in Williamsburg (800–753–7888), east of Traverse City; and The Bear at Grand Traverse Resort (800–748–0303), a Jack Nicklaus design—are rated among the nations's one hundred best public courses by *Golf* magazine. The Legend at Shanty Creek, 40 miles northeast of Traverse City, an Arnold Palmer–designed course, made the list at *Golf Digest.* The Traverse City area alone boasts almost twenty-five courses, while the Petoskey/Harbor Springs area is home to more than twelve. Call (800) 845–2828 in the Petoskey area for additional information on local tee time reservations and greens fees.

Orchards. Friske Orchards, on County Road 48, 10 miles south of Charlevoix (231–588–6185), is a 200-acre farm that's a great place to pick cherries, peaches, strawberries, and apples. The store is open all year.

top pick

Wineries. The Old Mission Peninsula is home to the finest regional wineries, among them the Chateau Grand Traverse, 12239 Center Road (231–223–7355), which has produced several award-winning Chardonnays and Rieslings. Chateau Chantel, 15900 Rue du Vin (231–223–4110 or 800–969–4009), is a combination B&B and winery—and easily the most romantic of the area wineries, while Boskydel Vineyards, 7501 East Otto Road on the Leelanau Peninsula (231–256–7272), specializes in excellent table wines. This is also the county's first bonded wine cellar, dating from 1965. All offer public tastings, but call ahead as hours vary during the seasons.

Zoo. The Clinch Park Zoo (231–922–4904), situated along the waterfront in Traverse City, is small but surely has some of the nicest views in the Midwest. The zoo has a selection of animals found in the wilds around Traverse City, and it's situated adjacent to the popular Clinch Park Beach. Admission is only $2.00, with reduced rates for children.

SPECIAL EVENTS

May. Blossom Days, Old Mission Peninsula. Morel National Mushroom Festival, Boyne City; (231) 582–6222.

June. Home Tours and Concerts in the Park, Petoskey. Classic and Custom Car Show, Cheboygan; (800) 968–3302.

July. National Cherry Festival, Traverse City; (800) 968–3380. Outdoor Art Fair, Traverse City; (800) 968–3380.

July. Fireworks Celebration and Harbor Days, Northport. Cheboygan Arts Festival, Cheboygan Ice Pavilion; (800) 968–3302. Little Traverse Historical Festival, Petoskey.

August. Boyne Falls Polish Festival, Boyne Falls; (800) 845–2828. Emmet County Fair, Petoskey. Annual Arts Festival, Sutton's Bay. Leelanau Peninsula Wine Festival, Northport. Harbor Springs Pow Wow, Harbor Springs. Renaissance Fair, Traverse City; (231) 632–3027.

October. Hemingway Festival Weekend, Petoskey.

December. Christmas Walk, Petoskey and Harbor Springs.

OTHER RECOMMENDED RESTAURANTS AND LODGINGS

Leland

Blue Bird, 102 River Road; (231) 256–9081. A longtime popular institution known for its homemade soups and cinnamon buns. Moderate.

Leland Lodge, 565 Pearl Street; (231) 256–9848. Offers quiet and elegant dining, with great views of the Leelanau Valley. Known for its excellent fish and steak. Expensive.

Leelanau Country Inn, 149 East Harbor Highway; (231) 228–5060. One of the area's best restaurants; noted for its superior and extensive Sunday brunch. As if that weren't enough, it also boasts the largest selection of local wines in the area. Moderate.

The Cove, 111 River Road; (231) 256–9834. Overlooking Fishtown; renowned for its famous Fishtown Stew. It's usually open only during the summer. Moderate.

Traverse City

Don's Drive Inn, 2030 U.S. Highway 31 North; (231) 938–1860. A fifties-style diner and an inexpensive stop for burgers, fries, and a Coke.

Mabel's, 472 Munson Street; (231) 947–0252. The best breakfast in Northern Michigan—so says *Traverse* magazine. It's served all day, so you have lots of opportunities to confirm this choice. Check your cholesterol at the door and succumb to plate-size omelets and, of course, sticky buns. Moderate.

Sleder's Family Tavern, 717 Randolph Street; (231) 947–9213. Claims to be the state's oldest tavern, dating from 1882. The menu features very good Mexican fare, and it's moderately priced.

Harbor Springs

Birchwood Inn, 7077 Lakeshore Drive; (231) 526–2151. A quiet location overlooking Little Traverse Bay. There's a communal fireplace room, outdoor pool, and tennis courts. Continental breakfast. Rates vary depending on the season and the view.

Boyne Highlands Resort, 600 Highlands Drive; (231) 526–3000. A full-service golf and ski resort that also features tennis courts, an outdoor pool, and summer dinner theater. It's closed from Labor Day to the opening of ski season. Rates start at about $150 and go way up from there.

Harborside Inn, 266 East Main Street; (231) 526–6238. An all-suite hotel located in downtown Harbor Springs. It's within easy walking distance of great shops and restaurants. Rates: $100 to $235, depending on the season.

The New York Restaurant, 101 State Street; (231) 526–1904. An authentic turn-of-the-century spot featuring an imaginative menu of pastas, salads, and Northern Michigan whitefish. Moderate.

Petoskey / Bay View

Apple Tree Inn, 915 Spring Street; (231) 348–2900. A small hotel with views of Little Traverse Bay. Indoor access to pool and spas. Continental breakfast. Rates: $80 to $160.

Bay Winds Inn, 909 Spring Street; (231) 347–4193. Another small hotel with great views of Little Traverse Bay. It's close to downtown and is very popular with families. Indoor pool and exercise room; continental breakfast. Rates: $90 to $160.

The Inn at Bay Harbor, 3600 Village Harbor Drive, Bay Harbor; (800) 462–6963 or (231) 439–4000. Offers 225 luxury suites, including one-, two- and three-bedroom suites. The setting is one of an elegant seaside cottage. Rates: $250 and up.

Stafford's Perry Hotel, at the corner of Bay and Lewis Streets in Petoskey; (800) 456–1917 or (231) 347–4000. Features eighty rooms and outdoor terrace dining overlooking Little Traverse Bay. It's within walking distance of shops, the waterfront park, and a fitness trail. Rates: $80 to $180.

The Terrace Inn, 1949 Glendale; (231) 347–2410. Another small hotel in Bay View, dating from just after the turn of the century. Features fresh country inn cuisine. How about a Michigan original—chicken with dried Michigan cherries? It's another popular haunt for vacationers. Moderate to expensive.

Latitude, 795 Front Street, Bay Harbor; (231) 439–2750. Chef Richard Travis carved out a name for himself at the acclaimed Tapawingo before striking out on his own. The menu is long on contemporary American fare. Don't miss the ultramoist barbecued duck with caramelized five-spice mango. Reservations highly recommended. Moderate to expensive.

Walloon Lake

Boyne Valley Lodge, 1712 South Shore Drive; (231) 535–2475. A small hotel with European-style lodging. Prices include meals, and there's a fireplace, gameroom, and year-round outdoor heated pool. Great for large family groups. Rates vary with the seasons.

Dickson's Lodge, U.S. Highway 131 and North M–75; (231) 535–2415. A family-owned and -operated hotel with more than seventy-five rooms (some cabins). New indoor pool and an indoor gameroom for the kids. It's a short drive to golf and skiing areas. Rates vary with the seasons.

Walloon Lake Inn, 4178 West Street; (231) 535–2999. A small inn and dining room on the shores of Walloon Lake. Of course, try any of the fish, including the Hemingway-inspired rainbow trout. Moderate to expensive.

FOR MORE INFORMATION

Petoskey–Harbor Springs–Boyne County Visitors Bureau, 401 East Mitchell Street, P.O. Box 694, Petoskey, MI 49770; (231) 348–2755 or (800) 845–2828; www.boynecountry.com.

Traverse City Convention and Visitors Bureau, 101 West Grandview Parkway, Traverse City, MI 49684; (231) 947–1120 or (800) 872–8377.

INDEX

ABOUT THE AUTHORS

BONNIE MILLER RUBIN is a reporter for the *Chicago Tribune*. She has spent twenty-five years working for daily newspapers, including the *Minneapolis Star Tribune* and the *Gary Post Tribune*. She is also a regular contributor to *Good Housekeeping* and *Ladies Home Journal*. Most recently she authored *Fifty on Fifty: Wisdom, Inspiration, and Reflections on Women's Lives Well Lived*. (Warner Books) Bonnie lives in the Chicago area with her husband and two children.

MARCY MASON is a Chicago-based free-lance writer. She is a regular contributor to the *Chicago Tribune* and has written for numerous publications, including the *Wall Street Journal, Essence,* and *Crain's Chicago Business.* Her subjects range from the arts, health, and food to travel, real estate, and finance.